LULWORTH SHARED MY PLAYGROUND

OCCOMORE SIBBICK

MINERVA PRESS
MONTREUX LONDON WASHINGTON

LULWORTH SHARED MY PLAYGROUND
Copyright © Occomore Sibbick 1996

ISBN 1 85863 955 7

First Published 1996 by
MINERVA PRESS
195 Knightsbridge
London SW7 1RE

Printed in Great Britain by
Antony Rowe Ltd., Chippenham, Wiltshire

LULWORTH SHARED MY PLAYGROUND

To Vera (my wife)
whose devotion has charted life's voyage.

REFERENCES

References to the following works are integrated into the text:

The King's Britannia	John Irving
Britannia *and her contemporaries*	Heckstall–Smith
The King's Sailing Master	Douglas Dixon
Great Years in Yachting	John Nicholson
A Hundred Years of Sail	Beken of Cowes
Minute by Minute	Gordon Fairley
Tom Diaper's Log	Tom Diaper
Cruise in Company	Small
Famous Yachts	Scott Hughes
Solent Yachting Scene	David Couling
Introduction to Yachting	Herreshoff
Splendid Book of Steamships	Gibbard Jackson
The Complete Yachtsman	Heckstall–Smith)
	Capt. du Boulay)
Memorials of the RYS	J. Atkins
Incidents and Reflections	J. Atkins
Enterprise to Endeavour	Ian Dear
Yachting Vol.II	His Grace the Eighth
	Duke of Beaufort
Victorian & Edwardian Yachting	Robert Simper
The Isle of Wight County Press	
Lloyds's Registers of Yachts	
Photographs – various	
	Beken of Cowes,
	Terry Davies and
	Capt. Phillip Wood

ACKNOWLEDGEMENTS

The author wishes to acknowledge the valued assistance of Wendy Gannon, whose talent and unfailing patience contributed substantially to the presentation of this manuscript.

His further appreciation is extended with gratitude to the following persons: Mr Lionel Willis of the National Maritime Museum, Greenwich; Mr Tom Ross, Librarian, Royal Ulster Yacht Club; Mr Nick Maris, Chairman, Camper & Nicholson (Yachts) Ltd., and his assistant Deborah Betteridge; Mr Trevor Davies of Swansea; Captain Phillip Wood, Deputy Harbour Master, Cowes and Marilyn Wood; Penelope and David Jefferson; Mrs Patricia Greenwood, East Cowes branch of the Isle of Wight County Library; Mr J. McCaig, Director of G.L. Watson, Naval Architects; Dominic Wood; Mr George Newlands; Mr Harry Spencer.

ABOUT THE AUTHOR

Born in the Isle of Wight, Occomore Sibbick served an indentured apprenticeship in marine engineering, following which he was engaged in the aerospace industry. His early career found him in the design offices of Westland Aircraft, Airspeed and Fairey Aviation.

He was variously engaged as a project engineer with Miles Aircraft, later becoming a divisional chief engineer of the Plessey Co., and served English Electric in a managerial capacity.

In 1973 he founded the Foreland Engineering Design Service, retiring in 1981. He is married to Vera and they have two daughters, Marilyn and Penelope.

CONTENTS

PART IV

PART V

APPENDICES

PLATES

Plate (1)

The Big Five: *Lulworth* (ex-*Terpsichore*), *Shamrock*, *Westward*, *Britannia* and *White Heather II*.

Plate (2)

Seal of Royal Yacht Club, Cowes.

Plate (3)

The auxiliary barque-rigged yacht *Fantôme II* (ex-*Belem*) owned by Col. The Hon. Arthur E. Guinness.
An early cruise in his ownership included a voyage around the world.

Plate (4)

The Royal Yacht Squadron Club House Premises.

Plate (5)

The steam yacht *Xarifa* built for Mr F. Morton Singer of New York by J. Samuel White & Co. Ltd., at Cowes in 1930.

Plate (6)

Mr Paxton's diesel engined yacht *Braemar II* immediately following her launch from the slipways of J. Samuel White and Co. Ltd., on the Medina River in 1929.

Plate (7)

The magnificent twin screw steam yacht *Liberty* of 1571 tons, 250 feet long, 35.6 feet beam, designed by Mr G.T. Watson for Mr J. Pulitzer and built by Ramage and Ferguson of Leith in 1901. She was owned and based in

Jersey by Sir Robert and Lady Fanny Houston, D.B.E., in the Twenties.

Plate (8)

A well-preserved relic of the nineteenth-century *Dolly Vardon*, pride of sailmaker Thomas Ratsey.
Her LOA and WL appear coincident.

Plate (9)

The 56,000 ton White Star liner, *SS Majestic* (ex-*Bismarck*), regular visitor to Southampton Docks.

Plate (10)

An unusual view of the very successful cutter *Nyria* in her earlier topsailed rig rounding a mark in light airs.
She was raced by the great sportswoman Mrs E.R. Workman in the early twenties.

Plate (11)

The cutter *Nyria* following her conversion to Bermudian rig in 1921.

Plate (12)

The famous ketch *Cariad* built for the Earl of Dunraven and later owned by Col. Gretton; six times winner of the King's Cup in 1905, 1910, 1912, 1921 and 1929.

Plate (13)

Sir William Portal's *Valdora* in her original yawl rig, later to be changed to ketch configuration. She won the King's Cup under handicap rating in 1922 and 1924.

Plate (14)

A fine study of King George V's cutter *Britannia* enjoying a "blow" to demonstrate her best behaviour.

Plate (15)

An imposing glimpse of Lord Waring's lovely cutter *White Heather II* with her lee rail uncomfortably awash.

Plate (16)

Lulworth sailing close-hauled past Ryde Pier with her vast spread of sail set to perfection heading for the Warner mark.

Plate (17)

The giant schooner *Westward* owned by Mr F.T.B. Davis from 1925 onwards. Without her pre-1914 contemporaries she raced under handicap with the big cutters, displaying a mastery in reaching winds.

Plate (18)

The picturesque schooner *Susanne* of 154 tons (T.M.) which occasionally joined the Big Class in the Twenties.

Plate (19)

The ex Kaiser's 400 ton schooner *Meteor IV* seen with Dr Krupp von Bohlen's contemporary yacht *Germania*. Both built in Germany. The earlier Meteors were from either British or American yards.

Plate (20)

Sir Thomas Lipton's twenty-three metre *Shamrock* of 1908 vintage, with her distinctive green topsides prettily posed for a classic photographic record.

Plate (21)

The Bermudian cutter *Astra* designed and built by Charles Nicholson for Sir Mortimer Singer in 1928.

Plate (22)

The Fife-designed Bermudan cutter *Cambria* of 1928 with a hitch in her mainsail.

Plate (23)

The Herreshoff schooner *Elena* of 1911 vintage, which appeared in the Solent in 1928 to sail with her pre-1914 rival double sticker *Westward*.

Plate (24)

The Nicholson cutter *Candida* built for Mr H.K. Andreae to compete in the big class with handicap allowance in 1929.

Plate (25)

The Great Cutter *Lulworth* showing a cloud of canvas leading her rivals whilst running through the Solent.

INTRODUCTION

As one whose boyhood was indelibly coloured by the Solent yachting scenes, embracing Cowes and Ryde Regattas in particular during the nineteen twenties, my narrative recalls the spirit of the great cutter *Lulworth* (ex-*Terpsichore*) which, despite her earlier tribulations, competed so brilliantly in the very select company of first-class yachts, especially in the years 1925, 1926 and 1930.

Schooldays at Cowes were inevitably enmeshed with the activities of the port, and my story recalling the visions of giant canvases in motion is offered as a background sketch of a lad's shoreside environment.

The collection of race summaries recalls many of the meetings joined by *Lulworth* (ex-*Terpsichore*) in competition with her most illustrious contemporaries of the big handicap class in the Twenties and further relates essentially a juvenile's vivid impressions, with notes of Solent activities taken during this period.

These notes provide a typically important series of this famous yacht's assignations in Solent regattas, revealing much of her rugged yet versatile character, complemented by those who sailed her to so many victories. The local influence upon *Lulworth* (ex-*Terpsichore*), and, indeed, her class rivals, deservedly gives a parochial bias in narration.

Boyhood impressions of the Cowes and Ryde Regatta atmosphere, with memories of the great personalities involved, combine to acknowledge the widespread pleasure which was provided by those who brought their most sophisticated models to the Solent playground for just a few precious appearances, year by year.

In setting out to relate some incidents in the racing life of *Lulworth* (ex-*Terpsichore*) these must, of necessity, include many allusions to her contemporaries and in consequence the presentation of these incidents becomes balanced against the outlines of her class, particularly in the 1924–30 era.

It is perhaps fitting that the retirement of *Lulworth* from the racing scene in 1930 coincided with the eclipse of traditional topsail apparel for the big cutters.

In retrospect, it was undoubtedly for me a unique bonus of life to be so privileged in witnessing the sights and actions of a handful of giant cutters year by year with their stately yarded topsails in the Over 100 Ton big handicap class. To see them from the shoreside, particularly in close company, heeling to windward, displaying their towering rigs with a vast spread of canvas, thundering through the surf with decks awash, manned by an extensive and dedicated crew, progressing in the region of twelve knots an hour – it was a thrill beyond literary expression!

The late Frank Beken's photographic masterpiece, generally known as 'The Big Five', exemplifies the atmosphere presented in 1925 by the elite class of yachts heading for the start line. *Lulworth* and her contemporary cutters *Britannia*, *Shamrock* and *White Heather II*, plus the schooner *Westward*, were the most expensive toys of yacht racing sport at that period, not merely in terms of their initial costs, but more in the long term with the employment of a competent skipper and mate with some thirty disciplined crew,[1] certainly for the yachting season, and in many cases the more able were retained from year to year. Additionally, modifications to hull and rigging to improve performance, gear replacements, slipway charges, mooring fees, cruising between racing venues of the British clubs, etc., must have swelled the luxury of ownership. The aggregate of these expenditures reflects the degree of enthusiasm displayed by the owners of such magnificent vessels.

For me 'The Big Five' represented the epitome of a recurring fantasy of all that yacht racing could offer. I have to confess a love affair with each of them in my boyish dreams, but my absolute devotion was centred upon *Lulworth* from a very early age.

These five yachts could fairly be described as the nucleus of the class during the nineteen twenties, although they were occasionally joined by others, and later by new Bermudan-rigged contemporaries before the forming of the 'J' class in 1931. This story is deliberately set to omit the racing events of the Jays, which are extremely well documented elsewhere and belong exclusively to the Thirties. There appears to be a great deal of confusion in local references, wherein one finds the Jackyarders wrongly described as 'J' class vessels. Two of the gaffers were converted, Bermudan fashion, to sail with the new class, *Britannia* in 1931 and *White Heather II* in 1932, but neither of these yachts was strictly Jays; further, not one of the sequential pure 'J' class yachts, *Shamrock V*, *Velsheda*, *Endeavour I* and *Endeavour II*, was to be seen with a topsail.

Whilst my schoolboy observations were limited to Solent events during the 1920–1930 period there were, of course, many other British Yacht Club regattas widely visited by the 'Big Five' during the summer season, giving pleasure to multitudes of yachting enthusiasts as well as the sponsoring clubs.

The summer yacht racing seasons around the coast during the Twenties usually began in late May and the giant yachts remained in commission through June, July and August, finishing competing in early September. During this period, fixtures were arranged for some forty-five races and, whilst individual yachts occasionally met for a full calendar, the Big Five were far from being fully represented at each and every club regatta. The average annual representations for each of the Five between 1924 and 1930 were as follows:

		Starts
White Heather II	7 seasons	34
Lulworth	7 "	30

Shamrock	6	"	28
Britannia	6	"	27
Westward	6	"	22

The usual racing routine commenced on the Thames Estuary, followed by visits to Harwich and Burnham, continuing to Deal and Dover, after which the competing yachts would sail along the South Coast, rounding Land's End for the Welsh coast and Kingstown. Sport was then joined on the Firth of Clyde for a fortnight's programme in July, after which the venue of Belfast Lough was enjoyed for a one day^2 appearance, returning via St George's Channel and the English Channel to meet at Cowes in early August for the Royal Southampton, Royal London and Royal Yacht Squadron regattas of the Week. The Royal Victoria and the Royal Thames events, conducted from Ryde, and the Southsea meetings of the Royal Albert concluded the Solent calendar, when the Big Five headed for the West Country to compete from Bournemouth, Weymouth Bay, Torquay, Plymouth Sound and Dartmouth.

Truly, such yachts were only built to sing and dance at the whims of signals from the Royal Yacht Squadron and other prominent locations, to the tunes and steps devised by such skippers as Captain Archie Hogarth (*Lulworth*), Fred Mountifield (*White Heather II*), Alf Diaper (*Westward*), Captain Sycamore (*Shamrock*) and the legendary Major Philip Hunloke (*Britannia*). It is on record that when the eminent designer, Charles Nicholson, was asked the secret of good yacht design the reply was, "Get yourself a good skipper." The experience of Archie Hogarth extended from the 1890s. He was skipper of *Calluna* in 1893, his first appointment to a first-class cutter, and became joint skipper of *Shamrock I* in 1899. Such men were, without doubt, amongst the greatest of their period. Charles Nicholson described yacht designing as something more of an art than a science and forecast that it should remain so. Whilst his philosophy cannot be entirely disputed, it could be said that the balance between art and science in yacht design has probably become reversed some seventy years onward.

Archie Hogarth's maxim was reputed to be 'Never look behind when racing'. The majority of his crew were recruited from the east coast, coming from such places as West Mersey, Tollesbury and Brightlingsea, although the team was supported by hands from the Itchen area of Southampton and the West Country. A good skipper had the ability to find a good crew, which was implicit in his terms of reference.

At the time when a new big handicap class challenger was launched from the stocks of Messrs H. and W. White Brothers' Southampton yacht yard with fevered haste, to bend her great spread of canvas and join the competition of a miscellany of pre–1914 vintage craft, the Solent had long established its claim as a top-ranking yacht racing venue, certainly in British eyes, if not the world's.

Nature had accidentally amassed a series of geographic criteria to allow a proportional expanse of relatively sheltered waters which not only provide a harbour for vessels of all tonnages and motivation, but contain a semi-enclosed playground for racing all classes of sailing yachts. The immediate southern shores of mainland England, with their unique harbour refuges, developed at Lymington, Southampton and Portsmouth, facing the northern shores of the Isle of Wight, with Cowes as a focal point, and a separating waterway of some three to four miles. These extensive waterfronts provided a most desirable series of observation locations, to the delight of many thousands of spectators who congregated to enjoy sightings of a literally royal sport – "free, gratis and for nothing".

Whilst the Solent–Spithead enclosure could not offer a facility for the conduct of strict comparative ultimate speed trials for the big class yachts, contests were enlivened by aggravated tidal influences and scattered shoals, accompanied by exaggerated variations in wind intensity and direction in combination with occasional steep seas.

In their pursuit of sporting rivalry, the tactical skills of skippers and seamen were tested to the extreme.

---

¹ A larger complement of seamen was carried on the schooners, numbering fifty ABs in the case of *Westward*. Conversely, the later Bermudan-rigged cutters *Astra*, *Cambria* and *Candida* could be sailed with a crew of seventeen ABs.

² The Royal Ulster Yacht Club Regatta was normally programmed for two days, but the Big Handicap Class yachts usually spent only one day at Belfast Lough, seeming to use the venue as a port of call while sailing from the Clyde events, making the return passage for participation in successive southern regattas.

PART I

THE ATTRACTION OF THE THRONE

It was an essential for the accepted 'success' of Cowes Week, certainly for those who lived on the fringe of the royal party, and to a great extent the loyal subjects of the local populace, that Their Majesties King George and Queen Mary should honour social events with their presence.

Indeed, it was such a favourable opportunity for so many islanders and mainland trippers to catch a glimpse of them. On some evenings Their Majesties would come ashore from the royal yacht *Victoria and Albert* moored in the Roadstead, to dine at the Royal Yacht Squadron where His Majesty was received as Admiral.[1]   Information about their scheduled movements would be circulated by 'bush telegraph' via one of the lower ranks of the yacht club fraternity, such as the signalman, becoming public property.

A precise time of arrival was seldom publicly known in advance of their landings, but the crowds used to wait patiently at the western end of the parade to witness the stately arrival from the royal yacht of an immaculately finished, dark blue steam pinnace, complete with a highly polished brass funnel, elegantly fluted at its top.   The small, smartly turned-out crew would dock the pinnace alongside the squadron landing with typical naval precision, whilst the royal visitors were hidden under protective canopies designed to fend off the sea spray *en route*.

A statuesque able seaman with a lengthy boat hook, poised ready, reached for one of the mooring rings on the landing stage and then the pinnace would be secured from the fore and aft cleats.   Meanwhile, a reception party from the squadron dutifully stood by as Their Majesties stepped from the deck of the pinnace on to the landing, to be welcomed not only by appropriate greetings and handshakes from the commodore and his entourage, but by the clapping and hearty cheers raised by their loyal subjects who had congregated so excitedly at the squadron end of the parade. Mission accomplished and, with the disappearance of the royal party into the exclusive environment of the castle, the crowds would disperse and on a fine evening saunter along the green in a westerly direction towards Egypt Point for a survey of the sunset, doubtless indulging in a series of conjectures as to the content of the club house menu[2] for the convivial feasting.

As a small boy, and before mastering the art of survival in the seaside waters, my stature substantially limited my ability to catch a glimpse of the event and I well remember being hoisted on to the balustrade of the sea wall by my father to obtain a view of the action, with a grim warning to hold on, otherwise I could fall overboard. The possibility of such an unhappy end to the evening blunted my enthusiasm for the 'pilgrimage', I have to confess.

On other occasions, when visits to Osborne House,[3] or Whippingham church,[4] were on the agenda, Their Majesties were received at the former by the governor, Major General Sir S. Guise–Moores, and the royal pinnace would ply from the *Victoria and Albert* to disgorge Their Royal Highnesses at the Trinity House Wharf at East Cowes, which was under the control of Captain F.G. Wynne, MBE, whose official title was superintendent. As the hired Daimler left the Trinity House premises Their Majesties were cheered by gatherings of loyal subjects along the tiny high street before turning into York Avenue to continue their mile-long journey uphill to Osborne, passing East Cowes Castle,[5] home of Lady Gort, to the left, and Kent House, the erstwhile residence of Prince Louis of Battenberg (later Marquess of Milford Haven and father of Lord Louis Mountbatten) to the right side.

Albert Cottage, an earlier home of Princess Beatrice, still stands at the top of the hill overlooking the King's Entrance to the Osborne Estate.

After spending an hour or two at Osborne House and the ornate Swiss Cottage, it was usual for the King and Queen to

extend the outing with a visit to Carisbroke Castle where HRH
Princess Beatrice was honoured by their call.

---

[1]   King George V was Admiral of the Royal Yacht Squadron from 1910
until his death in 1936.

[2]   Typical menu etc.:

Royal Yacht Squadron Dinner

Corne d'abondance de saumon fumé et caviar
Soupe de la tortue de mer
Sole à la mornay
Selle de Southdown rôti à la garniture
Cailles grandes à la glace vanille
Reginas
Champignons diablé
Dessert
Café

Vins:
Madeira (Sercial)
Champagne (Bollinger 1919)
Port (Cockburns 1912)
Brandy (de Gernon 1893)

Covers laid for sixty guests approximately.
Tables decorated with red and white carnations (colours of the R.Y.S.
burgee).
The one and only toast was "The King".

A choice programme of music was often rendered by The Royal Marine
Band or a hired orchestra.

[3]   Osborne House was purchased by Her Majesty Queen Victoria in
1845, to become a much coveted connection between the royal family and East
Cowes.

[4]   The church at Whippingham, known as St Mildred's, stands in an
idyllic location, high above the River Medina, about a mile from Osborne
House. Designed by Prince Albert, consort of HM Queen Victoria, in 1861,
it has a very distinctive aspect in its Teutonic architectural style, which
contrasts with other island seats of Protestant faith.

[5] East Cowes Castle, built on the site of a former residence, was designed by the famed architect John Nash, in 1798; it is a resplendent edifice on a prime site. He passed away in the year 1835 and was interred in the churchyard of St James, adjacent to the castle estate. The area has been sacrificed to the developers during the last four decades as a housing conglomerate and the lovely castle demolished. The ornate castellated entrance lodge in sympathetic detail met a similar fate.

I remember from the days of childhood a vision of Lady Gort, unhappily suffering from paralysis, propped up with cushions, taking the air in her beautiful, highly polished, open carriage drawn by two immaculately groomed black horses. She was accompanied by her maid and two horsemen with a footman perched at the rear. Her outfit included a heavy black veil to afford some protection against the dusty roadways of the period. Eleanor, Viscountess Gort lived with her second husband, Col. S.M. Benson, at the Castle in the Twenties.

THE ROYAL YACHT CLUB

The shoreside yachting fraternity of Cowes in the Twenties referred to the RYS castle as 'The Club House'. The original title for this elite body when it was formed under the seal embossed 'Dieu et mon droit', dated 1812 was The Royal Yacht Club, it being the first of its kind in the world. In making such a claim it is acknowledged that 'pleasure sailing' was the hobby of The Water Club of the harbour of Cork in the year 1720, but, as far as can be ascertained, the yachts did not compete at that time.

Another association of yachtsmen was formed in the year 1775 with the founding of The Cumberland Fleet on the River Thames, where carnivals were organised for public entertainment. Small boats were hired out for rowing contests and later some sailing races were conducted.

In the beginning, meetings of The Royal Yacht Club members were held at The Thatched House Tavern, St James's Street, London, under the chairmanship of Lord Grantham, who later built a resplendent residence on the West Cowes seafront, complete with landing stage, not far from the existing club house. This beautiful early Victorian residence later served as a hotel for many years and has since been demolished.

From 1815 The Royal Yacht Club had its meetings at The Medina Hotel near the waterfront at East Cowes and later at The Gloucester Hotel on the Parade at West Cowes, within a few yards of the castle.

The West Cowes Castle was built as a fort during the reign of King Henry VIII, designed to protect the harbour with its entrance to the River Medina, which is tidal to the centre of the Wight at Newport.

In the year 1834 The Royal Yacht Club title was changed to The Royal Yacht Squadron at the instigation of HM King

William IV, who was graciously pleased to accept the duty of admiral.

The castle was retained as a fort until the middle of the nineteenth century when the governor, the Marquess of Anglesey (hitherto a patron of yachting), passed on and the Marquis of Conyngham then leased the castle from the crown. In the year 1856 his occupancy was transferred to The Royal Yacht Squadron, as the club headquarters, in whose hands it has since remained. The RYS flag was first hoisted there on July 6th, 1858.

The Royal Yacht Squadron Castle commands a wide sweep of the Solent in what our lyrical twentieth-century advertisers might describe as a 'prestigious location'. The seascape includes Hurst Castle and Lymington Anchorage to the west, Calshot Castle and Southampton Water over to the north, with Portsdown Hill and Spithead Forts visible to the east.

Mr Joseph Weld–Blundell of Lulworth Castle in Dorset was a very keen yachtsman, as a founder member of The Royal Yacht Club in 1812 and it was a descendant of his, Mr Herbert Weld–Blundell, who became the owner of the yacht *Terpsichore* (built by Mr R.H. Lee), renaming her *Lulworth* in 1923.

In the year 1829 Mr Joseph Weld–Blundell owned one of the most advanced yachts of the time, which was appropriately named *Lulworth*, and which become a rival of Lord Belfast's cutter *Louisa*. Their crews were not particularly well disciplined or adjusted to the meaning of sport; in fact, their attitudes were grossly belligerent. It seems that the majority of the bigger yachts of the day were lightly armed for protection against piracy, equipped with brass cannon, ostensibly for firing salutes, and the crews had access to an armoury of rifles and cutlasses. One would have thought the latter to be doubtful assets in terms of security for the owners!

In the 1830 Royal Yacht Club event for the King's Cup at Cowes, Joseph Weld–Blundell's *Lulworth* and Lord Belfast's *Louisa* sailed a hard struggle for supremacy in a very light wind and, as the two yachts approached the finishing line in close company, separated by seconds only, the contestants collided. *Lulworth* was about to cross the finishing line on the port tack when she fouled *Louisa*, claiming starboard tack. The crew of the *Louisa* took up cutlasses and knives to slice at the rigging and sheets of *Lulworth*, resulting in the latter's complete disablement, whilst the crews continued in combat. The feud between the owners persisted until the following year, resulting in ruined yachting sport for the 1830 season.

A banker, Mr William Baring, who became an early member of The Royal Yacht Club, lent his name to Baring Road, Cowes.

The family tradition was carried on by General Charles Baring of the Coldstream Guards. He was elected to The Royal Yacht Squadron in 1856 when he owned the yacht *Caprice* of 56 tons, inherited from his father. The general suffered the loss of his right arm at Alma and as a consequence was granted a royal authorisation to wear his sword on the right hip. Except for those on active service overseas, life in the mother country was lived very much as in time of peace during the last century. The general, with his family, was to make the Cowes home of the Barings at Nubia House in the year 1871.

His son, Sir Godfrey Baring, Bart, later occupied Nubia House with Lady Baring in 1890. The house, since demolished, occupied an elevated location to the west of the Royal Yacht Squadron Castle. As an RYS committee member, Sir Godfrey held office for many years and it was well known in the Twenties that he spent as much time attending squadron committee meetings as his public duties permitted. Sir Godfrey chaired the Isle of Wight County Council,[1] having represented the island as a Liberal MP in the Edwardian Asquith parliament. Whilst he was a very popular guest of the Big Five owners in Solent regattas, his personal yachting pursuits were afforded by the ownership of a little 26 ton steam yacht named *Volante*, built at Cowes in 1899.

I recollect his occasional presence at school prize presentations when he appeared to follow the proceedings with a fatherly interest. Lady Baring devoted much of her time to the welfare of the local populace.

Another gentleman involved in the early proceedings of The Royal Yacht Club was Colonel Shedden, who built one of the finest marine residences facing the Solent at Spring Hill, on the east of the harbour, affording a truly magnificent view of yachting activities in the Solent. The building, which remains intact, is now occupied by nuns of the Convent of The Cross.

One of the colonel's descendants lived at Spring Hill in the Twenties with his family, namely Sir George Shedden, to be remembered as a most generous benefactor to the townsfolk. Midway through the decade he donated the whole of the shoreside of his estate to provide a half-mile extension to the somewhat limited esplanade as it then existed, thus permitting public access to Castle Point by road.

Stanhope Lodge, fronting the green in Queens Road, was the home of Lady Blanche and Lady Frances (Fanny) Stanhope[2] who graced the RYS with their presence in the Twenties.

A well respected local stalwart of the squadron, Lt. Col. Anthony Hickman Morgan, DSO, lived with his wife (also a member) at The Briary, west of Egypt Point, on the seafront. The ornate steam yacht *Boadicea* enjoyed their ownership and proudly occupied a convenient mooring west of Egypt Light during the Week.

The house known as Lower Holmwood at the foot of Egypt Hill was the homestead of the Percevals. Major Sir Philip Hunloke (sailing master of *Britannia*) was the son of Philip and Ernestine Perceval. Sir Philip Hunloke took the title when he was knighted in 1904, at the age of thirty-six. The house has since become a hotel cum restaurant.

Sir Philip Hunloke's twin sister, Kathleen Sophie Perceval, was an active member of the squadron. I well remember her when she appeared in the public eye, seated in a resplendent carriage with the 'cabby' up front and a top-hatted footman, complete with cockade, perched at the rear. In the early Twenties she resided at East Cowes in York Avenue, the house being named Yvery (after the family pedigree as the House of Yvery). She later built a home overlooking the Solent at Castle Road, West Cowes, still retaining the name Yvery. The building of the Osborne Court flats in the Thirties has since obscured an enviable view of the RYS starting line from the latter residence.

I recall the name of another distinguished resident of Queens Road, namely Admiral Sir Reginald de Horsey, whose father was connected with the original purchase of the squadron premises around the year 1855. Mr A.J. Hotham, coast guard officer for the island, was married to the admiral's daughter.

---

[1] Sir Godfrey Baring was Chairman of the Isle of Wight County Council from 1898 to 1949. He also chaired the Royal National Lifeboat Institution from 1923 to 1956.

[2] Ladies Blanche and Fanny Stanhope were prominent in racing the little 1 rater yacht *Mahatma* during the Solent Regattas of the 1890s.

PRELUDE TO THE WEEK

A typical Cowes Week, as I remember it, usually began at 4.00 p.m. on the preceding Friday, the moment when we were released from our studies for a whole month(!), after being lectured on the virtues of preserving the school image, with exhortations to behave during our holiday with the maximum of decorum for the honour of the school. And so with a short prayer and a couple of verses of the hymn 'Now the Day is Over', the assembly responded to the call of three cheers from our 'skipper, head master Mr Bertram Hallas.[1] We left the hall with a surge of excitement in anticipation of the fruits to be enjoyed on the days immediately following, as Cowes Week coincided with the first of our school holidays.

If the tide was favourable, the start of the holiday would inevitably be celebrated by my snatching my bathing costume and towel from the homestead to take a dip in the briny off the East Cowes shoreside, which provided an ideal vantage point for the Friday evening arrival of Their Majesties aboard the royal yacht *Victoria and Albert* some time around 6 p.m. The precise time varied from year to year, seemingly dependent upon the duration of entertainment provided for Their Majesties before leaving Portsmouth Harbour.

From Old Castle Point at the end of the esplanade, a splendid view of the approaching imperial squadron was enjoyed from the foreshore adjacent to Major Birkbeck's Norris Castle Boathouse. 'Pomp and Circumstance' was exemplified (sans musical accompaniment) with the stately 5,005 ton royal yacht *Victoria and Albert III*[2] (usually known as the *V & A* to the loyal local artisans) steaming majestically at some four or five knots, a vision of deepest blue and gold, with a grim and forbidding naval escort. The *V & A* was variously accompanied by a 30,000 ton battleship such as the *Barham, Rodney, Ramillies, Warspite, Royal Oak,* plus a destroyer and a minesweeper; the latter performing escort duty to the king's cutter *Britannia* on racing days, keeping a discreet distance astern, although the naval tender probably did more to assist her contemporaries from time to time, e.g. in the event of one of them typically becoming dismasted during Solent squalls, or possibly running aground.

After she had passed Castle Point, the *V & A* took a wide sweep to cruise through the Roadstead outside the numerous lines of yachts which had formed at their allocated mooring locations for the week. There were dozens of floating palaces, comprising steam and motor yachts, imposing schooners, and expensive sailing vessels of all types. The *V & A* dwarfed all of these as she proudly steamed westward beyond Egypt Point on the West Cowes Esplanade, to make a slow turn to come about past the RYS in an easterly direction. As the *V & A* eased by the guardship, the latter would then break the silence with a twenty-one gun salute which was repeated as a gesture of welcome for Their Majesties by the cannon of the RYS on behalf of Cowes and the other island subjects in general. The surrounding fleet of private yachts dipped their ensigns simultaneously. The salute was acknowledged by the *V & A* as she made the approach to her moorings with the admiralty flag, a golden anchor on a red ground, streaming from the foremast, the royal standard fluttering from the main, the Union Jack flying on the mizzen and the white ensign at the stern of the nautical treasure.

The ceremony continued with the hoisting of His Majesty's flag on his cutter *Britannia* to symbolise the admiral's authority over the Royal Yacht Squadron, whilst his racing yacht lay tethered to her mooring off the castle. Then followed a booming of another fifteen rounds from the squadron cannon as the admiral's salute.

It was usual for the commodore of the RYS to reach the *V & A* by pinnace at this juncture, conveying the yacht club's welcome to Their Majesties.

The proceedings were completed by the pealing of bells from the Holy Trinity church tower. With this majestic preliminary to Cowes Week fulfilled, the scene had been set for the appearance of The Big Five on the following Monday, sometimes to be joined by other sporting yachts which might offer a challenge. Big cutter racing on the Saturday preceding Cowes Week was normally the preserve of the Royal Southampton Yacht Club based at Calshot, on the western side of the Southampton Water estuary, although the RYS castle was the starting point for these races as a matter of convenience. For Cowes folk, the Week did not start until the following Monday simply because the local shipyards and other industries were not shut down until midday on the Saturday before the Week, although the dedicated 'shoreside yachtee' welcomed every opportunity to observe the giant cutters battling for supremacy.

Looking backward over some sixty years plus, Sunday was a day set distinctly apart from the rest. Whilst church attendance had declined to some degree since the Edwardian period, very little work was locally performed and neither was there a great deal of play on Sundays during the Twenties. This was the day when the chaplain of the RYS addressed both sinners and the faithful at the Holy Trinity church, adjacent to the castle. I remember the Rev. C.E. Paterson being appointed honorary chaplain in 1926, a vicar distinguished by a yachting cap worn with dog collar.

I vividly remember a most impressive sight which disturbed the Sunday observance code one bright and sunny morning when I was wandering along the beach at Cowes. I believe it was in 1928, when Captain Frogbrook delighted the crowds on the shore with a vision of the Hon. Ernest Guinness's auxiliary barque *Fantôme II* (ex-*Belem*) running through Roadstead with all canvas set. Normally the yacht cruised around under its diesel motors with the engine exhaust smoke issuing from the peak of the mizzen mast. This was my first sighting of a square rigger in full sail. Under a cloudless blue sky with just sufficient wind to fill the sails, the picture was quite a classic. The *Fantôme II* regularly appeared at Cowes each year and hence there could have been other occasions, but only once do I remember witnessing her fully canvased.

Through the kind offices of my dear maiden aunts, Bessie and Hilda, who lived at Shanklin, 'the nephew' was privileged to enjoy tea with the Frogbrook family at Sandown. The highlights included an introduction to Captain Frogbrook's parrot (a vicious character) and the inspection of a huge turtle shell which ornamented the lounge fireplace in the summer season. Photographs of the *Fantôme II* and its crew decorated the entrance hall.

I cannot remember any of the big cutters raising sails on Sundays for racing fixtures. Quite apart from religious considerations, the crews of the yachts were deserving of some relaxation from their labours. Their working days would normally commence at 5.30 a.m. when they either rolled hammocks or turned out of their cots to perform domestic routines and make preparations for sailing.

---

[1]   'Skipper' Hallas is remembered as a dignified gentleman of Yorkshire ancestry. He displayed that very rare quality of being both liked and respected at the same time.

There were a few occasions when his sense of humour was tinged with some light-hearted but never bitter sarcasm; always calculated to create amusement in the classroom.

The strictly unofficial title of 'Skipper' had no maritime connotation, although his vocational responsibilities otherwise extended to the control of a series of crews not unacquainted with perverseness.

He was a leading light in the local Brotherhood Movement which met in the East Cowes Town Hall on Sunday afternoons, and he also served on the local town council.

[2]   The 5005 ton twin screw royal steam yacht *Victoria and Albert III* was designed by Sir W.H. White, a one-time Director of Naval Construction, in 1889 (as a replacement for the earlier paddle steamer of 1855, bearing the title of *'V' & 'A' II*). She was 422 feet long, with a maximum beam of 50 feet and was fitted with triple expansion engines totalling 11,000 horse power, using coal-fired boilers.

The yacht was launched in the year 1901 by Admiral Meux and was manned by a naval crew throughout her service. Whilst she cruised south as far as Malta and northward to Reval, meeting the Tsar in pre-Revolutionary times, her usage was limited in the Twenties by King George V to visiting a few coastal regattas.

Her last recorded sailing was carrying King George VI and Queen Elizabeth, the current Queen Mother, to the Coronation Review in 1937.

[3] The Hon. Ernest Guinness's 611 ton (TM) yacht *Fantôme II* was built at Nantes in 1896 as a French trading barque named *Belem* in the yards of Dubigeon and was originally engaged on the South American nitrate service. She was purchased by the Duke of Westminster just prior to the First World War and converted to a luxury auxiliary yacht, when two large four cylinder diesel engines were installed.

This beautiful vessel cruised extensively in the Mediterranean and more widely, as far north as the Arctic Circle. *Fantôme II* was considered something of an extravagance, being most uneconomic in service and maintenance, but was handsomely matched by the fortunes of her owners.

COWES WEEK OF THE TWENTIES

During the Twenties Cowes Week was, especially for Cowes people, the greatest holiday event of the year, when the local artisans enjoyed a rest from their labours. No one ever considered leaving the island to take a holiday elsewhere at this time and, indeed, this was the one week when local industries closed down. For these people would have regarded it almost a duty to become a part of the shoreside scene; rigged in their best clothes, equipped with telescopes of diverse vintages, or binoculars which were family heirlooms left by seafaring ancestors. They held a conviction that this was the only show on earth worth watching and, maybe, they were close to the truth in this belief.

Whilst the regatta spectacle enjoyed royal and aristocratic patronage, with the wider support of the more successful captains of industry, as they were politely whispered, the population of Cowes, including the youthful members, expressing an interest, felt a genuine sense of involvement. This was particularly so during the days approaching the Week, as local excitement built up with expectations of what our society friends might provide for us. However, one could scarcely deny a latent desire, perhaps, to have been more closely associated with the action. Although the Weeks of this period were generally relaxed affairs, it must be said that a modicum of dignity was nevertheless in evidence.

Members of the Royal Yacht Squadron were the only people whose exclusive right it was to attend the proceedings of The Castle Club House and were frequently seen to arrive by steam pinnace or motor tender, from their cruising yachts moored in the Roadstead. The squadron landing jetty was but a few paces from the entrance to the Royal Yacht Squadron grounds, closely kept by a signalman, whose duty it was to vet the arrivals. Members could normally be distinguished by a

circular pale blue card badge suitably inscribed and worn on a
cord attached to the lapel of the navy blue serge jacket which
usually contrasted with their immaculate white flannel trousers.
It was generally acknowledged that squadron membership was a
male-dominated society, certain parts of the club being out of
bounds to the ladies.

When the weather was sufficiently fine (and on many
occasions in my recollection it was cruelly otherwise) members
would take tea on the lawn to the west of the castle and were
often provided with musical renderings by a military or marine
band from the sovereign's guardship.   The beautiful
wickerwork armchairs, with brilliant red cushions, made an
attractive outdoor furnishing feature, dotted against the slope of
the green velvet lawn, thus displaying a somewhat nostalgic
Victorian touch.   On the seaward side of the public walkway
was arranged a battery of twenty-two highly polished small
scale brass cannon,[1] located in an enclosure evenly pitched
around a gentle curve approximately following the castle wall
contour.   The racing signal flagstaff towered above the cannon,
just ahead of the starter's apartment in the castle.

It should not be forgotten that the Royal London Yacht
Club[2] exercised a great influence upon the activities of the big
class yachts as well as the Royal Yacht Squadron.   The Royal
London Cowes headquarters were sited a few yards distant
from the RYS along the parade, with their own starting cannon,
where they still occupy the lovely premises at the end of the
remains of a beautiful early Victorian terrace.   The flagstaff
carrying the club's exclusive burgee continues to tower over the
western end of the parade.   Using the RYS facilities, it was
usual for the Royal London Regatta to open the proceedings of
Cowes Week on the Monday.   The club accommodation is
much smaller and more compact than that of the RYS and does
not have the luxury of extensive garden accommodation.

During the 1920–1930 period, the Royal Yacht Squadron
was honoured to have His Majesty King George V as admiral; a

position which he had held since 1910, upon the death of his father, HM King Edward VII.

In 1920 the Duke of Leeds, RNVR, was elected commodore of the Royal Yacht Squadron, following the demise of Lord Ormonde in October 1919. Sir Richard Williams Bulkeley, Bart, KCB, RNR, stepped up to the position of commodore in 1927, having previously held office as vice-commodore since 1920.

In the early Twenties, the atmosphere was charged with a great deal of patriotic fervour, with the nation licking its wounds after the 1918 victory; Cowes was hosting HM King George V with Queen Mary, who was not enthusiastic about sailing but, nevertheless, added much to the festival. She was known to be taxied around the Island by the manager, Mr W. Caws, of the Fountain Garage, Cowes (owned by the Groves family) to meet her friends, the Oglanders of Nunwell House, Brading, Sir Godfrey and Lady Baring of Nubia House, Cowes, and Lord and Lady Mottistone of The Manor. Visits to Princess Beatrice at Carisbroke and to Osborne fitted into the itinerary, not forgetting those where she met the Earl and Countess Jellicoe at St Lawrence. Major General and the Hon. Mrs Seely of Brooke House were often honoured by Her Majesty's visits, in addition. Queen Mary occasionally sailed on *Britannia* but her time spent aboard the royal cutter was alleged to have been spent almost exclusively below deck.

Naval support from the guardships surrounding the royal yacht, moored in the Roadstead, with crews visiting the town, added a great deal to the regal tone for most of us who had spent much of our school lives studying the geography and virtues of empire. Our loyalties were stimulated by organised marching in the school playground carrying individual Union Jacks on Empire Day, May 24th, in successive years, struggling to walk in step to Elgar's *Pomp and Circumstance* and *King Edward VII Coronation Marches* howling from a wind-up gramophone perched at the top of the school entrance steps.

Later we became versed in the chanting of Sir Henry Newbolt's renowned verses, 'Vitai Lampada', but the recitation of Allan Cunningham's poem 'A Wet Sheet and a Flowing Sea', although inspired by the tall ships of historic memory, alternatively contrived to stimulate us to imagine topsailed cutters racing through the classroom! And so I quote:–

> A wet sheet and a flowing sea,
> A wind that follows fast,
> And fills the white and rustling sail,
> And bends the gallant mast;
> And bends the gallant mast, my boys,
> A while like an eagle free,
> Away the good ship flies and leaves
> Old England on the lee.

One's imagination extended without poetic continuity to visions of the island on the weather side!

It was not unusual for local folk to speak of visiting 'England' in contemplation of a visit to Portsmouth or Southampton, although an earlier reference commonly used by island dwellers to describe mainland folk as "overners" had fallen into disuse after 1918.

---

[1] In the year 1833, a miniature 50 ton toy frigate named *Royal Adelaide* was built for King William IV and his wife, Queen Adelaide. Its exclusive function was that of 'cruising' Virginia Water, on the shores of which the sectioned-off vessel was finally assembled.

This little royal yacht fell into disuse and was eventually dismantled in 1877. The small-scale artillery pieces have since served as signal cannons for the Royal Yacht Squadron.

[2] The Royal London Yacht Club grew from what was originally known as the Arundel Yacht Club, since members' boats were kept on the shores of the Thames at the bottom of Arundel Street, off the Strand. It was founded in the year 1838.

In 1845 the club became known as the London Yacht Club, and received recognition by Queen Adelaide, which authorised a further change of title, becoming the Royal London Yacht Club.

It was not until 1882 that Cowes hosted a branch HQ. The RLYC was amongst the first British clubs to adopt the YRA (Yacht Racing Association) rules in 1892, when the Duke of York was elected admiral.

REGATTA DAY

The Friday of Cowes Week was the final day of the regatta, when the first class yachts sailed to delight an enlarged multitude of spectators. The movements of the big cutters were not always easy to follow, as the Solent was strewn with yachts dressed with masses of bunting, presenting a panorama of nautical carnival. The scene was further interspersed with racing yachts of the second class dicing in the 35 to 100 TM. category, rigged inevitably as smaller gaffers, some bearing unforgettable names such as *Moonbeam IV, The Lady Anne, Sumurum, Norada, Mariquita, Corona, Dorina, Thanet* etc. At a long distance it was sometimes difficult to distinguish between the first and second class cutters where, for instance, the profile of the smaller *Moonbeam IV* with her topsailed rig bore a remarkable resemblance to that of *White Heather II* of the first class. In addition, the classes of twelve metres, eight metres, six metres, Solent One Designs, West Solent Restricted, Solent Sunbeams, Seaview Mermaids, Bembridge Redwings, Yarmouth One Designs, 'X' One Designs, fourteen foot National Dinghy competitors shared the waterway with the Lymington Scows, these being the smallest boats. Just to ensure that all of the locality was fully utilised, there were twelve man and coxswain rowing contests between naval cadets in whalers from Portsmouth and also races for oarsmen in lighter rowing gigs representing the local firms of Messrs J. Samuel White and Co., S.E. Saunders, Groves and Guttridge, Lallows Yard, Ratsey and Lapthorn etc.

I felt that the progress of smaller class events were easier to, follow always provided that a programme listing names and numbers was to hand, as the yachts were closer in shore for much of the time and, unlike the big handicap classes, they were usually more concentrated. Of course, first over the finishing line took the winning flag. However, the giant gaffers were the undoubted prime favourites.

There were many events arranged for individual participation, such as diving contests, offshore swimming races, surfboard riding behind fast motor launches as well as children's competitions on the green. The Cowes Town Band obliged with such soothing accompaniment as the *Overture to Poet and Peasant*, *Heart of Oak* and *Rule Britannia*, plus gems of Vivaldi and Mascagni, issuing from an early Victorian bandstand situated on the green.

The Friday atmosphere on shore built up into a crescendo towards the evening with a brilliant and extensive display of Pain's fireworks to round off the Week's events. The first rocket with an ear-shattering bang claimed the immediate attention of the huge crowds gathered on the west and east sides of the port at 9.30 p.m. People travelled from all parts of the island to be in at the grand finale, by buses, charabancs, or in private cars of diverse vintage, also on pony and traps, bicycles, tandems, tricycles, with others having hiked substantial distances. During the day the populace had further swollen with visitors from Southampton, Lymington and Portsmouth arriving at the Cowes pontoon by steam packet paddle boats. I remember there being a wide discrepancy in actual passage times claimed; for example, a billed crossing from Cowes to Southampton in sixty minutes, allowing twenty minutes from the Royal Pier at Southampton to the Western Docks Station for the Waterloo–London train, could by no means be guaranteed. If you were fortunate enough to find the paddle steamer *Princess Elizabeth* making the passage you might be reasonably sure of fulfilment of the timetable, unless your transport was dogged by a stiff nor'wester in combination with a foul ebbing tide in the eight mile stretch of Southampton Water. The *Princess Eleanor* was notoriously slow in crossing, as also was *Her Majesty*, but I think the slowest journey which I experienced was made on the twin-funnelled *Solent Queen*, taking ninety-five minutes during a Sunday afternoon! I counted an average of twenty-eight crankshaft revolutions to the minute in the rotation of her paddles.

For those whose journey from the Southampton Royal Pier to the West Railway Station was timewise imperilled, as a function of a normally extended sea crossing, a traveller's gambling instincts enjoyed a stimulus. The choice lay between boarding a bus of doubtful reliability with a random departure schedule, or hiring a horse-drawn cab.

The Regatta Day events on shore included such scarcely professional entertainments as climbing the greasy pole by an enthusiastic band of local clowns, the shared prize consisting of a leg of gammon strung to the top of the pole, which was erected on the beach by the green.

Another party would perform the Duck Hunt from a punt, giving a display of all manner of aquatic antics.

Punch and Judy[1] never failed to entertain les enfants as well as more senior observers. I shall never forget the sight of a legless great war veteran who regularly attended each year, taking a pitch on the esplanade west of the RYS.

It was with the greatest admiration combined with pity which prompted charitable contributions to his welfare by those whose fortunes in life had proven infinitely kinder. I believe that he was decorated with the Mons Star, together with a host of other decorations. The yearly attendance of this old soldier seemed somehow to radiate a message of hope and courage.

A little distant was the stand of the organ grinder, complete with pet monkey chained to the music box. The peace of the afternoon was shattered by an inevitable rendering of *It's a Long Way to Tipperary* being emitted from the portable instrument which competed with the brass on the squadron lawn, where members were soothed with excerpts of the *1812 Overture*. To suffer deafness in one ear might have been a distinct advantage in this situation.

A uniquely talented occupier of a pitch on the public walkway, seaward of Colonel Gretton's residence, was a prolific pavement artist whose favourite subjects, attracting much attention, included Osborne House, Carisbroke Castle, Godshill Church and views of Alum Bay, all extremely topical.

There were normally at least two very enterprising longshoremen offering trips in thirty foot open motor boats "'round the royal yacht and battleship" for the princely sum of one shilling from the public slipways between the Victoria Pier and the RYS landing. These motor launches were officially restricted from carrying over a given number of passengers but they were not required to wear life jackets. Whether or not the skippers were covered by insurance was never disclosed – one pinned one's faith under a mythical Board of Trade umbrella!

Lining the edge of the esplanade opposite the entrance to the Victoria Pier were the barrows of vendors selling carnival novelties such as hydrogen-filled balloons, paper hats and masks, not forgetting large bags of confetti. There was a small concert hall on the pier providing nonsense entertainment for sixpence. One typical musical rendering springs to mind:

> If I were the Royal Yacht Squadron
> I would, I would,
> I'd chuck those guns upon the beach and serve
> up teas at a tanner each,
> I would, I would...

The Victoria Pier was a favourite docking location, enjoying the patronage of evening trippers who braved the crossing from the mainland on one of the diminutive Portsmouth–Gosport Harbour ferries during summer evenings when the weather was favourable.

The Solent–Spithead Cruise was embellished by the facility of a bar serving copious jugs of Brickwoods beer, thus allowing unlimited scope for revellers intent upon a fluid orgy, the inevitable distractions at Cowes being catered for by local inns such as The Globe or The Union!

In the middle of the parade there was usually a huge set-piece of a complex firework pattern draped with tarpaulins to protect it from the elements, which invariably threatened the proceedings, but seldom caused any serious interference. I seem to remember only one occasion when the firework display was postponed and held on the Saturday evening following.

As with 'prom' concerts, the crowds loved to participate in firework displays. Just prior to the finale a series of rockets would be fired at appropriate intervals, each with a hearty bang. When a rocket reached its zenith, it would discharge a number of differing colours in ascending order, whilst the crowd, almost with one voice, chanted delightedly at maximum volume from one upwards to seven.

Some of the rockets were discharged from the esplanade and others from a barge in the river estuary, the latter emitting a dull thud produced by the recoil of the missile as it thumped the deck of the vessel.

The day's jollifications were concluded by the firing of the set-piece on the parade, shedding its light upon a sea of merrymakers, many of whom subsequently sought to slake their thirsts at the local inns if they were successful in elbowing a position close enough to a chosen bar.

It was always surprising when viewing the Solent on the following Saturday morning to find such a high proportion of yachts had disappeared overnight, some of these having moved on to the Royal Victoria Yacht Club events at Ryde, where the Big Five again became highlights of a few days in 'another week'.

---

[1] With reference to the popularity of Punch and Judy for numerous decades, an American summary can be commended:

'This Mr. Punch is altogether the strangest and least comprehensible hero who has ever trod the boards, and indeed, it is difficult to appreciate his claim to heroism.

'In addition to the fact that he is a criminal – which would not of itself disqualify him for belonging to the class, let us say, of Shakespeare's *Macbeth* – he is a coward, a braggart and a fool. He never says or does a witty thing and his chief activity is to knock other people on the head. The question may be asked, what has he got to have endeared himself to millions and which draws an indulgent smile from the stern-browed moralist? The answer is simply his most amazing success.

'Mr. Punch behaves exactly as he wishes in his tiny wooden world and the things he delights in doing are one and all atrocious, but he is never punished for them, except for an occasional knock on the head – and yet he emerges triumphant from every encounter. Out of nothing but tragic material he creates a roaring farce, thus putting the whole world in his debt.'

SOMETHING ABOUT WEST COWES

Convivial evenings were the norm for crews which celebrated race victories and they fraternised with ample bar accommodation at The Globe on the parade, The Union at the top of the watch house slipway, The George (which was opposite the 1914–18 War Memorial, only to be permanently removed by enemy action in 1943), The Three Crowns, The Fountain, The Pier Hotel, The Vectis Tavern, The Britannia Inn, The New Inn, The Anchor, The Painters' Arms, The Duke of York and The Falcon Bar along the main thoroughfare *en route* to the floating bridge connection with East Cowes, the site of The Bell Inn.

I was, of course, too young during the Twenties to sample the delights of supping ale in such establishments, but how I envied those seamen, not for their liquid capacities, but their entitlement to wear blue guernseys, generally with white or sometimes red lettering proudly announcing the names of sailing yachts to which they were appointed, e.g. *Terpsichore* RYS in white. Their wages averaged some £3 per week, with a bonus of £1 for a win, 10 shillings for a second and 5 shillings for third place. In addition to these earnings, a food allowance of 2 shillings 6 d was paid daily, plus two pints of beer (valued at 4 old pence a pint). A clothing allowance for uniform was normally made.

Some owners were, inevitably, more generous than others in facilitating opportunities for the ABs to acquire legitimate perquisites. Human nature obviously motivated crews to augment a modest living by taking advantage of any such bonuses of their profession. Whereas the term "perks" was commonly used by landlubbers, the vocabulary of seamen substituted a reference to "stet"[1] in comparisons of fortune.

The big cutters usually carried two masthead men, plus a bowsprit man and one responsible for the yacht's gig (or cutter).

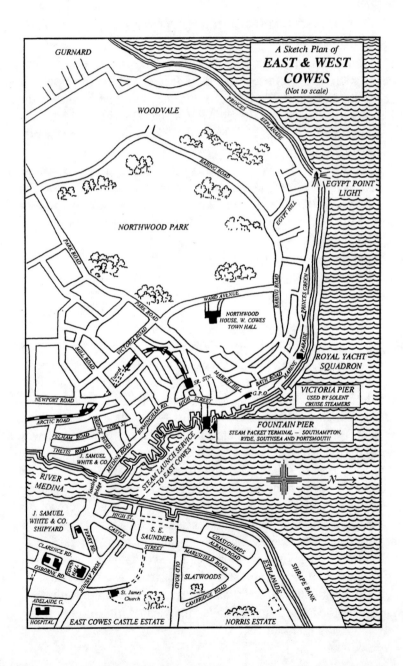

A Sketch Plan of
EAST & WEST COWES
(Not to scale)

These four each enjoyed the increased remuneration of one shilling per day above that of the able seamen (ABs) as compensation for greater responsibility.

West Cowes was remarkably well endowed with shops offering services and wares of the highest standards, alongside those which competed to meet the needs of townsfolk of more modest means. It may be of interest to recall the names of leading grocery and provision merchants whose businesses were conveniently situated along the narrow High Street, within easy reach of public slipways, providing temporary berths for yacht tenders. These stores were granted a special licence during Cowes Week, enabling them to supply bottled alcoholic beverages outside normally permitted hours. The two largest were Dear & Morgan at the Sun Hill intersection and Brown's Stores at the eastern end of the High Street. Both of these establishments were luxuriously scented with oriental spices, bulk teas blended on the premises, freshly ground coffee, dried fruits tempered with the aroma of smoked bacon; all literally reeking with quality. Hewitt's Stores and Shergold's were also grocers of repute, occupying a much smaller floor space.

Other competitors for the grocery trade included Lipton's, World Stores and The Maypole. Next door to the last-named was a very competitive fishermen's outfitter by the name of Whitcher, who dealt in fishing nets, rods and deep sea tackle, complemented by clothing stocks of somewhat coarse texture to withstand the rigours of the trade.

Island-grown vegetable produce, in combination with numerous varieties of unblemished bouquets of flowers, were obtainable from Miss Hatch's greengrocery store situated at the head of Watch House Lane. At the lower end of this lane, local pilots and customs officers were accommodated and these were establishments were recognisable by the aroma from their inhabitants' coronas. Marshall's greengrocery store (near The Pier View Hotel) suffered the disadvantage of tidal invasions, as the floor was two steps below street level, requiring the service of pumps at spring tide. Near the junction of Denmark

Road with the High Street was situated yet another top quality greengrocery, owned by the Randall family, where fresh cream was also sold.

There was no lack of choice in butchers' shops, with Abram's at the top of Shooters Hill, Cole's, Slade's and Prangnell's in the High Street, the last-named being famed for pork butchery, including the most delicious brawn, cooked pigs' trotters and chitterlings.

Paskins & Sons were the fishmongers of distinction, having their own oyster beds at Newtown River in the West Wight and a mini trawler to fish the Solent at nights for the following day's business. A less pretentious service was provided by Corke's of Medina Road on a more modest scale, but, nevertheless, their enterprise extended to evening peddling of such delicacies as freshly caught Sandown Bay herring and sprats in season. Their delivery facilities consisted of a handcart with scales on board, business after dark being conducted by the light of an oil lamp, aided by vocal entreaty to alert potential customers.

The world-renowned ship chandlery and ironmongery business managed by the Pascall Atkey family stood opposite The Fountain Hotel (where they both remain) conveniently close to the town quay for the sailing fraternity. Other ironmongery emporia included Timothy White's and Taylors, and Fearon & Son, which specialised in high-class tools for most trades, not forgetting Paddy Dean's (he was practically stone deaf) midget ironmongery, a classic *multum in parvo*. Never was there so much stock displayed in so small an area!

Morgans were the tailors of distinction, patronised by yacht owners and others with local society pretensions in yearning to achieve recognition of credit worthiness. Woodyear's, which traded in female apparel of matching quality, offered a companion service for ladies of good taste, many of whom visited West Cowes all the year round, the shop being within a few yards of the "Siwepaco" pontoon (i.e. Southampton and Isle of Wight, South of England, Royal Mail Steam Packet

Company, Ltd.) now occupied by Red Funnel. For those rather less well endowed with life's bonuses, Compton's Clothing Hall in Birmingham Road provided a surprising range of boys' and men's outfits. An excellent made-to-measure tailoring service was offered by Jim Warne who had crafted costumes and suits for a more fastidious clientele in competition with the Russell family, whose renowned little sewing business operated from less conspicuous premises, in the front room of their dwelling, at the western end of Medina Road. The main ladies' gown shop, known as F.J. Phillips's, was a star attraction for the housewives of local artisans. The Singer Sewing Machine depot was situated on the side opposite to Phillips's Beckford Road display windows. The local Salvation Army band and choir occupied a pitch on the pavement outside F.J. Phillips on Friday evenings, with a repertoire largely consisting of 'Moody and Sankey' vintage. The Angels subsequently followed with a visit to the local inns, peddling *The War Cry*.

Another ladies' outfitters of moderate status was Hillyer's Stores, situated in the middle of the High Street, with a toy department on the first floor. The town's classic toy shop, by the name of Caws, was situated behind the Westminster Bank. Stock included such desirable acquisitions as model yachts, toy forts, lead soldiers, clockwork and wooden trains, stationary steam engines, magic lanterns etc.

Boots and shoes of top quality were sold by Mr Gladstone Jolliffe in Shooter's Hill. I have happy memories of his associations with our youth club, when he contributed accompaniments on his cornet to swell the praises of Sunday afternoon meetings, whilst we sang in choral unison *Will your Anchor Hold in the Storms of Life?* Other footwear specialists were Lee's in Bath Road, Stead & Simpson, Olivers and Wearwell, not forgetting the Government Surplus Stores (opposite The Royalty Cinema) where the less delicate army boots and clogs were dangling, undeterred by the elements, outside the premises. A range of items from hurricane lamps to pith helmets was housed inside!

The chemists, Beken & Son,[2] proudly displayed a 'By Appointment' royal insignia, part of the shop being allocated to the extremely successful marine photographic interest. Their premises in Birmingham Road backed on to the harbour where Frank Beken kept his 'camera pursuivant motor launch', named *Rosabelle*. Bostock's, the chemists, were sited in the High Street at the opposite end of the shopping centre. The owner followed the spiritualist rituals of Sir Arthur Conan Doyle.

There was yet another chemist shop, somewhat dilapidated, with a unique window display. Here were two huge ornate jars tapering towards their tops containing vividly coloured fluids, surrounded by faded packages of patent medicines, complemented by examples of Mr Cole's achievements in taxidermy to capture freaks of nature, such as animals with two heads! This gentleman was reputed to have had considerable prowess in bygone years in the extraction of teeth without the refinement of an anaesthetic for the modest sum of one shilling per tooth.

There were at least two marine photographers[3] other than Beken which spring to mind, namely Debenham's and Kirk's, which were honoured to receive instructions in taking pictures of the royal visitors in addition to practising their outstanding skills in yacht photography.

First-class furnishings for yachts and homes were supplied by Wadham & Son at the top end of the High Street. Silverman's and Wyatt's, both of Shooters Hill, catered for the supply of family quality furniture, the latter including mangles, perambulators and linoleum. For real bargains in second- to twentieth-hand furniture, Charlie Paul's was a must, the Assembly Rooms being sited well below street level and backing on to the harbour opposite the Methodist chapel in Birmingham Road. An auction was regularly held there, the dates being announced slightly in advance by the town crier, who would systematically perform his duties, street by street, in both West and East Cowes. I seem to remember that pianos changed hands from fifteen shillings upwards. The auctioneer's commission must have left the vendor with a very modest gain in such instances! Charlie Paul's was treated largely as a place of entertainment by the locals, or more specifically as a 'kaleidoscope museum'.

The brothers Charlie and Bill had pretensions to the musical arts, the former claiming a modicum of tuition in pianoforte renderings and the latter "delighting" visitors to the premises with a variety of tunes played by ear, on one or other of the off-key sale bargains.

For anyone rather more seriously showing an interest in music, patronising a barber, Mr (Shiner) Moon, combined a dual service with shearing and shaving by providing pianoforte solos interpreted from the works of J.S. Bach. On Sundays he performed at the organ of the Holy Trinity church in Queens Road.

Westbourne, a beautifully proportioned eighteenth-century house which occupied a waterside site (and still does) in Birmingham Road, was once the home of Captain William Arnold, who was the Collector of Customs for the Isle of Wight during the years 1777–1795, before he took up residence at Slatwoods Estate in East Cowes. The house at West Cowes has since been regarded as something of a memorial to his intellectual offspring, Dr Thomas Arnold, who was appointed head master of Rugby School in 1827. A permanent circular plaque recording this distinction was displayed on the front wall of the building.

Benzies, trading under the pennant of The Yachtsman's Jeweller, were substantially stocked with yacht racing trophies and specialised in an ingenious array of beautifully fashioned gold and silver accessories, vividly adorned with exquisitely enamelled flags. Alternative sources for the acquisition of jewellery were Hurst's and Tom Taylor's, whose trade was perhaps targeted to provide the extravagances and needs of local residents, the latter shop specialising in a wide variety of timepieces.

In the shop windows of J.C. Airs, situated in mid-High Street, was an imposing display of exotic cigars favoured by the upper ranks of the yacht club patrons. In addition, every conceivable geometric variation of tobacco pipe, from long stemmed clay to the finest briar, swelled the array, in company with Virginian, Turkish, Russian and Egyptian cigarettes. Tobacco from a huge selection behind the counter might be blended and weighed for the connoisseur. Rugg's at the bottom of Shooters Hill were in competition, with a very much reduced range of smoking requisites.

To the best of my recollection there were three banks serving the High Street patrons: Westminster Bank, Midland Bank and Lloyds Bank, where they remain. (Westminster has now joined with the National Provincial, of course.)

Marvins Yacht Agency had a wonderful display in its windows, situated at the bottom of Bars Hill, of pictures of vintage craft, some of which might have been rusted and ripe planked hulks to judge by the state of their photographs!

Another branch of the Marvin family specialised in yacht furniture in some rather outwardly dull premises in Medina Road.

Ice cream of a distinctive flavour could be purchased from Donato's Sweet Shop in the High Street next door to Marshalls. An extension to the business was operated from a kiosk along the green, where steaming hot cups of tea were also dispensed, usually to the accompaniment of buzzing from a myriad of aggressive wasps!

In the late Twenties ice-lined box tricycles under the UNIC ice cream label were pedalled around by youths beneath the slogan 'Stop me and buy one'.

The green was patrolled at regular intervals by a familiar and dedicated old gentleman named Patey, who continued his duties long past retirement. He carried a walking stick with a nail protruding from the bottom end, which was used to stab and pick up items of litter dropped on the grass by untidy holidaymakers.

The major hotels housing visitors for the Week consisted of The Gloucester on the esplanade, adjoining the Royal London Yacht Club, The Marine Hotel, where my cousin, Alan Ross,[4] and his charming wife May used to spend the Week, The Globe Hotel, also on the parade, where in a misspent youth I later trifled with the art of billiards, and The Fountain Hotel adjacent to the pontoon, which was popular with travellers to and from the mainland, and enjoyed the dual advantage of close proximity to the former Cowes Railway Terminal. There were many larger private houses along the seafront made available for entertaining parties of privileged guests, and boarding establishments in the upper regions of the town, together with a number of enterprising smaller homes offering accommodation at 'peppercorn' rates for the impecunious sightseer.

The whole of the shopping area and esplanade was festooned with mixtures of every conceivable design of flag, e.g. national flags of friendly powers, imperial flags, international code signals, yacht and yacht club burgees hanging from the first floors of buildings and criss-crossing the streets. This extravaganza of decoration was enjoyed for some ten days, to quite suddenly be lowered and only be re-hoisted at twelve monthly intervals.

Afternoon teas closest to the action were served at Rush's Cafe near The Marine Hotel, on the parade. Other locations offering tea and cakes were the bakers' shops of Teddy Baker, Weeks and Leftwich's through the High Street.

The Gloster Restaurant (not to be confused with The Gloucester Hotel), offering sustenance of first quality, was situated opposite the former George Hotel, at the bottom of Market Hill.

The local newsboys occupied a pitch at the eastern end of the esplanade, usually bawling themselves hoarse to attract the curiosity of passersby who might be prepared to part with one or two coppers in order to be regaled with the drama of a yachting mishap. A special version by *The Daily Telegraph*'s yachting correspondent was assured by the evidence of a nearby lurid poster.

The town was well provided with bookshops/newsagents, with W.H. Smith & Son inevitably pitched at the Cowes Railway Station terminal, the Misses Rowes in Birmingham Road, Chiverton's on Shooter's Hill and Neale's, which combined a small printing works, just off Bath Road.

Holmes's Garage, below The Duke of York Inn, had an agency for Rover cars and also incorporated a bicycle shop in Mill Hill, as well as a franchise for that wonderful series of model products created by the genius of Frank Hornby.

Another small garage of high repute was that of Clark & Blatchford on Market Hill, largely engaged in servicing a heterogeneous collection of tradesmen's vehicles and belt - driven motor cycles, not forgetting the maintenance of a plethora of post office and trade pedal cycles.

Attrills of Birmingham Road occupied a purpose-built shop in a prime position, catering for the supply of bikes and trikes ranging from tandems to steeds of junior proportion.

It seemed to be the norm in those days, before general acceptance of arresting tooth decay, for the local people to visit a dentist only for an extraction when nature signalled dire toothache. In this connection, the practices of Mr Mountain at the bottom of Bars Hill and Mr Lowein, near Bekens in Birmingham Road, were favoured, under duress of course. The latter displayed a prominent sign inviting customers to 'Please Walk In'. The inevitable query arose from an elderly relative, "Does he really think that people would want to run in there?"

The Alexandra Hall[5] in Birmingham Road (now converted to dwellings) was used for local charity dances and events such as the Annual Lifeboat Ball and church bazaars. I remember attending three plays presented at the hall by the Cowes Operatic and Dramatic Society during my school days, one being *Miss Hook of Holland* and another *The Only Way*, based upon Dickens's *A Tale of Two Cities*; a third being Gilbert & Sullivan's *H.M.S. Pinafore.*

There was one activity which steadily gripped the local populace in the decade of the Twenties, more particularly when the yachts and boats were safely berthed during the winter and that was, in common with the rest of the nation, listening to wireless broadcasting. Some emphasis was undoubtedly contributed by the regular appearance of Signor Guglielmo Marconi's magnificent yacht *Elettra* in Cowes Roads during the Week, with its red, white and green bunting. An early successful wireless communication was accomplished between the island and the mainland by Marconi before the First World War. In almost every household DIY crystal receivers were experimented with and Dominey's, at the eastern end of the High Street, did much to boost interest by supplying components and receivers of progressively advancing sophistication. The ability to tune in to '2.L.O.' was enjoyed by the owners of the big steam yachts, which were rigged with the then fashionable twin aerials, reaching fore and aft. These might have served as status symbols initially but would have been a trifling indulgence compared with the owners' alternative extravagances. Another competitor by the name of Sherrat later appeared, opening premises close to Morgan's, the marine outfitters in the High Street.

All these enterprises were interlinked to weave a pattern of continuing services which, either directly or indirectly, reflected the status of Cowes as a yachtsman's mecca from the last century. For those who came to Cowes to enjoy the relative safety of sailing in Solent waters or merely to subscribe to the social scene, the cream of yacht clubs was to be found and the talents of the local populace were unsurpassed in the techniques of building and maintenance of yachts in all categories.

Cowes was not exactly well endowed with art shops, probably on account of the fascination implicit in the study of marine photographic presentations. However, some fine pictures together with artists' materials were offered by Warne's of Shooters Hill. There was also another studio opposite the Midland Bank which seemed to specialise in dramatic scenes depicting stormy seas, including sailing ships in the agony of perishing; all masterpieces luxuriously executed in oils of the deepest shades. I regretfully admit an inability to identify with such heart-rending samples of art in my tender years, but I learned to appreciate that sailing in waters outside the Solent was not all beer and rum. The anger of the deep was duly impressed upon me some years later, when I was travelling steerage over the propeller shafts of an ancient packet steamer crossing the Irish Sea during an October gale.

---

[1]   From the Latin STET: let it stand.

[2]   Frank Beken, who had inherited the well-established chemist business from his father, enjoyed the patronage of a broad spectrum of local society. He was tall and distinguished in appearance with a confident, if subdued tone of voice, and prescribed patent remedies for a wide range of ailments, being readily trusted by sufferers who preferred to patronise him rather than visit a doctor's surgery. His reputation was deservedly unsurpassed.

[3]   The title 'photographer' bore a much too sophisticated sound for the tongues of many yacht hands, who cheerfully referred to such members of society as "fotoggers".

[4]   Alan's father, uncle Jim, managing director of a London manufacturing chemical business, was a member of the Royal London Yacht Club, which he regularly attended during the Week at Cowes.
I must confess the absence of any recollection of his local sporting activity, but Cowes Regatta was, of course, equally a social event. To the best of my knowledge his sailing yacht never ventured far from its mud-bound port of registration at Southend-on-Sea.

[5]   Alexandra Hall, with its pleasing stone facade, was built in the last century as a Wesleyan Methodist chapel. It was subsequently forsaken, to be replaced by a red brick edifice of dubious taste on the opposite side of Birmingham Road.
In the year 1901, the building became the site of a virtual bridgehead for the invasion of a Thames-side boat-building entrepreneur, Mr Samuel Edgar Saunders, who specialised in river launches at Goring. He sought to expand

his activities to include saltwater craft, powered by internal combustion engines, which were at that time steadily improving in reliability, and to replace steam pinnaces as yacht tenders for a growing market. Whilst some of the early Saunders products employed steam prime movers, the business rapidly expanded to meet a demand for the convenience and economy of the motorboat. From this modest foothold 'Sammy' Saunders, assisted by a wealth of local boat-building and engineering expertise, subsequently created one of the major British aircraft design and manufacturing concerns in parallel with a thriving motor yacht yard, with its main offices on the eastern banks of the Medina River.

TENANTS OF THE PORT AND THE RIVER

Between the eastern end of the West Cowes Parade and the floating bridge western disembarkation point was a miscellaneous series of waterside business premises lining the harbour, with the customs watch house in a commanding position and the island sailing club buildings next door. Other waterfront activities were those of the GPO and Ratsey & Lapthorn, the world-renowned specialists in yacht sails. Tom Ratsey and his son Chris were familiar Solent figures who sailed the green-hulled cutter *Dolly Vardon*, which was of typical nineteenth-century design, equipped with immaculately cut tan sails. She was built by J. Samuel White & Co., at Cowes in 1872. *Dolly Vardon* was occasionally seen to be sporting white canvas. Earlier activities, long since discontinued, included a very successful yacht-building business in the last century.[1]

The yacht construction branch of the Ratsey enterprise competed in the late Victorian era with other distinguished little Cowes yards, such as C. Hanson & Sons and that of Charlie Sibbick, whose legendary skills attracted the patronage of Prince Edward of Wales in the building of his most successful Gunter-rigged 1 rater, named *White Rose*. (This pretty example of the class was claimed to have evolved from drawing board to building, painting and rigging in the short span of a mere eight days!) Lallow's Yard built yachts of superb quality for the smaller classes, on a site which was and is entered from Medina Road. William White & Sons specialised in brass and gunmetal castings, finished to perfection, for all manner of yacht fittings. As a supplement to their main business on the other side of the river, Groves & Guttridge provided a repair and maintenance service for smaller yachts. Albert Guttridge divided the time between his business interests and those of the county council, of which he was a greatly respected member. The penetrating smell of dope (cellulose) pervaded the atmosphere for the greater length of the waterside premises of S.E. Saunders in Medina Road, where metal flying boats were built and launched from the slipways. The Twenties heralded the introduction of light alloy stressed skin construction for aircraft, the science of which had been established for yachts in the last century with alternative materials.[2]

Wharves operated by Shephard Bros. for the docking of their barges shared a prime position of the harbour installations. The island builders merchants, Hooper & Ashby, shared a quayside warehouse.

Medina Road boasted a third-rate cinema by the name of Poole's Picture Palace, where local urchins paid one penny for the privilege of watching the show with necks craned whilst seated on the floor at the front of the theatre!

A specialist marine painting service was operated by Edward Watts & Sons with stores situated at the junction of Medina and Bridge Roads, whilst mobile teams carried out their artistic assignments either shipboard or from dock environments, sometimes varnishing cabins and furnishings, otherwise treating keels with copper or mercurial oxide paints to express the maximum loathing of barnacles and weed.

Ropes of the highest marine quality were produced by Henry Bannister & Sons in the ropewalk entered from Mill Hill Road.

Rowe's of Mill Hill Road manufactured a wide range of hardwood and metal pulley blocks, which were finished to perfection and supplied worldwide for vessels of all types.

The principal activities of the largest employers in Cowes, notably J. Samuel White & Co. Ltd., were sited immediately upstream of the floating bridge crossing the river. The company was founded in 1857 by John Samuel,[3] although the site was originally developed by Thomas White, who moved from Broadstairs in Kent to establish a ship repair business immediately following the defeat of Napoleon at Waterloo in 1815. The engine works on the west bank were set behind an extensive quayside, whose chief landmark was and is in the form of a gigantic eighty ton hammerhead crane. Family history records that my grandfather, Ned Sibbick, who was a master builder, had the contract in 1911 to provide the foundations for this crane and to rebuild the dockside where dry dock facilities once existed. The shipyard on the opposite bank of the river accommodated the stocks for the simultaneous building of four 320 ft destroyers, with a number of small vessels, in the 1914–18 conflict, and also a covered facility where submarines could be constructed.

With the cessation of hostilities on the high seas, a drastic reduction in the output of British naval vessels was signalled, which inevitably meant the refocusing of outlook to generate alternative business activities for the survival and progress of J. Samuel White & Co. As the firm no longer enjoyed the luxury of John Samuel's helmsmanship, it passed into public ownership, appointing two very able overseers who succeeded in widening the scope of the organisation through the Twenties. Mr Frank Shearman headed the restructured company as chairman, assisted by Peter Ewing CBE[4] in the office of managing director, a post he held until 1932.

Of naval contracts, I recall the building of HMS *Wolverine* and HMS *Worcester*, both destroyers for the British Admiralty. In addition, three destroyers, *La Rioja, Mendoza* and *Tucuman* were completed for the Argentine navy and the modernisation of four Greek naval vessels named *Ierax, Aetos, Panther and Leon* was undertaken, utilising White's basic techniques.

A miscellany of civil marine activity embraced a number of coastal cargo vessels in the order of 2,000 tons, such as the colliers *Argonne*[5] and *Auvergne* for French coastal service, an oil-fired paddle steamer, *Crested Eagle*, built for the General Steam Navigation Co., operating from London Bridge, a little paddler, *Freshwater*, for the Southern Railway's Solent Services, motor yachts *Noneta* and *Taifun,* the motor vessel *Sea Belle II*, ordered by the crown agents for duties in the Malay states, the Woolwich ferries *Gordon, Squires, Will Crookes* and *John Benn*, the laying of keels for two Adriatic coastal passenger ships, *Rab* and *Bakar*. I well remember the launching of yachts built for Mr F. Morton Singer (a wealthy American): his *Xarifa* in 1927 and a second, larger, *Xarifa* in 1929. The diesel-engined yacht *Braemar* was launched in 1929 for Mr George Paxton. Chain ferries for the Cowes and Swanage river crossings provided examples of diversity. Dozens of lifeboats and small motor launches were constructed for civil and defence usage. (The wartime seaplane design and manufacturing facility was discontinued shortly after the cessation of hostilities.)

These memories are by no means claimed as a comprehensive summary of the yard's output during the period, but are recalled as typical enterprises of the decade.

Amongst the earliest recollections of my childhood was that of attending a peace festival with my parents in the spring of 1919, held in the Aviation Department of J.S. White's, this facility later being used exclusively for the construction of lifeboats for the Royal Naval Lifeboat Institution. At that time my mother supported the local choral society, the members of which appeared uniformly dressed in dazzling white gowns, ornamented with red, white and blue ribbon sashes worn diagonally.

Whilst the rendering of Elgar's *Land of Hope and Glory* echoed in the hangar, my father, sensing my infant inability to identify with such rejoicings, sought to provide a distraction by hoisting me into the pilot's cockpit of what was probably a Short Bros. type 184 string-bag float-plane parked on the slipway outside. In truth, I was much too young at that moment to fully appreciate the gesture, but it left a lingering chord in my memory. As we returned, the choir was heartily indulging itself in a burst of patriotic fervour with *The Soldier's Chorus* from *Faust*, suitably substituting the word "Motherland" for that of "Fatherland". At least I enjoyed an early, if somewhat odd, impression of the interior of a place where "things were typically made" to join the sea. Alas, this world-renowned organisation, which so successfully competed with the Scottish, northern and Ulster shipyards for many years, finally lost its identity in 1972, the last ship delivery being effected in 1965.

Whilst relating some of the business activities on the banks of the Medina, a rather extraordinary, if not bizarre, operation comes to mind, associated with the years 1926 or 1927. A certain very enterprising gentleman acquired the use of a slipway situated on the west bank southwards of J. Samuel White & Co.'s premises, although obviously not associated, the purpose of which was to break up old steamships in order to deal in scrap metal. It happened that his enterprise was based upon a free supply of suitable vessels which were obtained from the harbours of Dieppe, Le Havre and Cherbourg. A skipper with a skeleton crew, including engineers and stokers, would cross over to these ports armed with fictitious papers, wasting no time in coaling and raising steam, in order to limp across the channel for a final resting place at Cowes, where the vessels were dismantled. A number of local men enjoyed employment with this concern for a while, quite unaware of the illegality of their labours, until one or two of the staff found to their cost that the greed of their employer had extended to the printing of counterfeit bank notes as a gesture of remuneration. The entrepreneur paid a protracted visit to Parkhurst as a holiday for his ingenuity!

On the west bank further upstream, Marvin's Yacht Yard prospered in servicing yachts owned by many well-heeled clients. George Marvin was the owner of a smart little steam yacht named *Undine* which was occasionally seen to be cruising the Solent and visiting its harbours. My wife's grandfather, Walt Wakeley, exhibited an extraordinary skill in the layout and construction of yacht furnishings, tailored and finished to perfection for the most fastidious clients of Marvin's. Yacht furniture was practically all hand-crafted and built in place. Owners more liberally endowed with the necessary funds would often have all the furnishings ripped out and replaced to satisfy a whim, or as a matter of rival ostentatious display. Lord Tredegar's (and later Lady Fanny Houston's) magnificent steam yacht *Liberty*[6] was frequently berthed there. The chief engineer, Will Johns, was married to my Aunt Alice. My uncle, Albert Sibbick, performed an equally responsible engineering service to Lord Inverclyde of Castle Wemyss on his diesel-engined yacht *Beryl*, which sometimes wintered at Cannes in the Mediterranean. Its owner was at one time the Commodore of the Royal Clyde Yacht Club.

Other examples of the most imposing cruising yachts seen around the Solent, haunting Medina dockyards, were the SY *Alacrity*[7] and SY *Sapphire* owned by Lt. Comm. Montague Graham–White.

A long coaling jetty with tidal access lying parallel to the river bank accommodated colliers and barges to discharge 'black diamonds' for domestic heating into the awaiting trucks, which were shunted into a branch line of the Southern Railway Company (user of anthracite – Welsh steam coal). The quayside grab bucket could handle in excess of 100,000 tons of steam and domestic fuel annually. Supplementary supplies of household coal arrived by sailing barges at various wharves, to be winched by hand from the holds in huge wicker baskets which were laden by the shovels of brawny local gangers, their corduroys secured below the knees and suspended with the aid of four inch wide leather belts!

The principal riverside works of S.E. Saunders (incidentally, before he joined forces with Sir Alliot–Verdon Roe in 1929 to become Saunders–Roe Ltd.) were on a prime site to the east side of the harbour between the esplanade and the present Red Funnel terminal.

This site was formerly occupied by The Medina Hotel and the waterside residence named Seaholme. The business was mainly concerned with flying boats, whilst small land planes were built on the premises by an offshoot company known as Spartan Aircraft Ltd., during the Twenties. 'Sammy' Saunders lived in a beautiful old house named Padmore high above the river level near to Whippingham church. The house has since become a restaurant.

Smaller riverside premises on the east bank were tenanted by Miss Marion B. Carstairs, a millionairess indulging her fancy in fast motor boats with such names as *Estelle* and *Newg* (the reversed name of her actress friend, Gwen Farrar). *Estelle* was raced against the *Gee Whiz*, owned by the American commodore, Gar Wood.

The East Cowes Sailing Club was enthusiastically organised and conducted by those of modest means, seeking sport with a heterogeneous collection of mainly open sailing dinghies, most of which used either dipping lug or gunter rig. The inevitable gas works were situated next door, the other side of which the little boatyard of Groves & Guttridge built life boats for the RNLI and small motor yachts. The flying boat specialists, S.E. Saunders Ltd. built motor boats at their Cornubia Yard further upstream. The genius of Sammy Saunders manifested itself in the construction of the record-breaking motor craft *Miss England II*, averaging 98 m.p.h. over the timed distance. Unhappily, its pilot, Sir Henry Seagrave, subsequently lost his life at the wheel, reaching a peak speed approaching 120 m.p.h. at the instant of fatality.

Before the turn of the century, my grandfather and grandmother lived with their family in a house bordering the Medina River, mooring boats at the bottom of the garden. I used to be regaled with stories of grandpa's exploits in wild fowling to supplement the larder, when he would cast off in a dinghy, before morning light, with his muzzle-loading guns.

A delightful, little olde world boatyard with premises of eighteenth-century slatted wooden construction, set in a copse fringing the Medina, was operated by George Suter and his family. My Aunt Rose was one of his heirs. Small dinghies were built there and much of the business was based upon yacht maintenance. It was here that I gleaned the rudiments of small boat construction, becoming acquainted with the relative techniques of 'clinker' and 'carvel' construction for dinghies, which were lofted on the floor of a draughty shed, internally bordered by wood shavings, emitting delightful aromas heightened by the blending of yacht varnish.

Outside the building the Medina River waters might be heard on a still day gently lapping at a rather unstable staging which reached out across the mud to an extreme low tide mark. Sometimes a brazier fuelled by coke would be alight on the shingle by the entry to the boat shed where a cauldron of bubbling pitch was being rendered sufficiently fluid to achieve the watertightness of a leaky veteran dinghy. The quaint little boatyard was equipped with a covered slipway, at the head of which stood a heavy, rusting old winch where two brawny men occasionally operated the crank handles, turning a pinion meshing with a big spur wheel to the accompaniment of a ratchet, which hiccoughed and clanked in sympathy.

A visit by the Luftwaffe in 1944 extinguished this charming old established enterprise.

Naval cadets from Osborne College[8] used a site named Kingston, where rowing skiffs were kept until the seat of instruction was moved elsewhere; the location later providing the amenity of a conventional electric power station. The kingfishers no longer nest there.

For a schoolboy with his heart inevitably sharing in all these activities, the locality was something akin to an Aladdin's cave during the Twenties; somehow the local atmosphere has since become much more streamlined and perhaps less fascinating, with changes accelerated by the events of 1939–45, plus the effects of a revolutionary economic climate.

---

[1] During the early 1870s, the Ratsey Yacht Yard was in its prime when two beautiful clipper-bowed schooners (built for Mr James Ashbury), firstly the *Cambria* and secondly the *Livonia*, each sailed the Atlantic, making separate, but unsuccessful bids for the Americas Cup.

[2] As a matter of historic technological interest, the use of light aluminium alloy was adopted for the topsides of Sir Thomas Lipton's first challenger *Shamrock I* for the Americas Cup, sailing against *Colombia* in the year 1899. The bottom skins were formed from manganese bronze riveted over steel

frames and stringers. The prospective onset of early corrosion problems seems to have been disregarded, bearing in mind the substantial differential in electrolytic potential employing a combination of such skin materials in contact with saltwater! In fact, this erstwhile challenger made a second visit to the USA as a trial horse for *Shamrock III*, tuning up for Lipton's third Cup bid in 1903.

[3] The legendary John Samuel White crossed the bar in 1915.

[4] Peter Dewar Ewing, CBE, was a member of the Royal London Yacht Club.

[5] A most imposing and very detailed scale model of *Argonne*, some five feet long, sheltered by a glass case to protect it from cigar fumes, was on display for many years in the J.S.W. board room of the Medina Road offices. Its pristine aspect, with a light grey hull and pink enamel below the waterline, defied that of its ultimate full-scale parent, whose inevitable grimy fate was to become blemished with coal dust!

[6] *Liberty* was one of the most elegant of the British-built steam yachts, designed by G.L. Watson and launched from the yards of Ramage and Ferguson of Leith in the year 1908. She was constructed for an American newspaper magnate, Mr Joe Pulitzer, who enjoyed a rags to riches success but unhappily became almost totally blind in his evening years. She was acquired to serve with the British Auxiliary Naval contingent during the Kaiser's ambitious expansionism, becoming known as *Glencairn*.

Renamed *Liberty* when passing into the hands of Lord Tredegar after the conflict, she subsequently came into the ownership of Sir Robert and Lady Houston. Her ladyship is affectionately remembered for her generosity in setting up a fund for the continuance of the 1931 British entry in the series of Schneider Trophy races which led to the winning of the cup outright, in three contests, 1927, 1929 and 1931.

[7] The lovely steam yacht *Alacrity*, 1,797 tons, designed by G.L. Watson, was built for Mr A.J. Drexel at Greenock on the Clyde, in the year 1900, bearing the original name *Margarita*. After passing through the hands of the Marquess of Anglesey, she was often seen at Cowes in the Twenties, then being owned by Lieut. Commander M. Grahame-White. Her overall length was 288 feet and her maximum beam was approximately 37 feet.

[8] My uncle, Arthur Towle (married to my aunt Elizabeth), was a strict disciplinarian, performing as an engineering instructor to the cadets stationed at the Osborne and subsequently Dartmouth Naval Colleges.

During an inspection of a British Legion parade in the summer of 1928, His Royal Highness Edward, Prince of Wales chanced upon a link with his former Osborne cadet days (pre-1914) and kindly acknowledged an earlier mentor with the query, "You're Towle, aren't you?" This most treasured anecdote enjoyed the maximum exposure both within and without the family!

WATERWAYS AND LINKS BETWEEN
WEST AND EAST COWES

There has, from time to time, been much confusion in the use of the title "Cowes". The residents occupying the west side of the harbour, in the main, claimed to be under the umbrella of the town of Cowes, which gave its name to the premier yachting festival widely known as Cowes Regatta,[1] dating from the last century. The elite members of local society would never use the term "West Cowes" unless they resided on the "East Cowes" side of the harbour. There seemed to be no hard and fast ruling, as it was often necessary to quote a clear definition as to whether one was domiciled on the east or west bank of the river.

However, historically, or by legend, it was understood that two fortresses were built to guard the harbour in the time of King Henry VIII (one of which was the original site of the Royal Yacht Squadron) the designations being West Cow(e) and East Cow(e). The precise location of the latter is still a subject of conjecture. Where some emphasis is desirable, this narrative shows a preference for the geographical division which is used on earlier local charts of the harbour.

In the early Twenties, these two towns were governed by entirely separate local councils under two distinct chairmen, which had proven for many years to be a perfectly satisfactory system, giving at least an acceptable service to the respective bodies of residents. The individual elected councillors were far from unanimous in their outlooks, which provided local residents with ample entertainment material gleaned from reports of council meetings publicised by the Isle of Wight County Press!

The West Cowes Council eventually gained control of the East Cowes Council, to the detriment of the latter, which has indisputably suffered ever since. In contrast to the thriving business centre which East Cowes once was, it has become a site for the convenience of Red Funnel car and lorry traffic; in fact, a place where transport lands and passes through.

The nearest land crossing of the River Medina remains as it was in the Twenties, at Newport, some four and a half miles distant, and the established Cowes Harbour link since the last century is by means of a floating bridge or chain ferry. The 1920–1930 ferries of which there were two, one in service and the other undergoing maintenance, were propelled across the twin chains by a compound steam engine which, of course, needed a boiler inevitably fired by coal; on occasions the passengers were subjected to a shower of soot from the funnel! Skipper Charlie Hayden, a rather nervous little chap, controlled the ferry from the open deck (often clad in oilskins) using a pukka Chadburn's engine room telegraph system to signal to the engineer below.

Bearing in mind the imprecise response factor inherent in the system, it resulted in the ferry running aground periodically, aggravated quite understandably by the bogey of an ebbing tide. Passenger transport was continued in such circumstances by a substantial rowing boat with a pair of eighteen foot sweeps, often providing the boatman with an unhelpful challenge as tidal movements retarded progress by drifting the ferry boat leewards with both the fall and rise of the swift current.

Immediately following these admittedly rare mishaps, Charlie was summoned to the office to suffer the indignity of a censuring from the floating bridge committee manager, which only served to reduce his skipper's flagging morale.

A luxury of diesel-electric propulsion for the floating bridge was not introduced until some time later, in the Thirties.

The normal public alternative mode of transport was by steam launch, already mentioned elsewhere. This was considered an extravagant indulgence by local residents, as the one way fare was double that of the chain ferry, i.e. one penny against a half-penny! Shipyards with premises based each side of the river operated their own private work-boats for the crossings. The J. Samuel White *Falcon* was powered by a four stroke single cylinder petrol/paraffin motor which might have been audibly detected turning its propeller at around 100 r.p.m!

River traffic in the Twenties consisted mainly of transport barges of various ages and types. We saw the prime sights of the tan sailed[1] spit- and mizzen-rigged, shallow draft, Thames barges often beating up and down the river narrows (minus the refinement of auxiliary motors) and crewed by one genius of a sailing master with the assistance of an ex-schoolboy apprentice. Without the slightest touch of borrowed drama, the fact that they voyaged regularly from places such as Gravesend to the Cement Mills near Newport on the Medina River, in all seasons, was nothing short of miraculous. The sheer ability to navigate the local river, tacking against wind and tide with such a large and heavily laden vessel, sluggish in stays, additional to meeting the hazards of the open sea, demanded the greatest admiration. There were from time to time innumerable obstacles around which to navigate, such as various barges and lighters moored in the river, also steam and sailing yachts, pilot boats and the Trinity House vessel *Warden* (which serviced the local navigational buoys and lightships). In the early Twenties I recall the presence of flying boats of wood construction at their moorings off the slipways of the Folly Works of S. E. Saunders Ltd., sited midway between Cowes and Newport Harbours. Incidentally, a rather bluff but kindly character named Bob Savage was licensee of the nearby Folly Inn, where the employees and bargees found agreeable refreshment.

On the western bank of the Medina River, down from the Folly Inn and almost opposite, a series of evenly spaced oak stumps indicating the skeleton framing of a once-proud ship was visible. This old hulk, which seemed to have lost a name, was identified by local legend as having served Lord Nelson in the capacity of a victualling vessel with an historic attachment to Trafalgar.

Between the Folly Inn and Newport Quay, a flour mill of substantial proportions was operated by tidal displacements. It was owned by the Roach family and locally known by the name of the Black Mill, possibly on account of its tarred finish. Collections of grain from island farms and the subsequent delivery of milled products was performed by Foden steam wagons, which were basically traction engines with a built-on trailer, but they had a vague resemblance to lorries incorporating internal combustion engines. The Fodens appeared to be very powerful in the haulage of freight, if somewhat low-geared. In consequence, they were painfully slow and one had little difficulty in overtaking a wagon by pedal cycle or even Shanks pony while it was mounting a rise!

I have vivid memories of an October gale sweeping the island one Sunday evening in 1928 when the force of the wind passing through the air vents of my home caused the sitting room carpet to be raised by several inches in some places. It was learned on the day following that Roach's mill was sans roof and otherwise substantially damaged by the elements, and from that time onwards business was seriously affected. A marina with the attraction of an old paddle steamer now occupies the site.

There was always a substantial commercial fleet of oil-engined barges, both diesel and hot bulb types, plying between the island and mainland, such as those owned by the Newport brewers, Mew Langton & Co., taking their fine ales to slake the thirsts of mainland imbibers. In addition, the motorised commercial barges of Pickfords, Crouchers and Shephards, together with the most memorable island transport company's vessels the mvs *Arreton*, *Brightstone* and *Calbourne*, provided a daily link with the mainland in a mutual exchange of life's necessities, as well as bringing in the raw materials used in the construction of ships, flying boats, dwellings etc. Timber-carrying vessels from the Baltic and coaling barges from the north of England and South Wales were frequent visitors. Tramp steamers regularly limped in and out of port to discharge miscellaneous cargoes or seek repair.

The burden of responsibility for the berthing of many luxurious vessels during the Week at Cowes during the Twenties, in addition to the movement of competing yachts from the various clubs and the normal flow of transport to and from the port was shouldered by the harbour master, Capt. G.F. Goodenough, whose office was adjacent to the town quay. Without the assistance of modern shortwave VHF radio and mobile telephone handsets, the task during the festivities must have been something of a nightmare, but he gave impeccable service, issuing a hearty vocal command, amplified in its turn by a giant loudhailer trumpet!

The little harbour of Bembridge to the east of the island, fronting the waters of Spithead, was controlled by my father's cousin, Herbert Occomore, for many years. The crews of the adjacent Bembridge Lifeboat Station gave a selfless service to yachtsmen and merchant seamen alike when distress flares were sighted and a maroon alert sounded in defiance of nature's occasional wrathful intrusions. A complementary lifeboat service based on Yarmouth Harbour courageously responded to traumatic signals from vessels in the western Solent channels.

Southampton was the principal terminal for worldwide ocean-going liners plying to New York and the Colonies in those days and the Cowes waterside provided an ideal observation platform to become acquainted with the outline characteristics of the White Star Line's floating palaces such as the *Majestic, Homeric, Olympic*, competing with the Cunard ships bearing such titles as *Mauritania* (which was for many years holder of the Atlantic Blue Riband) *Aquitania* and *Berengaria* springing readily to mind. The familiar dove-grey hulls of the Union Castle Line ships with their bright red funnels, such as *The Windsor Castle, Cape Town Castle, Athlone Castle* or *Dunnotar Castle* conjured up visions of sunny South Africa. Ships of The Peninsular and Oriental Line, the British India Steamship Company and Shaw Savill line variously appeared in the Solent Roadstead, perhaps awaiting a pilot or high water before proceeding to, or returning from, the extensive Southampton docks.

Another giant visiting liner appearing on its way to and from the Southampton terminal was the United States Lines *Leviathan* (ex-*Vaterland*), with an overall length of 907.6 ft. between perpendiculars, in comparison with that of the *Majestic* (ex-*Bismarck*), quoted as 915.5 ft. The American vessel claimed greater tonnage on account of structural modifications engineered in the States.

During the late Twenties, Solent sightings included the passage of the north German Lloyd Motor ships *Bremen* and *Europa,* each with its truncated pair of funnels. Both of these vessels succeeded in stealing the Atlantic Blue Riband held by the steamship HMS *Mauritania* since 1907.

It was in 1928 that I was privileged to view the staterooms of the then largest liner in the world, the *Majestic*, which left me relatively unimpressed as I had been expecting to look over the source of power, some decks below. However, a subsequent tour of the docks and a close-up view of the giant floating crane did much to mollify my disappointment. The mighty vessel was not only majestic in name but was also a majestic vision, with a slowly measured rate of progress, accompanied by tugs and a seagull escort, to and from her terminal. The deep-throated ship's siren, reverberating across the Solent waters, was sounded with uncanny authority as the displacement swell temporarily destabilised the regatta competitors and the beaches became washed with the breakers.

Quite apart from the obstructions which littered the Cowes Roads during the Week, in the form of numerous steam and motor vessels, not forgetting cruising yachts, passenger ferries with paddle propulsion, coastal barges and the competing yachts of the smaller classes, the big class cutters had to share the waterway, particularly around the Brambles Bank,[2] with ocean-going liners of considerable bulk and tonnage in the Twenties. I seem to remember that the skill of the pilots was such that it was very seldom a liner went aground in the Solent.

There were, of course, the smaller obstructions of the island forts between Bembridge and Southsea to be circumnavigated, although presenting little obstacle except in fog.

On one occasion during a race, I recall the giant cutter *Lulworth* became involved in a near *contretemps* with the 56,000 ton White Star liner *Majestic*, (formerly the German *Bismarck*, acquired as part of the 1914–18 War reparations) to become a prominent representative of the trans-Atlantic fleet, for the luxury of visitors to the New and Old Worlds. On this occasion *Lulworth* was sailing close-hauled, heading in the direction of the *Majestic*, which was anchored in the Solent Fairway. *Lulworth* had the schooner *Westward* close under her lee and, the former counting the liner to be an obstruction (there was scarcely any argument about that), hailed the schooner for room to tack, which could only be sensibly accorded, as safety took priority over any other matters of rule book protocol. One could quite imagine Mr Davis's rejoinder, bearing in mind his reputation as a linguist!

Sir William Burton, who was in charge of *Shamrock* at this time, expressed the opinion that he saw nothing illegitimate in *Lulworth*'s taking advantage of an obstruction when Mr Davis consulted the YRA for a ruling on whether *Lulworth* had been entitled to put *Westward* about after hailing.

Sir Charles McIver concurred with Sir William Burton, saying that, in meeting with a buoy or something similar, one should not hail. Surely upon encountering a mass as large as the liner *Majestic* one has every right to hail.

The committee was far from agreement, being practically equally divided on this issue. However, the day was carried by those who took the view that *Lulworth* should never have put herself in such a position, but could have given herself sea room by sailing clear of the obstruction at an earlier opportunity. In retrospect, it does seem a rather desperate attempt at stealing a march on an opponent, if not a very risky one had it been deliberate, but, in *Lulworth*'s defence, the rules were not specifically compiled to accommodate the mooring of the White Star Company's monsters. An obstruction was an obstruction, whether it be ship or rock. Another possible condition might quite easily have arisen, supposing the wind to have eased, with *Westward* under *Lulworth*'s lee, coincident with a strong flood tide producing an embarrassing leeway, then an original intention to clear the liner could have become frustrated, leaving the latter with no option but to hail.

Incidentally, it was not unknown for collisions to occur between racing yachts and ocean-going liners at anchor in the Roadstead during the Week. In 1925 the 94 ton yawl *Harbinger*, belonging to Sir Alan Garrett Anderson, fouled the P&O Liner *Ranchi* at anchor. *Harbinger* lost her topmast but fortunately there were no more serious consequences.

Of course, it was quite usual for a sailing yacht to lose her wind almost entirely if she was close enough to be screened by the freeboard of a liner under her lee.

In all fairness, it has to be remembered that skippers were employed to provide the very best possible results for their owners when racing and it was in the unwritten terms of reference of the former that every possible advantage should be taken over a rival outside the written code, provided safety provisions were wholly met.

---

[1] In the early days of The Royal Yacht Club, shortly after its formation in 1812, the Sailing Matches were known by the title of The Isle of Wight Regatta, later to be localised as Cowes Regatta, which embraced West and East Cowes.

[2] The Brambles Bank, as it is termed, is a widespread shoal to the east of the estuary to Southampton Water and an 'island' becomes revealed for fifteen minutes or so when there are ultra-low tides during periods of the equinox.

A TRIFLE ABOUT EAST COWES

East Cowes High Street, as I remember it, has virtually disappeared, except for two remaining landmarks: the Trinity House premises, which have been uprated over the intervening years, and The White Hart Inn. The buildings formerly on the eastern side of the street have been completely demolished (assisted by the Luftwaffe in 1943) to provide a car and lorry ferry terminal for Red Funnel shipments. Even in the Twenties the street had long since lost its function as a major shopping location, the traders having developed the area further onshore. Nevertheless, the old High Street, shabby though it became and narrow in concept, with a Dickensian character, was at that time a truly fascinating relic of the eighteenth century. At the southern end, facing a wharf mainly used by coal barges, stood a beautiful, half-timbered, double-fronted alehouse named The Ship and Launch, tenanted by a retired boat-builder named Frederick Reed. Next door was a grocery business run by George Weeks, who could supply from its dim interior rare items of which even Fortnum & Mason were probably unaware, but one could not say that it was outwardly prosperous, although trade was discretely boosted by a wine and spirit delivery service.

In the vicinity stood The Trinity Arms Inn, a one-time thriving establishment, which was tenanted by my Aunt Polly during the Kaiser's War and into the early Twenties. She was the widow of my uncle, Charles Coles, who paid the supreme sacrifice in the 1914–18 conflict when his ship, the minelayer *Princess Irene*, was blown up in the Medway, coincident with the day upon which I was born. My Aunt later retired to live at Denmark House, next door to The White Hart Inn, at the northern end of the High Street. Denmark House no longer stands, but the inn remains to greet the weary travellers from the mainland. A gentleman named Mortlock was the keeper in bygone days, who very public-spiritedly held a little unofficial regatta during late August of each year for the benefit of the local street urchins – aspirant skippers of punts!

Opposite the Trinity Wharf entrance was a gloomy, second-hand furniture emporium. I cannot recall seeing anyone entering or leaving the premises, but business seemingly flourished, as the establishment persisted for many years.

On the waterfront opposite to The White Hart alehouse was the SIWEPACO pontoon where the paddle steamer *Lord Elgin* docked daily with cargo (only), often including horses and carts or carriages, cattle, sheep and live poultry. Freight might occasionally boast of a lorry.

A regular service by a steam launch named *Precursor* crossed the harbour for the convenience of voyagers leaving from the West Cowes pontoon for Southampton. This sooty little vessel was commanded by one Captain Matthews, who stood at the semi-exposed wheel 'up for'ard' behind a canvas screen. His crew consisted of a teenager inevitably answering to the nickname of 'Steamboat' and whose duties included mooring the launch as her skipper skilfully navigated alongside the respective pontoon piers on either side of the waterway. Steamboat's duties extended to collecting tickets and stoking the boiler. A horse and cab rank was located nearby the East Cowes landing which afforded a leisurely service to Osborne principally, or wherever a taxi ride might be needed. During the Week festoons of faded bunting were rediscovered from old sea chests to decorate the street as a welcoming gesture to Their Majesties while going to and from the Trinity House premises.

The street, though indisputably bearing the hallmarks of neglect, had tremendous character, with odd gas lanterns here and there, attended by a professional lamplighter at dusk and dawn. Public docking facilities existed at each end of the High Street for the convenience of coal barges, yacht tenders and dinghy yachtsmen.

For locals wanting to purchase really fresh fish from an overnight catch, a visit to Oatley's fish shop, tucked away on the adjacent Shephard's Quay, was always rewarding. Of the same trade Francis (Fran) Hollis was a keen competitor, with a one man business inshore.

TONS, TONS, TONS AND TUNS

I seem to recollect an immense amount of confusion and indeed argument about what was implied by quoting the tonnage of a yacht in the Twenties. My youthful outlook had been fashioned by the appreciation of objects being placed on kitchen scales to produce an answer in pounds. 2,240 of these constituted one ton. It followed that the displacement weight of a vessel gave a scientific assessment of a given number of these said tons.[1] This appraisal, however logical it appeared, was not the accepted definition, of course, because the expression "Thames Tonnage" was normally quoted in Lloyds's Register as a basis of comparison and, to the best of my knowledge, figures of tonnage quoted in the text belong to this category. They are not, in fact, a function of avoirdupois.

To find Thames tonnage for a typical vessel, the length of a yacht measured on the deck from the fore end of the stem to the stern post is nominated in a typical calculation as L for length, B to specify the maximum beam in the formula:

$$TM = \frac{L - B \times B \times \frac{1}{2}B}{94}$$

Obviously this derivation has no scientific status, being an empirical rule to establish a basis of relationship between vessels.

A third quotation of yachts' tonnage occasionally used in connection with sailing yachts, but more frequently with barges and larger cargo vessels, adding spice to the conflict of intelligence, was that of "Registered Tonnage". Unlike "Thames Measurement Tonnage", the British Board of Trade established a comparative formula based upon a ship's internal cubic capacity, i.e. simply that one hundred cubic feet of space should be nominated as a "one ton register" (once again, this cannot bear any relation to displacement weight considering the variations of specific gravity of any cargo filling the volume). Just to further complicate matters, the BoT sometimes used its discretion in reducing the said calculated volume to make allowances for crew accommodation, sail lockers and galleys. To discuss tonnage of yachts was commonly regarded as a subject suited to comic opera, certainly not one for the regatta sightseers. I must confess that it took many years for me to put all these tonnages into some sort of perspective, such knowledge being omitted from my formal education, but the picture still remained incomplete when I discovered a tun of wine equals 252 gallons!

Only yacht masters and the more experienced longshoremen were privy to these secrets of the trade.

---

[1] A displacement ton is approximately equal to 35 cu.ft. of saltwater.

PART II

TERPSICHORE TESTS THE WATER

Since the end of the century and up until August 1914, the big cutter class was fragmented: HM King Edward's yacht *Britannia*, after her brilliant debut in 1893–95, passed into private ownership and was later repurchased, to be used for cruising with a cut-down rig. Alterations to the hull included the fitting of bulwarks and it seemed that her racing career was at an end until she passed as a legacy into the enthusiastic hands of HM King George V, who decided otherwise. In her cruising rig *Britannia* was raced in 1913 and also in the early part of the 1914 season, until the balloon went up.

The main focus of attention in the racing of giant sailing yachts was the privilege of the big schooners in the immediate pre–war era, with contests between the Herreshoff-designed 338 ton *Westward*, built for Mr A.S. Cochran, Charles Nicholson's masterpiece named *Margherita*, owned by Major Whittaker (which, incidentally, took five first prizes in six races at Kiel in 1913), Kaiser Wilhelm's 400 ton *Meteor IV* and the *Germania*, owned by Dr Krupp von Bohlen. The big class of cutters survived mainly due to the enduring enthusiasm of great sportsmen such as Mr Myles Kennedy, who owned the Fife-designed *White Heather II* (179 tons) dating from 1907 and Sir Thomas Lipton, with his 23 metre Fife-designed *Shamrock* (175 tons), built in 1908. In this connection, credit is also due to Mr R.W.N. Young, who engaged Charles Nicholson to design a slightly smaller cutter named *Nyria*, of 169 tons. These cutters were often joined by yawls and ketches of lesser tonnage which sailed with substantial handicap time allowances. In his book *The King's* Britannia, John Irving records the activities of the ageing 143 ton yawl named *Wendur* built in 1883[1] as one of the royal cutter's principal opponents in the 1913–14 seasons. Bearing in mind the difference in tonnage of the two vessels, it can be conceded that Mr Richard H. Lee, who owned *Wendur*, was to be congratulated for his gamely stance. When the 1914–18 conflict was over and the prospect for a big handicap class revival was in serious doubt, Mr Lee's enthusiasm for the sport remained undimmed.

The situation was given substantial stimulus following the débâcle of attempts to revive the sport in 1919 by the actions, firstly, of an announcement from Buckingham Palace to the effect that His Majesty was prepared to fit out the 221 ton (TM) cutter *Britannia* for the 1920 season and, secondly, Mr Lee (who, incidentally, hailed from Bovey Tracey in Devon) decided to order a new first class competitor for the royal cutter. And so it was that a 189 ton rival named *Terpsichore* was far too hastily contracted to be built by the White Bros. of Itchen, Southampton at a cost of £24,000 which might compare with a sum of £3,000,000 in 1990 terms. Her basic construction followed the traditional composite practice and, incidentally, that of the contemporary cutters, using timber planking fastened to steel frames. *Terpsichore* was named after the Greek muse of dance.

Following these post-war moves the 1907 *White Heather II,* formerly owned by Mr Myles Kennedy, was purchased by Sir Charles Allom, who fitted her out to join a new assembly of first class cutters.

For many years big class yacht racing had been a male-dominated sport and it was a refreshing act on the part of Mrs Workman (a member of the Royal Ulster Yacht Club) to purchase the 1906 *Nyria* from Sir Charles Allom, who sailed her under ketch rig in 1919. In 1920 Charles Nicholson reconverted *Nyria* to topsail cutter rig with a Marconi mast to add a fourth competitor.

Of the big schooners, the 1910 *Westward* owned by Mr Clarence Hatry took part, with *Margherita* remaining on the sale list. The 154 ton schooner *Susanne* of 1904 vintage, owned by Mr W. Brookes, sailed in a few races with some success during this season.

The 1920 season was the only one by Mr Hatry in racing *Westward* and it was not until 1925, under the new ownership of Mr T.B.F. Davis, that she reappeared to race with the cutters. Unhappily, Mr Hatry became involved in a financial scandal in the City which earned him a custodial sentence.

Mr Warwick Brookes (a member of The Royal Thames Yacht Club) was a so-called financier whose talents were rumoured to provide him with an enviable standard of living, by reputedly creating fortunes and going broke.

The 1908 cutter *Shamrock* did not take part in the racing for the 1920 calendar as her owner, Sir Thomas Lipton, the Scottish grocery magnate, was very much occupied with his long-postponed fourth challenge for the Americas Cup, *Shamrock IV* having just made her voyage to the USA at the time of the outbreak of hostilities in 1914 to sail against the American cutter *Resolute*. In order to provide some competition to *Shamrock IV* in tuning-up trials, Sir Thomas Lipton's skipper took the 1908 23 metre *Shamrock* across the 'pond' after the conflict. It was not until 1924 that the 1908 *Shamrock* entered the over 70 ton handicap class in local regattas, when she presented a very distinctive picture, displaying emerald green topsides with a sometimes visible black keel, and a contrasting white boot top division. Upon her return, she raced each year with the big yachts until 1930, when *Shamrock V* went on trial.

Of course, the designation 'over 70 ton handicap class' permitted the inclusion of many smaller vessels (in addition to those already mentioned), some of which had distinguished records from earlier years. These yachts consisted of cutters, yawls and ketches and the problem of devising fair handicap ratings for such a diversity of types and tonnage was practically insoluble. Following bitter criticism of the handicapping applications for the 1920 season, the system was later revised but obviously there could never be a perfect approach for, where a slight bias in the number of seconds per mile allowed could produce almost any result the handicapper desired, it still remained very much a discretionary science. In those days the *Homo sapiens* computer took all the flak.

It can be truthfully stated that much but not all of the criticism was quite undeserved at the time, in view of the fact that an abundance of changes to YRA rules were an underlying cause of dissent. It is doubtful whether anyone other than Major B. Heckstall–Smith (whose nickname, incidentally, was 'Bookstall') could have measured up to the responsibility. His experience as the yachting editor of *The Field* and later *Yachting World* commenced in 1894 and was unsurpassed as he had acquired a unique feel for the sport, sailing as a guest in so many races on different types of yachts over twenty-six years.[2] Moreover he had ingratiated himself with all those associated with the sport and his opinions were internationally respected at that time. For the 1921 season the YRA recognised that the mainstay of the association was provided by interest in the big handicap class and busied itself in amending the handicapping system, firstly by adopting the new international time scale and, secondly, by the adoption of an entirely new method of handicapping. The revised system introduced a theoretical figure for a yacht's speed, tabulated against a variety of ratings, the figure equivalent to the time taken in seconds for a yacht of a specified rating to cover a nautical mile at maximum speed in tideless water. To the 'theoretical speed of the vessel' a handicap figure in seconds would be added, this latter being decided by a handicap committee and, when applied to the tabulated speed figure, it resulted in a 'handicap speed figure' for any particular yacht. In such projections the difference between the handicap speed figures for entrant yachts would be the time allowance in seconds per mile between them.

It could be argued that the number of miles sailed over a given course, with straight line measurements taken from mark to mark, must vary considerably depending upon the yacht's quality, for instance, in pointing to windward, when it is generally conceded that well-balanced cutters must have a windward advantage over schooners, ketches and yawls in sailing shorter resultant distances. Moreover, the cutters always appeared more responsive to the helm in coming about. Obviously, the rule could not take account of the prevailing conditions at any specific time, where wind direction and velocity plus tide variations introduced such a strong element of luck to the outcome of a race, relative to the disparity in sizes of competing yachts. Accepting the relationship of a yacht's speed to an immersed waterline length, it so often proved hopeless for a small yacht to compete in certain conditions when following a larger one, despite any considered fairness of handicap allowances. Where, for example, the latter had a substantial lead, advantaged by slack water on the approach and rounding of a mark, then to subsequently enjoy the bonus of a flooding tide, the former often had to suffer a formidable and enduring battle with a foul current to fetch the buoy. These odds were typical in early handicap events but such was the spice of competition, especially with a fluky wind!

Smaller contemporaries of *Terpsichore* in the 1920 revival consisted of three cutters, almost half her tonnage, the very pretty little cutter *Moonbeam IV* of 92 tons, a new vessel built for Mr C. Johnston; the 92 ton cutter *Zinita*, owned by Mrs de Rothschild built in 1904, bearing a distinguished pre-war record; also of 1904 conception was Mr Wylie's 80 ton *Vida VI*, the smallest yacht to take its place in the big class racing with such a wide band of ratings.

In addition, the company included the 94 ton yawl named *Harbinger*, of 1913 vintage, newly owned by Sir Thomas Dunlop, the 92 ton yawl *Sumurun*, constructed in 1914 and belonging to Lord Sackville, the 106 ton ketch *Valdora*, well preserved since it was built in 1904, owned by Sir William Portal, and Col. Slade's 89 ton *Joyette*, another ketch-rigged competitor constructed in 1907.

The first appearance of *Terpsichore* at Cowes Regatta in 1920 was, for her, a complete fiasco. The brand-new cutter scarcely made the start line on Monday, the first day of the Week. Her debut proved a complete anticlimax not only for her owner, Mr Lee, but those who gathered with such expectations of *Terpsichore*'s challenge to a field of competitors which had distinguished themselves in pre-1914 regattas such as *Britannia, Nyria, White Heather II*. Before *Terpsichore* could cross the line, she was seen from the shore to be in some difficulty when her throat halyards were carried away; forced to abandon her entry, she returned to her moorings.

However, Monday's setback was quickly rectified and *Terpsichore* arrived at the start line for the King's Cup Race on Tuesday, the day following. *Terpsichore* was the only big class yacht competing and sailed scratch, allowing Major Lionel de Rothschild's cutter *Zinita* 22 mins 44 secs, Mr C.P. Johnston's cutter *Moonbeam IV* 28 mins 36 secs, Lieut. Col. A.E. Gage's ketch *Julnar* 27 mins 52 secs, Lord Sackville's yawl *Sumurun* 30 mins 4 secs, Sir William Portal's ketch *Valdora* 33 mins 44 secs and Capt. C.W.P. Slade's yawl *Joyette* 44 mins 44 secs. The queen's course of twenty-two miles twice round was sailed. The start was particularly ragged, owing in part to the calm conditions, the yachts appearing to be substantially without the hint of a breeze. *Terpsichore, Zinita* and *Valdora* were first over the line, with *Julnar* lamely distinguishing herself by being seventy minutes late in getting away! *Terpsichore* led at the weather mark, rounding the East Lepe buoy well ahead of the rest and progressively stretched her lead to the Warner. The prospect of her redeeming the ill fortune suffered on the previous day looked likely at this stage, particularly as the wind began to freshen. Unhappily, another stroke of misfortune was visited upon her when a fault in her gear forced her into retirement at the end of the first round. It seemed that insufficient investigation had been exercised in the determination of design loadings for sheets and halyards and their anchorages, over a spectrum of elements to carry some 10,000 sq.feet of sail.

In the event, Mr C.P. Johnston's new Clyde-built cutter *Moonbeam IV* took the honours on this day, winning by seven minutes on corrected time; *Zinita* was placed second, with *Sumurun* third.

Obviously it seemed pointless for *Terpsichore* to take her place at the start line again until the details of her gear had been properly looked into. But time was insufficient to allow a thorough investigation in the middle of a regatta schedule. It is, of course, only to be admitted that rival yachts were sometimes sailing close to the limit of their spars and riggings, but with an established advantage derived from trial and error. The faults experienced in the case of *Terpsichore* were relatively minor, although their effects became most pronounced and in retrospect one is obliged to concede the embarrassment of yacht designers on such occasions in the absence of nylon ropes, stainless steel forgings and rigging wires!

It will be noted that only *Terpsichore, Britannia, White Heather II* and *Nyria* formed the nucleus of cutters which might have been expected to race on something like level terms, although there was considerable disparity in tonnage between *Nyria* and *Britannia*. Unhappily for Mr Lee, his sporting gesture must have proved a bitter disappointment for, in its debut on the Solent scene, *Terpsichore* came nowhere in 1920, participating in only four events and failing to gain a flag, and so the stock of prize burgees remained in the locker; in truth she had not yet entered the competition, as she was completely lacking in readiness for battle.

Clearly, *Terpsichore* needed to be thoroughly investigated in detail for her design shortcomings and lack of performance by an independent authority. There was no one better than Charles Nicholson for Mr Lee to consult and so, in the winter of 1920–21, the fatherly hand of the Gosport Wizard began to exert a beneficial influence upon *Terpsichore*, later *Lulworth*, which extended to the end of the yacht's racing career in 1930.

It had to be acknowledged that Messrs White Bros. of Itchen, Southampton from whom *Terpsichore* was ordered, were very experienced in the design of smaller classes of yachts, having the monopoly of business with, for instance 'The

Solent One Design' class before 1914 and a few larger vessels in addition. These included the yawl *Coral* of 63 tons, built in 1902, and which, in Mr Frank Chaplin's ownership, won the King's Cup Race in 1926, also in 1928, at Cowes. John Nicholson (the son of Charles Nicholson) records in his book, *Great Years in Yachting*, that *Terpsichore* had beautiful lines and was a very well-balanced design. In consequence, one concludes that the White Bros. original concept was substantially endowed with latent merit. Although mounting criticism was levelled against the White Brothers at this time, it was later established that they possessed considerable flair[3] in yacht design, but for *Terpsichore* much of the detail was hastily conceived in the absence of background data. It was late in the yachting season, when still somewhat 'tender', that she reached her first starting line to earn the early *nom de guerre* of '*Terpsichore* the Unlucky' when she might have been more deservedly referred to as '*Terpsichore* the Unfinished'.

In 1920 there was a shortage of essential high quality materials, where for instance, the market was scoured for a seasoned mast of suitable proportion without success and *Terpsichore* was fitted with an improvised 'stick' in the form of a steel tube,[4] which in turn necessitated rigging modifications away accepted conventional practice. She was, however, fitted with a Marconi-style mast, unlike *Britannia*, which retained the antiquated fidded topmast construction until 1927. For some unknown reason *Terpsichore* emulated her royal contemporary initially by adopting the built-in handicap of high bulwarks. Bearing in mind that *Terpsichore* had been designed for racing essentially, admittedly with an ability to sail between racing venues around the coast, it does seem odd that a designer should accept for a first-class racing cutter the penalty of trapping some tons of water against the lee rail when taking it green. At the time when *Britannia* had undergone her conversion to cruiser in 1912, the object had been (in combination with a substantially reduced sail area) to increase her freeboard, allowing dryer conditions for the ship's company.

One supposes that there could have been something nostalgic in the choice of black topsides for *Terpsichore*, remembering the racing days of the 1890s when the big class trio of *Britannia*, *Meteor* and *Satanita* were in uniform colouring.

Terpsichore was clearly distinguishable from *Britannia* at close range, firstly on account of the former's very aggressive semi-spoon bow, which seemed to suit her very much better when she took on the white mantle of *Lulworth*. Secondly, as *Terpsichore* sailed within range of The Glasses the No.2 figure which appeared either side of her mainsail could scarcely be confused with No.1. I seem to remember *Britannia* as No.1, *Shamrock* No.3, *Nyria* No.4, *Westward* No.5 and *White Heather* labelled No.7. Late in 1927, when Sir Mortimer Singer disposed of *Lulworth* and she was acquired by Mr A.A. Paton, her mainsail bore No.6 for the 1928/29/30 regattas. Her former owner retained the No.2 identification for his new cutter *Astra*.

One rather odd feature of *Terpsichore*'s design was the inclusion of chain plates, which were not found on her contemporaries. Obviously the White Brothers had set out to maximise the athwartship base for the staying of the towering mast, whilst accepting any drag penalty resulting from these protrusions when heeled to leeward. At close range the sight of those chain plates presented something of an historic aspect, hardly consistent with practice of the times. (Strangely enough, Charles Nicholson incorporated this feature on *Shamrock V* some ten years later.)

Terpsichore, in her entry to the field and later as *Lulworth*, carried a magnificent suit of sails drawn tightly with scarcely a wrinkle in evidence whilst beating to windward, and a reference to this quality is made in the caption under the picture of *Lulworth* in the Beken Collection of Yachts *A Hundred Years of Sail*. John Nicholson records that *Lulworth* was remarkably close-winded, to cite an incident somewhat later, in the 1930

Clyde Regatta, when sailing with Ted Heard aboard *Shamrock V* before she left for the USA.

Skipper Hogarth got the better of Skipper Heard at the start and, after some twenty minutes had elapsed, *Lulworth* was holding *Shamrock V* nicely under her lee. Several times Hogarth was seen to leave the helm to give instructions for trimming the head sheets. John Nicholson further relates that Hogarth proved his skill in combination with a complete knowledge of *Lulworth*'s capabilities year by year. His preference was for a flat-cut mainsail. John Nicholson had great opportunities to sail upon and to study the character of all the big class yachts at different times, including *Lulworth*. In particular he mentions *Lulworth* as a virtually hard weather vessel, although there were times when she went like a train in light airs. He explains this by suggesting that she had the tide under her in coming on a wind!

The great cutter always appeared to be so finely balanced and she displayed an ability to respond with the minimum of leeway in answering the helm when coming about in a foul tide. This characteristic was especially evident when rounding a mark in close company; the whipcrack of those thousands of square feet of canvas would shatter the peace of the Solent for a brief second or so, as the crew leapt into action for the next follow-on manoeuvre.

In 1920, when *Terpsichore* joined the racing scene for Cowes Week, I remember being escorted by my father to observe the 10 o'clock start from the promenade fronting the Royal Yacht Squadron, which was crowded with onlookers whose opinions regarding revival of the sport were legion, inevitably charged with emotion, fell short of any logical expression. There was, of course, no reason to doubt their conclusions, many having "seen it all" from the "good old days" when Her Majesty Queen Victoria was on the throne and Prince Wilhelm came seemingly to torpedo the proceedings for Prince Edward.

The daily yacht-board routine was usually heralded by the activity of the watchman, who attended the galley fire at 5.30 a.m. before arousing the crew from slumber, tumbling out of their cots and hammocks. Following performance of the morning ablutions, the company would concentrate on their allotted duties, such as polishing the brass fittings, leathering varnish work, stoning and swabbing the deck, all painstakingly performed by dedicated crew members sharing with an owner a pride in his possession and, incidentally, to remind him of the many services loyally contributed beyond their main assignments. Meanwhile, the gig would have been launched and manned by fellow shipmates, to make the all-important victualling errand. After toiling with the oars for some twenty minutes, the gig would have fetched up on the Sun Hill slipway, conveniently located for a shopping visit to Dear and Morgan's grocery stores, where the staff awaited such early morning patronage. Following a return with the sustenance, a steward, supported by some of his more domesticated team mates, prepared breakfast and filled a hamper, usually with cheese or bacon sandwiches, together with bottled beers, for the lunchtime repast. The opportunity for this indulgence during a race usually took place when the yacht might conveniently be running free.

At 7.55 a.m. naval tradition was observed by the *V & A* when the raising of a blue and white flag defined an 'official sunrise', timed for eight bells, heralding the start of the 'forenoon watch'. The ceremony was then pursued on the naval guardship as its 'outdoor orchestra' then burst into melody. Sequentially, those yachts which were to remain at anchor for the day hoisted their over-all dressings, in parallel with the exhibition of white, blue or red ensigns to meet their appropriate entitlements.

From this point onwards, the day's regatta programme received its deserved attention from the seamen, who commenced the rigging of contestant vessels. Firstly, the skipper would have to decide the likely immediate weather prospects and choose his canvas to suit his 'hunch'. This would be divined from the consideration of the immediate intensity and direction of the wind, morning overtures of the skies and possible influences derived from the portents of the last evening's sunset. In comparison with modern forecast facilities, it all added up to an imprecise 'feel'. For those who had toiled on the deck with fishing fleets in earlier times, the skipper's intuition was invariably reliable, but the Solent weather often exhibited a fickle nature.

The normal drill in the raising of sails usually started with removal of the mainsail cover, which was rolled and spirited below deck. The first jib, jib topsail and the working staysail (sometimes referred to as a foresail) were carefully rolled and tied with rotten cotton yarn in readiness for breaking out of its respective sheet by a jerk, after setting it in position. Attention was then concentrated on the hoisting of the mainsail, which was quite a protracted drill. With the mainsail uncovered and the mainsheet secured, the boom had to be lifted from its nocturnal support crutch, involving the efforts of many stout hands whilst the load became carried by the topping lift. With the ship pointing into the wind, all hands formed a chain to walk up the deck, with unified efforts applied to the throat halyards and the topping lift, whilst keeping the gaff on a relatively horizontal plane as the giant sail was raised. Some juggling usually took place to set the sail with the minimum of wrinkle when the throat and peak were finally belayed. And then the challenge of raising the topsail followed. The setting of a jib header in deference to a threatened blow was slightly less of a task than that of handling the jackyarder used in less boisterous weather. Without proper teamwork, there could be a danger of either the jackyard or topsail yard ripping into the mainsail *en route*. A hauling team was usually employed to concentrate their efforts on the halyard with their eyes on the progressive movement of the sail, whilst another assembly of deckhands attended the sheet haul to the mainsail peak. The masthead man was employed in guiding the topsail assembly into position aloft, subsequently attending to the lacing of its luff close by the topmast. His technique was practised to ensure that the topsail could be lowered without jamming in the event of an emergency.

After tidying the deck clear of the halyard falls and attending to the final belaying to set the sails fair, the mate took over the wheel whilst the jib and trysail stops were broken, leaving the moorings astern as the yacht headed for open water.

By 9.45 a.m. a yacht would have left its moorings and could be seen performing a series of directional gyrations to the downside of the start line. With fifteen minutes in hand, the majority of the class would be jockeying well behind the line, particularly if the tide was flooding over it. At times when the wind eased before the starting gun, a yacht would occasionally be carried by the tide ahead of the line, subsequently finding the greatest difficulty in getting back into position before the starting signal, which obviously resulted in the loss of much valuable competitive time. Even using the best chronometer that money could purchase, the art of getting the weather position and simultaneously nosing over the starting line immediately after the puff of smoke appeared from a gun, was the achievement of an ace.

At 9.50 a.m. the preparatory flag would be hoisted by the signalman at the squadron flagstaff.[6] The signal flag used for the first class yachts exceeding twenty metres rating in this period was international code flag letter 'A' (white and blue) and this remained aloft until the starting gun fired.

At 9.55 a.m. the 'Blue Peter' was hoisted, coincident with the 'Get Ready' gun being fired.

If one had arrived well in advance of the starting time behind the RYS battery and found a location directly below the starter's office (preferably to windward of an old seadog's clay pipe) the stentorian voice of the race officer above would bark out the approach instruction to the artilleryman: "One minute to go... fifty seconds... twenty seconds... ten, nine, eight, seven, six, five, four, three, two, one fire!" The word "one" and command "fire!" were uttered in the same breath.

At 10 a.m. the 'Blue Peter' would be lowered, as also would code flag 'A' simultaneously, the firing of the starting cannon thundering its message to the anxious captains on duty at the wheel of their respective charges. The mounting excitement onshore reaching its crescendo, it was relieved by a mutual utterance of, "They're off!"

The foregoing starting system was standard practice throughout all British yacht clubs to avoid any confusion. There had to be a duplication of signals, visual and sound, in case a cannon misfired, in which event the master helmsman, with watch in hand, would fix his sights upon the 'Blue Peter', which had to be lowered strictly to time by the sailing committee. In other words, time was reckoned by the flag and not by the gun.

Invariably a second gun report could be heard close on the heels of the starting signal if one or more of the competing yachts happened to have made to cross the start line before the 10 a.m. signal. The offending vessel would have her number run up immediately at the yacht club flagstaff to signify an appropriate recall. Occasionally two or three yachts might find themselves transgressing, leading to a great rattle of canvas when such vessels were obliged to come about to recross the line. On average, one to four minutes could be lost as a penalty in this manoeuvre and sometimes a great deal more, dependent on wind/tide conditions, not to mention the potential hazards vis-à-vis the other competitors where delay was dictated by safety considerations. Meanwhile the advantage gained by the rest of the field could be very substantial, more so in cases where these were favoured by wind and tide.

When Terpsichore joined the class in 1920, I was just beginning to distinguish between a cutter and a schooner; the subtleties of difference between yawl and ketch had yet to be mastered and came later when I learned the art of focusing a

98

pair of binoculars to locate wheel and mizzen whilst appraising the proportions of the latter.

The relative simplicity of sail plan, even accepting in those days, as it did, a variety of topsails, drew me into early recognition of *Terpsichore*, with sympathy for her early misfortunes and rejoicings for her later achievements.

---

[1] *Wendur*, classed as a 40 rater, was owned and raced by Col. T.C.B. West towards the end of the last century. Built in 1883 by D.& W. Henderson of Glasgow, to the design of George Watson, the yawl *Wendur* measured 89 feet on the waterline with a maximum beam of 18 feet (ratio 4:94).

[2] In the year 1928 Major Brooke Heckstall–Smith was appointed yachting correspondent to *The Daily Telegraph* whilst he retained his post as editor of *Yachting World*.

He was for many years secretary of the Yacht Racing Association (YRA) and also the International Yacht Racing Union (IYRU).

[3] A privileged observation of the stern wake generated from a big cutter on an eastbound reach past Old Castle Point could be appreciated from an elevated position of the Norris Castle Farmstead. A surprisingly modest turbulence from the outflow of *Lulworth*'s displacement served to provide some confirmation of her designer's flair. Bearing in mind the haste of her building programme, there could have been scarcely any time available for the testing of experimental hull forms. Such a relatively clean wake gave testimony to substantial imagination in the preparation of her lines.

[4] The adoption of steel tubular masts on Big Class cutters was not exactly a novelty at this time, as such were employed with varying degrees of success in the last century; for example, *Shamrock I* carried a steel 'stick' in 1899.

[5] The 300 ton topsailed cutter *Satanita*, designed by J.M. Soper and built at Harwich for Mr A.D. Clarke in 1983, enjoyed a nostalgic reputation as the fastest cutter ever sailed on a reach. She measured some ten feet longer than her immediate rival *Britannia*, whose own racing history was substantially prolonged.

[6] The Royal Yacht Squadron flagstaff, raised in the year 1914, was formerly the mast of a famous old 40 ton cutter named *Bloodhound* which was laid down in 1873 for the Marquis of Ailsa, later passing through the hands of a variety of owners until the Marquis repurchased the cutter in 1907 to prevent

her threatened butchery. Around that time, *Bloodhound* had suffered the indignity of being sunk by the yacht *L'Esperance* off the Shrape Shoal, and her consequent resuscitation was entrusted to the genius of William Fife. He had been impressed by the early experiments of Charles Nicholson and as a result *Bloodhound* was very successfully endowed with a longer stick to carry a redesigned rig of high aspect ratio. The yacht was finally destroyed by fire in 1922.

1921

THE SEASON'S HONOURS WON BY MRS WORKMAN'S *NYRIA*

The traditionally royal atmosphere of Cowes Week was rekindled by the enthusiastic attendance of Their Majesties King George V and Queen Mary, who were joined by many distinguished visitors, to the delight of those who came to participate and others in their multitudes to observe the sport. The local people had striven hard to preserve the continuity of the great yachting festival and they were amply rewarded by the encouragement of the royal entourage. Support for the big handicap class continued, but a great deal of anxiety was felt for its future in successive seasons. Events of the intervening years had unhappily left the regatta without the pre-1914 attendance of other crowned heads of Europe. Moorings were no longer needed for the Russian royal yacht *Standart*, the German *Hohenzollern*, King Christian's *Dannebrog*, King Alfonso's *Giralda* and Archduke Stephen's *Ul* (interpreted 'Hive') and which flew their national standards in earlier times, but a Republican American presence lent welcome support to the Solent scene in the summer of 1921.

During the Saturday immediately prior to the Week, the royal yacht *Victoria and Albert* steamed from the Portsmouth Naval Base in a westerly direction, through the waters of Spithead, with Queen Mary on board, to reach its allotted location off the West Cowes esplanade, arriving at 1.30 p.m. The customary twenty-one gun salute from the Royal Yacht Squadron battery boomed out its loyal signal from the port. It was not publicly known at this time that His Majesty had arrived earlier to sail on his yacht *Britannia* in the company of Captain Sir Charles Cust, RN, to participate in the opening event of the Royal Thames Yacht Club Regatta from Ryde.

Escorting the *V & A* was the imposing sight of the guardship HMS *Resolution*, an up-to-date example of a British battleship of the period, which was lavishly bedecked with acres of multi-coloured bunting, contrasting its inherent menacing aspect, and offering sympathy with the jolly mood of the revellers ashore. The Cowes Roadstead was privileged this year to further accommodate the little twin screw turbine-engined royal yacht *Alexandra,*[1] dwarfed by the *V & A*.

The local yacht clubs and the seafront were strewn with flags of seemingly infinite variety to welcome those afloat and to contribute a carnival touch. Nature had smiled upon the day by providing brilliant sunshine tempered by a gentle breeze.

The British naval contingent was augmented by the arrival of the destroyers HMS *Valhalla* and HMS *Rocket*, providing a further protective air to the proceedings. The collection of armour in the Solent in 1921 was very substantially enlarged by the visiting naval vessels of our American cousins. Vice-Admiral A.P. Niblack, commander of the American squadron stationed in European waters, brought the US battleship *Utah* to the scene. She was unmistakable from the sight of her 'braced girder' type masts, carrying huge crows' nests, such features being typical of American naval architecture of the times. The US destroyer *Sands*, commanded by Captain Gormley, was anchored close to the battleship, both flying the Stars and Stripes. The panorama was further complemented by the imposing outline of the huge White Star Liner *Teutonic* with its black-topped buff funnels, anchored to the eastward of the men o' war. She provided a magnificent grandstand from which privileged spectators could follow the racing of the bigger classes of yachts.

Queen Mary was accompanied on the royal yacht *Victoria and Albert* by Princess Mary, the Duke of York and Field Marshal the Duke of Connaught. Her Majesty was attended by the Countess of Shaftesbury and Mr Harry Verney. Captain the Hon. Francis Needham was in attendance upon the Duke of Connaught.

His Majesty King George V arrived at Cowes later in the afternoon aboard *Britannia* following a day's sport, at approximately 4 o'clock. A salute of fifteen guns boomed out from the Royal Yacht Squadron Castle when the admiral's flag was hoisted, to receive the acknowledgement of *Britannia*.

On the completion of the ceremony the King joined the *Victoria and Albert* where he was received by the Duke of Leeds, RNVR, commodore of the RYS, Sir Richard Williams–Bulkeley, vice-commodore, and Mr T.H.S. Pasley, MVO, secretary. The party left in a steam pinnace for the club house around 5 o'clock, to be cheered by those loyal subjects whose patience had been stretched for their monarch's arrival.

Whilst the big handicap class took its deserved share of the spectators' attention, the town enjoyed the novel distraction of entertaining American sailors on shore leave from their warships, and a common interest became centred upon the international sporting contests between the elite six metre yachts of British and American design and build, manned by their respective national crews. Both visiting and local brass bands indulged their odd fortissimo renderings of Souza's *Hands Across the Seas*, offering a lively signature tune to augment the facilities of the Royal Yacht Squadron. The weather was uninspiring, being cloudy, and exhibiting odd showers for most of the day, to the accompaniment of a steady south-westerly breeze. The course was programmed twice round the Solent Bank and North East Middle buoys, a distance of thirty-nine sea miles, with a 10 a.m. start. *Britannia* sailed scratch to allow Mr R.H. Lee's *Terpsichore* 1 minute 18 seconds, Sir Charles Allom's *White Heather II* 3 minutes 15 seconds, Mrs E.R. Workman's *Nyria* 3 minutes 54 seconds, Mr J. Swann's yawl *Brynhild* 18 minutes 51 seconds, Mr C.P. Johnson's *Moonbeam IV* 25 minutes 21 seconds, the Earl of Dunraven's *Cariad* 26 minutes 39 seconds, and Capt. C.W. Slade's *Joyette* 42 minutes 54 seconds. All the yachts carried jackyarders with the exception of *Terpsichore* which cautiously set a jib header.

A spectacular start, without recalls, was witnessed with the first five yachts approaching the line on the starboard tack and then coming about as the signal boomed from the battery. *Terpsichore* led the fleet on the weather side, followed in order by *Joyette* to leeward, *Britannia*, *White Heather II* and Nyria in the outer position. *Valdora* led *Moonbeam IV* with *Cariad* under her lee, leaving *Brynhild* at the tail of the fleet.

The beat to the Solent Bank buoy in a westerly direction was assisted by an ebb tide and the light breeze threw up a slight chop. Spinnakers were set for the return past the RYS castle and, as the yachts veered in the direction of the North-East Middle Mark, the scene developed into a reach to finish round one by a reverse reach back to the start line. During the run from the Solent Bank buoy *White Heather II* was seen to be setting the pace, enjoying her own special weather, to lead in order *Britannia*, *Terpsichore* and *Nyria*.

At this stage the smaller yachts, with their generous handicap allowances, trailed in the formation of *Brynhild*, *Moonbeam IV*, *Cariad* and *Joyette*.

As the yachts completed the first round, *White Heather II* led *Britannia* by 2 minutes 34 seconds clear of her time concession, followed by *Nyria* and *Terpsichore*, which was 4 minutes 28 seconds behind the leader. The smaller yachts were a long way astern in their earlier order, with *Moonbeam IV* and *Brynhild* still well within time allowances.

The corrected finishing times at the completion of the second round confirmed the prospects for the fleet at the end of the first. In such light air the big cutters *Britannia* and *Terpsichore* had little chance to save on their respective times, with the ample handicap donations accorded to the vessels of lesser rating. Whilst *Britannia* just managed a sixth placing on this day and *Terpsichore* was distinguished by being placed last, it was for the latter something of a red letter day – completing a race without mishap! Her troubles were by no means at an end and, apart from enjoying a third flag on Thursday of the Week, her Solent appearances substantially served to augment an incredible catalogue of misadventures.

Monday's official results for the over 70 ton class read:

Moonbeam IV (winner)	1 hr 49 mins 54 secs
Brynhild (second place)	1 hr 54 mins 3 secs
White Heather II	1 hr 56 mins 13 secs
Nyria	1 hr 58 mins 31 secs
Joyette	1 hr 58 mins 51 secs
Britannia	2 hrs 0 mins 3 secs
Cariad	2 hrs 0 mins 7 secs
Terpsichore	2 hrs 1 mins 44 secs

Tuesday of the Week at Cowes saw the 10 a.m. start of the King's Cup race as the first on the Royal Yacht Squadron programme. Heavy rain was earlier experienced, followed by fitful sunshine and showers through the day. A stiff westerly breeze generated a very rough sea, which found some weaknesses in competing yachts. Happily, none of the accidents proved to be of a serious nature. The first casualty of the elements, just after the starting gun was fired for the Royal Cup contest, came when *Terpsichore* collected yet another mishap to her plague of troubles. Her peak halyard deck hook failed, forcing an early retirement from the event. Seeing her plight, a picket boat from HMS *Resolution* stood by in case of a need for assistance, but the unlucky cutter was seen to lower her flaying canvas and make for her mooring under a trysail.

However, *Terpsichore* did not earn the distinction of misfortune on this day as *Nyria*, which had been preparing for her entry in the second handicap event, sympathetically ran into trouble. Her boom had sprung and she was unable to participate in the race. The unkind elements later conspired to reveal a weakness in the boom of Mr Johnston's little cutter *Moonbeam IV* during the second round of the King's Cup contest, when running back from the westward. The hollow spar had snapped off close to the mast, tearing her mainsail in the process, making continued participation impossible. A picket boat from HMS *Resolution* took *Moonbeam IV* in tow to her anchorage.

Cariad, owned and sailed by the Earl of Dunraven, was the winner of the King's Cup. The corrected finishing times were:

Cariad	2 hrs 33 mins 26 secs
Valdora	2 hrs 42 mins 6 secs
Joyette	2 hrs 43 mins 47 secs
Sumurun	2 hrs 45 mins 59 secs

In *Terpsichore*'s absence *Sumurun* became scratch to allow *Cariad* 2 mins 12 secs, *Valdora* 5 mins 52 secs, *Joyette* 11 mins 44 secs.

In the second race for yachts of 70 tons upwards, competing for prizes of £80 offered by the RYS, only two competitors made the start line. The king's *Britannia* and Sir Charles Allom's *White Heather II* sailed in a stiff breeze, which was in favour of the royal cutter. A time allowance of 1 minute 34 seconds was donated to *White Heather II* by *Britannia*. The conditions were too severe for the white cutter, which crossed the line without a topsail, seemingly a self-imposed handicap which cost her dearly. *Britannia* was the winner with some 14 minutes to spare.

The day was not without its share of adventure for *Britannia* when a member of her crew narrowly escaped slipping overboard. This might have proven quite serious as a rescue would not have been easy from that sea. He lost his footing and fell on to the yacht's windward freeboard, but with prompt assistance from a fellow crew member was hauled back to the safety of the deck.

It could have been some consolation to Mr Lee, joining his admiral and fellow members at the Royal Yacht Squadron dinner in the evening, burying the morning's disappointment by sampling the delights of a classic menu. Popular music of the period rendered by a hired orchestra conducted by a certain Mr Filer, included: a march, *Children of the Regiment*, a waltz, *On Miami Shore* (Jacobi); a selection *Cavalleria Rusticana* (Mascagni), *Preludium* (Jarnefelt), *Indian Love Lyrics* (Findon), *Humoureske* (Dvorák): selection from *Gipsy Princess* (Kalman). Following this soothing repertoire, the king presented his trophy, with hearty congratulations, to *Cariad*'s owner, the Earl of Dunraven. One is left to imagine the later atmosphere of the club house scented with rich Havanas rivalling the density of an Irish snug.

Wednesday's race for the big handicap class added yet another chapter of disappointment, for Mr Lee in particular. Dismay was earlier caused for the spectators on the parade and afloat by the absence of five entrant yachts at the start as the cutters *White Heather II, Nyria* and *Moonbeam IV*, together with the ketch *Valdora* and the yawl *Sumurun*, were unable to fulfil their entries.

The royal cutter sailed scratch, allowing *Terpsichore* 2 mins 21 seconds, the ketch *Cariad* 38 minutes 23 seconds and the ketch *Joyette* 48 minutes 34 seconds. Both *Britannia* and *Terpsichore* came to the start line reefed down, whilst the ketch and the yawl set jib headers, respecting the squally conditions which were accompanied by heavy rain.

Joyette was first over the line as the starting signal was fired, to be closely followed by *Terpsichore*, which jeopardised her prospects almost immediately by passing to the wrong side of the Fairway Buoy. This entailed a loss of some five minutes in coming about to restart. (Oddly enough, the same error was made by the little cutter *Cyra*, sailing in the 10 to 70 ton handicap class on this day.)

Britannia had the race all her own way when *Terpsichore* retired in the first round, leaving *Cariad* to take second prize whilst *Joyette* came third, completing a forty-seven nautical mile course.

On Thursday of the Cowes Regatta Week, the opening race for the town prizes of £100 was joined by yachts exceeding 70 tons sailed under handicap allowances. *Britannia*, the scratch yacht, gave *Terpsichore* 2 mins 21 secs, *White Heather II* 1 min 34 secs, *Cariad* 38 mins 23 secs and *Joyette* 56 mins 24 secs. The day was favoured by a fresh westerly breeze with occasional heavy squalls and all the skippers, with the exception of *Cariad*'s, prudently hoisted jib headers and reefed their mainsails. The course was programmed to follow that of the previous day with a beat to the Lymington Spit buoy and then running eastwards to the North-East Middle Mark. Sir Godfrey and Lady Baring were Mr Lee's guests on *Terpsichore*. A strong flooding tide from the Needles Channel prompted the fleet to make towards the north shore, where the current slackened. *Britannia* was first over the start line, marginally ahead of *Joyette*, followed by *White Heather II*, *Terpsichore* and *Cariad*. There were a number of changes of position in making the first mark, with *White Heather II* taking a lead from *Britannia* and *Terpsichore* in third place. The little ketch *Joyette* was overtaken by her competitors to find herself last in the procession but, with a generous time allowance ahead, her fortunes were by no means diminished. In rounding the Lymington Spit buoy, *Britannia* passed *White Heather II* and the two leaders enjoyed an immense struggle for first place on the eastward run. As the yachts approached Cowes Roads fate intervened with the prospects of Sir Charles Allom's lovely white cutter when her boom failed under the peak loading of a gusting breeze in a gybe, and so *White Heather II* was forced to retire from the contest.

Terpsichore was unable to match *Britannia* initially in this weight of wind and the latter steadily drew ahead to lead by some 10½ minutes at the close of the first round. The times noted were:

Britannia	1 hr 12 mins 49 secs
Terpsichore	1 hr 23 mins 28 secs
Cariad	1 hr 50 mins 50 secs
Joyette	1 hr 56 mins 36 secs

In the second round, *Terpsichore*, whilst failing to close the gap to the royal cutter, nevertheless matched the leader mile for mile to finish practically the same 10½ minutes distant as recorded at the end of the earlier round.

The actual finishing times were:

Britannia	3 hrs 45 mins 1 sec
Terpsichore	3 hrs 56 mins 26 secs
Cariad	4 hrs 34 mins 27 secs
Joyette	4 hrs 49 mins 49 secs

The corrected times, however, favoured the gallant *Joyette* with her generous time concession, although she was unable to save her time from *Britannia*; the second place was stolen from *Terpsichore* by 1½ minutes, the results being:

Britannia (winner)	3 hrs 45 mins 1 sec
Joyette (second prize)	3 hrs 52 mins 25 secs
Terpsichore (third prize)	3 hrs 54 mins 5 secs
Cariad	3 hrs 58 mins 4 secs

The weather on Friday (Regatta Day) proved ominously treacherous, with heavy squalls predominating. Fears for sails and gear caused the majority of entrants in the over 70 ton handicap class to forgo the privilege of participation. Only *Britannia* and *Joyette* appeared at the start line, well reefed, for the challenge. Oddly enough the race was braved by the largest yacht, *Britannia*, at 221 tons, and the smallest, *Joyette*, at 89 tons, in the Week's competitive series. With such diminished support, the contest proved very disappointing to the spectators, whose eyes became feasted on the events of the smaller classes. *Joyette* was hardly sufficiently weatherproof for racing in such rough climatic conditions and it seemed likely that *Britannia*'s gear was being tested close to its limit from time to time, in roundly beating her spirited little opponent. Sailing on *Britannia* were HM the King, Princess Mary, the Duke of Connaught, the Marquis d'Hautpoul and Capt. Sir Charles Cust.

Deferring to the elements on Regatta Day, Mr Lee had kept *Terpsichore* at her moorings in sympathy with the prudent attitude of the majority, but although the wind had eased to some extent when *Terpsichore* ventured to join the Royal Southampton Yacht Club Regatta on the following day, Nemesis once more intervened. The reservations of Friday on the part of Mr Lee unhappily proved to be of little or no consequence on the Saturday following. The unfortunate *Terpsichore* suffered the ultimate agony of the 1921 Solent events, with the loss of her topmast, off Calshot Castle on the Southampton Water Estuary. Not only did this prove a blow to the immediate prospects of the yacht for this contest, but entries programmed by the Royal Thames Yacht Club Regatta during the following week at Ryde could not be joined; such continuing ill fortune seemed incredible!

In the event, only *Nyria* and *Britannia* came to the line on Monday to sail a course of 46½ miles for yachts exceeding 110 tons (TM). A strong westerly wind, reaching gale force at intervals, whipped up a choppy sea, presenting a formidable challenge to the ultimate capacity of spars and riggings. A last-minute withdrawal, to acknowledge discretion as the better part of valour, saw *Nyria* remaining on the downside of the start line, leaving *Britannia*, fully reefed and minus topsail, to make a sail-over.

Despite *Terpsichore's* misadventures during her 1921 participation in Solent regatta events, much essential data was collected to eliminate relatively minor but otherwise significant weaknesses which could have shown to serious disadvantage on subsequent occasions. The weather in Cowes Roads was some of the roughest likely to be experienced on consecutive days, resulting in conditions which adversely affected many of *Terpsichore's* contemporaries in diverse ways. In later years *Terpsichore* as *Lulworth* proved as rugged as any of the big cutters in the foulest weather. At least *Terpischore's* performance for the season, whilst far from outstanding, was not entirely without some merit, as she gained two first, two second, and one third flags in only thirteen starts. On a points for flags assessment, proportionate to the respective numbers of starts, Mrs Workman's *Nyria* made the star showing, seemingly profiting from her change to Bermudan rig. A comparison of performance figures for the big cutters sailing with marginal time concessions reads:

Yacht	Tonnage	Length o/a	Starts	Perf.Fig.
Nyria	169 TM	98.00 ft	35	2.25
Britannia	221 "	100.00 "	28	1.71
White Heather II	179 "	95.60 "	24	1.58
Terpsichore	186 "	95.50 "	13	1.00

Note: Performance figures calculated by 4 points for first flag, 2 points second flag and 1 point third flag, divided by number of starts.

Following the bitter disappointment of his first season with *Terpsichore*, Mr Lee took the logical step of consulting Charles Nicholson, OBE, RDI, MRINA, an acknowledged leader in the design of big cutters and schooners. His company, Messrs Camper & Nicholson of Gosport, was founded in 1855 by William Camper and his father, Benjamin Nicholson. Charles Nicholson's experience extended over the building of seventy-five schooners, seventy-three cutters and sloops and over fifty yawls and ketches, some of which were constructed after the time of Mr Lee's approach for assistance.

Quite apart from a number of detailed shortcomings with which *Terpsichore* had been plagued in the 1920/21 seasons, it was very obvious that she was far from fulfilling her potential speed capability. Her lines were well conceived for a top-class competitor and there seemed to be no obvious reason why a thorough investigation should not come up with some explanations. Charles Nicholson was amongst the most experienced helmsmen of his day, in addition to his design accomplishments, which made him the ideal or, if not, a uniquely qualified investigator to resolve Mr Lee's problems.

John Nicholson relates in his book, *Great Years in Yachting*, something of the substantial influence which his father exerted upon *Terpsichore* (later extended to *Lulworth*) over the years. In fact, it could be said that Charles Nicholson virtually adopted her and, had Mr. Lee not consulted him, the yacht subsequently known as *Lulworth* could have missed fulfilling her potential as a formidable competitor in later years.

During the Solent regattas Mr Lee invited Charles Nicholson to sail aboard *Terpsichore* and investigate the reason for a sluggish windward performance.

Following a lengthy sail, with much of his time around the foot of the mast, Charles Nicholson arrived at the conclusion, following a study of her bow wave, that the yacht was sagging forward to leeward. It seemed more than possible that someone had either erred in calculation or overlooked a fundamental design concept, to arrive at inappropriate dispositions of the CG (centre of gravity) and the CB (centre of buoyancy) in consideration of the midship sections with the cutter heeled.

Bearing in mind that the high bulwarks gave *Terpsichore* an exaggerated freeboard, which could be used to advantage, Charles Nicholson suggested, as a preliminary, sending the vessel to his Gosport yard for the stowage of additional ballast, which he calculated to be in the order of 9 tons, before racing again. This was no mean adjustment in relation to her displacement weight, but, nevertheless, the innovation proved most effective.

To the delight of Mr Lee, his ambition to build a yacht capable of beating *Britannia* was fulfilled by *Terpsichore*'s improvement in the next racing fixture, resulting in a substantial win over His Majesty's yacht. Whilst one seagull does not make a summer, Mr Lee was greatly encouraged and was subsequently happy to take the further advice of Charles Nicholson on modifying *Terpsichore* by fitting a new and deeper keel.[2]

Hitherto, all of the big cutters (with the exception of *Britannia* which, until 1930–31, was serviced by George Marvin at his East Cowes yard) were laid up and maintained by Charles Nicholson at Gosport. However, the proposed keel modifications exceeded the draft capacity of the Gosport facility and, in consequence, *Terpsichore* was taken to Camper & Nicholson's Southampton yard, where the work could be conveniently handled.

Although Charles Nicholson was involved to a limited extent with certain servicing needs of the schooner *Westward*, she was, whilst in the ownership of Mr Davies, maintained at her home port in Jersey, in the Channel Islands, during the winter.

Terpsichore was the only one of the giant cutters to join the big handicap class in 1922, when she met yachts of lesser tonnage with differing rigs.

Nyria made just one more seasonal appearance in the racing scenario, i.e. during 1923, after which she was lost to the class.

White Heather II was laid up until the 1924 season, when she took the class honours.

Britannia returned to take part in the 1923 season onwards.

---

[1] The smaller royal steam yacht *Alexandra* of 2157 tons (TM) was built for King Edward VII in 1908, designed mainly for cross-Channel visits. Her screws were driven by two Parsons turbines fed from three Yarrow boilers to achieve a top speed of nearly 20 knots. She passed from royal ownership in 1925.

[2] Whilst the introduction of the keel modification was seen to pay off in terms of improved trim without portable ballast, the handling of the yacht in Solent waters inevitably imposed some handicaps. There were times when *Lulworth* (ex-*Terpsichore*) could have profited by sailing an inshore course to cheat the tide whilst her contemporaries gained this advantage. At other times, when leading the fleet and with victory apparent, she grounded and robbed herself of the honour.

1922

TERPSICHORE BEARS THE TORCH

This was the year when the arrival of the royal yacht and her escorts for Regatta Week followed an alternative programme. Instead of making the traditional approach to Cowes Roads from Portsmouth Harbour through Spithead, their Majesties King George V and Queen Mary, on board the *V & A*, cruised 'down channel' in fair weather, with a detour to reach the usual mooring, by sailing through the Needles Passage. The customary boom of welcoming artillery gave a stamp of authority to the pageant arriving from the west as the sovereign's ships claimed their normal anchorages.

The guardship HMS *Barham* (flagship of the First Battle Squadron of the Atlantic Fleet commanded by Robin C. Dalglish, RN) and the destroyer HMS *Versatile* joined to stamp His Majesty's authority upon the festival. The men o' war relieved their aggressive silhouettes of deepest grey with myriads of bunting, seemingly competing with the lavish decorations of the yacht clubs and seafront generally, where thousands of loyal subjects had congregated to greet the royal party, which included Prince George and Field Marshal the Duke of Connaught. Of the many distinguished visitors, this occasion included the presence of Princess Margaret of Greece.

Following enthusiastic attempts by the Royal Yacht Squadron to revive first class cutter racing in the 1920 and 1921 seasons, the torch burned very dim in the year 1922. The King's favourite toy was out of commission, undergoing some essential renovation and refitting in the hands of George Marvin on the River Medina slipway. These were on the recommendations of Watson's surveyor, Mr J.R. Barnett. His Majesty's indulgence in the sport was sustained by two of his most loyal subjects at the club house. The King sailed firstly in the 28 ton cutter *Mavoureen*[1] with Major Philip Hunloke and later, accompanied by the Duke of Connaught, on the magnificent black-hulled 292 ton (TM) auxiliary schooner *Magdalene*[2] (owned by another squadron member, Mr W.G. Jameson), to cruise the Solent and observe the racing.

Neither *Nyria* nor *White Heather II* were fitted out, which left only Mr Lee to maintain big cutter interests, more particularly as the further necessary development of his yacht was dependent largely upon extended racing experience. The competition in 1922 provided scope for only a limited number of starts, from which *Terpsichore* enjoyed a fair share of success.

During Cowes Week of 1922, *Terpsichore* kept the big handicap class standard flying as a sole representative of the big cutters. However, she found some good sport with four smaller opponents which she had already met in the 1921 events. On Monday, the first day in the calendar, she joined the handicap event for yachts of 70 tons and over, with any rig, the course being twice round the Solent Bank and N-E Middle buoys, a distance of 39 nautical miles, starting at 10 a.m.

The starters were Mr R.H. Lee's *Terpsichore*, 186 tons, Capt. Cecil W.P. Slade's ketch *Joyette*, 89 tons, Sir Thomas Dunlop's yawl, *Harbinger*, 94 tons. *Terpsichore* allowed *Joyette* 36 mins 24 secs and *Harbinger* 39 mins. A most uninspiring start was made when the Blue Peter was lowered. Both *Joyette* and *Terpsichore* were over the line with the signal and as the recall gun was fired they came about, joined by *Harbinger*, not sure whether she too had transgressed! The Clyde-built yawl quickly recovered and took the lead. *Terpsichore* and *Harbinger* sported jib headers and *Joyette* a jackyard topsail. The beat to the Solent Bank Mark was soon headed by *Terpsichore* and she was 18 minutes ahead of *Joyette* as she rounded to run back to the westward with spinnaker set. *Terpsichore* pulled further ahead as she left *Joyette* astern, which in turn increased her distance from *Harbinger*.

The first round times were:

Terpsichore	12 hrs 22 mins 52 secs
Joyette	12 hrs 51 mins 26 secs
Harbinger	1 hr 2 mins 13 secs

The positions remained unchanged until some minutes after the start of the second round, when *Joyette*'s bobstay failed, resulting in her bowsprit snapping off short. This misfortune obviously necessitated her retirement, thereby losing the prospect of second prize. *Terpsichore* added yet another mishap to her previous year's catalogue of ill luck by losing her spinnaker boom, but she was fortunate in being able to carry on to a successful finish with 14 mins 9 secs to spare beyond her time allowance to *Harbinger*.

The resulting times (corrected) were:

Terpsichore (winner)	2 hrs 15 mins 53 secs
Harbinger (second prize)	3 hrs 46 mins 2 secs

The first prize of £70 was awarded to Mr Lee's cutter.

Terpsichore was entered for the King's Cup race on Tuesday of the Week. Mr Lee was entertaining the Marquis of Ailsa and a number of Sir Godfrey Baring's guests from Nubia House on board his cutter. The race was sailed over two rounds of the 46 mile Queen's Course, exclusive to yachts of 30 tons TM upward belonging to members of the Royal Yacht Squadron. Competing yachts at the 10 a.m. start included Mr Lee's *Terpsichore*, Lord Sackville's yawl *Sumurun*, Sir William Portal's 106 ton ketch, *Valdora*, Capt. C.W.P. Slade's ketch *Joyette* following an overnight bowsprit replacement, and Brigadier General Sir Hugh Drummond's yawl *Coral*.

Terpsichore was the scratch boat, allowing *Sumurun* 28 mins 36 secs, *Valdora* 53 mins 32 secs, *Joyette* 60 mins 52 secs, *Coral* 98 mins 16 secs. A strong westerly breeze was blowing at the start, heralding some spirited racing. Outside the Cowes Roads a fairly heavy sea was running. All of the yachts were fully canvased with yarded topsails. *Terpsichore* and *Joyette* were over-anxious to get started, being across the line once more when the gun fired, earning a recall. Neither of them wasted much time in making a renewed get-away. *Sumurun* led the little fleet with *Valdora* just astern, followed by *Coral* some way behind. It was not *Coral*'s day, however, as her bobstay plate fractured immediately after crossing the line, thereby forcing her retirement. *Sumurun* sailed astonishingly well, holding off the challenge from *Terpsichore*, which had overtaken *Valdora* and *Joyette* before rounding the first mark. Following a beat to the East Lepe buoy and a run to the Warner Lightship, and with a further beat to the line at the end of the first round, *Terpsichore* was eight minutes astern of *Sumurun* and shortly afterwards gave up. *Terpsichore* had been plagued by trouble with an experimental power-assisted steering gear, consisting of an electric actuator. Mr Lee had a wish for his grandson, Master Roger Leech, to take an active part at the wheel and, whilst the proposal was admirable in many ways, the equipment lacked adequate development.[3]

Sumurun extended her advantage over *Valdora* and *Joyette* during the second round, finishing 21 mins 21 secs ahead of *Valdora* but, in having to concede the ketch 25 minutes, the yawl *Sumurun* had to be content with second place.

Corrected times were:

Valdora (cup)	2 hrs 52 mins 39 secs
Sumurun	2 hrs 57 mins 14 secs
Joyette	3 hrs 0 mins 6 secs

On the Wednesday of the Week, in a handicap race for yachts exceeding 70 tons (Thames Measurement) for a squadron prize of £100 over a 42 mile course, *Terpsichore*'s opponents were *Sumurun*, 92 tons (Lord Sackville), *Harbinger*, 94 tons (Sir Thomas Dunlop), *Joyette*, 89 tons (Col. Slade).

No entry was received from Sir William Portal's yacht *Valdora* and Mr Warwick Brookes's 154 ton schooner *Susanne*, although entered and on station, was withdrawn from the event.

Terpsichore allowed *Sumurun* 30 mins 33 secs, *Joyette* 65 mins 4 secs, and *Harbinger* 67 mins 30 secs. They all came to the line on the starboard tack carrying jib topsails and jack yarders, with the exception of *Joyette*, which had nothing aloft. There was a moderate westerly breeze blowing at the start, which dropped later. *Terpsichore* distinguished herself once again by qualifying for a recall gun, being marginally over the line at the start! As she came about *Harbinger* slipped into the lead. With such big margins of time allowances to overcome, this additional handicap was obviously deserved but most unwelcome. *Harbinger* had the windward position, closely followed by *Sumurun* whilst *Joyette* was some way astern and to the leeward of *Sumurun*.

Terpsichore recrossed the line with a minimum of delay and made the Lymington Spit buoy before her competitors. As she passed through the Roads on the return leg to the eastwards, she led *Sumurun* by approximately eight minutes, with *Joyette* and *Harbinger* following in that order. They made use of their spinnakers against a foul tide to round the N-E Middle buoy.

Times at the end of the first round were:

Terpsichore	1 hr 28 mins 30 secs
Sumurun	1 hr 41 mins 13 secs
Joyette	1 hr 55 mins 42 secs
Harbinger	1 hr 59 mins 32 secs

Terpsichore forged ahead to increase her lead in the second round (during which *Joyette* and *Harbinger* gave up) and won by a comfortable margin of some 18 minutes. Finishing times were (corrected) as follows:

Terpsichore (winner)	5 hrs 13 mins 9 secs
Sumurun (second)	5 hrs 31 mins 50 secs

The programme for the Thursday of the Royal Yacht Squadron Regatta again drew the support of Mr Lee's *Terpsichore*, Lord Sackville's yawl *Sumurun*, Sir Thomas Dunlop's yawl *Harbinger* and Col. Slade's ketch *Joyette*. This was a more closely contested race than the one sailed on the day before. Prizes presented by Cowes Town were £70 for the winner and £30 for second place.

The 10 o'clock start for the little fleet was the finest of the Week, coming up to the starting line on the starboard tack in a faint air with very little distance separating them. *Terpsichore* allowed *Sumurun* 28 mins 36 secs, *Joyette* 60 mins 52 secs and *Harbinger* 63 mins 4 secs. As they crossed the start line *Harbinger* was just showing ahead of *Terpsichore*, followed by *Joyette* and *Sumurun* in that order. On the beat to the East Lepe buoy *Terpsichore* took the lead, rounding the weather mark 1 min 14 secs ahead of *Sumurun*, with *Joyette* only one minute later and *Harbinger* trailing astern. For the run back to the Warner, spinnakers were set and the results at the completion of the first round show *Terpsichore* nearly 13 minutes ahead of *Sumurun*, the times being:

Terpsichore	1 hr 21 mins 30 secs
Sumurun	1 hr 34 mins 24 secs
Joyette	1 hr 52 mins 11 secs
Harbinger	1 hr 58 mins 15 secs

Terpsichore doubled her lead in the second round but both *Sumurun* and *Joyette* had their revenge over the previous day's placings by taking first and second prizes respectively, each having saved her time on *Terpsichore*, a tribute to their sportsmanship. The final results based upon corrected times were:

Sumurun (winner)	3 hrs 49 mins 43 secs
Joyette (second)	3 hrs 51 mins 25 secs

| *Terpsichore* | 3 hrs 51 mins 53 secs |
| *Harbinger* | 4 hrs 4 mins 0 secs |

These results are most interesting, being something of a compliment to the handicapper, as they are relatively close considering the differing rigs and tonnages of the competing yachts. Here we find *Terpsichore*, a cutter of 189 tons, just an artificial 2 mins and 10 secs behind *Sumurun*, a yawl of 92 tons, sailing a course of some 44 miles with wind forces at compass points which could scarcely be anticipated. The resultant time separation between *Terpsichore* and *Joyette* of only 28 secs shows an even greater tribute to estimates of sailing performance.

On Friday of the Week, otherwise known as Regatta Day, the royal yacht *Victoria and Albert*, the guardship HMS *Barham* and the attending destroyer were dressed overall, with the fleet of cruising yachts belonging to the loyal subjects being similarly festooned in line with customary drill. The opening race of the day was a handicap for yachts exceeding 70 tons sailing a course of 47 miles, the prize being £100 first (only).

Terpsichore, the lone representative of the big cutters in 1922, sailed scratch, allowing the mixture of competing rigs the following times:

Lord Sackville's yawl *Sumurun*	30 mins 33 secs
Sir William Portal's ketch *Valdora*	57 mins 11 secs
Captain Slade's ketch *Joyette*	65 mins 1 sec
Sir Thomas Dunlop's yawl *Harbinger*	79 mins 7 secs

Full light weather canvas was carried by all competitors on this day as the wind was disappointingly frugal. All the yachts were well behind the start line as the 10 a.m. gun boomed. *Terpsichore* was first to cross, followed in order by *Harbinger*, *Sumurun*, *Valdora* and *Joyette*. The last two ketches had misjudged the timing very badly and their skippers found themselves substantially behind, although *Valdora* did well to make up the distance, eventually taking second place.

Terpsichore, with spinnaker set to port, was first to round the Lymington Spit Mark and continued, not unexpectedly, to increase her lead over *Sumurun* as the beat was made to the North-East Middle buoy against a foul tide and with a paucity of air. The winning gun was received by *Terpsichore* at the end of the first round. Due to the conditions, it was considered unlikely that any of the other competitors might be able to overhaul her as she was, even at half distance, comfortably in hand with the fulfilment of her full time donations. The final result gave *Terpsichore* her third win of the week, with *Valdora* taking the second flag and *Harbinger* third.

The results were:

Terpsichore (winner)
Valdora
Harbinger

The 1922 programme of the Royal Victoria Yacht Club did not include any events to invite *Terpsichore*'s participation at Ryde.

---

[1] Sir Philip Hunloke's 28 ton cutter, named *Mavoureen*, sailing at Cowes in the Twenties, was built at Fairlee on the Clyde in 1909, her original name being *Chameleon*.

[2] Mr W.G. Jameson's auxiliary schooner *Magdalene II* was a robust steel yacht; a typical product of the American Herreshoff yard. With a deck measurement of 130 feet, her dark hull with classic lines presented a most striking appearance, both at anchor and with all fabric bent. She was launched under the name of *Elfay*, later being given the title of *Katoura* before her post-war appearance at Southampton.

[3] In retrospect, it seems extremely odd that an electric power-assisted steering installation should have been specified for *Terpsichore* without some provision for a manual override in case of mechanical failure. Without such a facility the vessel could have become a serious danger to itself and shipping using the Solent waters generally.

The Yacht Racing Association Rule No.22, which was mandatory at this time, states 'Manual power only may be used for hoisting and working sails, or for working a centre board or plate', and it was subsequently decided that the use of any power except 'manual' during a race, such as steering, was contrary to the spirit of the rules. It seems likely that, had the electric steering aid been successful and *Terpsichore* won, she could have been disqualified, although Rule 22 did not at that time specifically refer to power-assisted to steering, even if it had been implied.

Plate (1)   *The Big Five*– Lulworth (*ex* Terpsichore), Shamrock, Westward, Britannia *and* White Heather II.

Plate (2)

Seal of the Royal Yacht Club, Cowes.

Plate (3)

The aux. barque-rigged yacht Fantôme II *(ex* Belem*) owned by Col. the Hon. Arthur E. Guinness. An early cruise in his ownership included a voyage around the world.*

Plate (4)
The Royal Yacht Squadron Club House premises at Cowes.

Plate (5)
The steam yacht Xarifa *built for Mr F Morton Singer of New York by*
J Samuel White & Co Ltd, at Cowes in 1930

Plate (6)
Mr Paxton's diesel engined yacht Braemar II *immediately following her launch from the slipways of J Samuel White & Co Ltd, on the Medina River in 1929*

Plate (7)
The magnificent twin screw steam yacht Liberty *of 1571 tons, 250 feet long, 35.6 feet beam, designed by Mr G T Watson for Mr J Pulitzer and built by Ramage and Ferguson of Leith in 1901. She was owned and based in Jersey by Sir Robert and Lady Fanny Houston, DBE, in the twenties*

Plate (8)
A well preserved relic of the nineteenth century Dolly Vardon *pride of sailmaker Thomas Ratsey. Her L.O.A. and W.L. appear coincident.*

Plate (9)
The 56,000 ton White Star liner, S.S. Majestic (ex Bismark). A regular visitor to Southampton Docks.

Plate (10)
An unusual view of the very successful cutter Nyria *in her earlier topsailed rig rounding a mark in light airs. She was raced by the great sportswoman Mrs. E.R. Workman in the early twenties.*

Plate (11)
The cutter Nyria *following her conversion to Bermudian rig in 1921.*

1923

BRITANNIA TAKES THE SEASONAL HONOURS

On Saturday, August 4th 1923, prior to Cowes Regatta Week, the King and Queen arrived aboard the twin screw steam yacht *Victoria and Albert III*, under the command of Rear Admiral Henry Buller ADC. She was escorted by the battleship HMS *Barham* (which attended previously in 1922), commanded this year by Captain Percy Noble, RN, and the destroyer HMS *Vesper*, under Commander R.V. Holt, whose duty it was to escort the King's cutter *Britannia* throughout the racing season at the various coastal regattas. The royal party was joined by the fourth son Prince George, Princess Victoria, Field Marshal the Duke of Connaught, the Marquise d'Hautpoul, the Countess of Shaftesbury, the Earl of Mount Edgcumbe, the Hon. Sir Derek Keppel and the Hon. Sir Harry Stonor. Of the great fleet of magnificent steam and motor yachts, which mostly boasted British ensigns, there were a few foreign visiting craft such as Brig. Gen. Cornelius Vanderbilt's[1] three-masted schooner *Atlantic* (winner of the Atlantic race for the ex-Kaiser's Gold Cup in 1905) flying the Stars and Stripes; the steam yacht *Elettra*, the property of Senator G. Marconi was bedecked with the Italian national flag, together with the RYS burgee at the foremast to indicate his club membership, and the gigantic steam yacht *Goizeko–Izarra* belonging to Sir Ramón de la Sota flying the Spanish pennant. On a few of the smaller vessels the Tricolore appeared, giving the scene something of the air of an international pageant.

Cowes Week had yet to re-establish the sparkle of its illustrious pre-war past. It seemed that continued enthusiasm for big cutter racing was all-important in the maintenance of long-established popularity. For the yachtsmen there was everything to enjoy by competing in the ranks of varied class events, but for the spectators, many of whom had scant knowledge of the sport, the apparent confusion of the scene could be undoubtedly bewildering. Recognition of a handful of giants was therefore easier and almost always provided greater excitement for the lesser-informed onlooker, whilst equally riveting the attention of more mature students of the sport.

During their absence from the Summer Regatta of 1922, *Terpsichore*'s contemporaries *Nyria* and *Britannia* had been undergoing updating modifications and refits for the following season's racing calendar.

The future of the class still hung in the balance, for *White Heather* did not fit out, which left the three big class cutters *Terpsichore*, *Nyria* and *Britannia* as mainstays of the events. *Terpsichore* participated in only fourteen races in the 1923 season, whilst *Nyria* and *Britannia* took part in twenty-five and twenty-six respectively.

With improved rigging and hull renovations, *Britannia* narrowly led the league over *Nyria*, each having eleven first prizes, with the former taking two more second flags.

Terpsichore managed just three first prizes and two seconds. A crew which takes part in fewer races is often at a substantial disadvantage *vis-à-vis* its contemporaries. Not only is there a reduction of practice in working together, thereby restricting the master's opportunity to train a crew, there is, equally, the loss of opportunity to study rival tactics and reactions under a greater spread of tidal and climatic influences. Whilst *Terpsichore* had at this stage made odd appearances, thereby assisting in bolstering support for the big class, she had not nearly completed a full calendar during the earlier seasons of the decade. She had yet to demonstrate convincing competitive capability.

In order to complete a full season's round of the premier yacht clubs, a competing yacht would have to sail something like four thousand, five hundred miles under all sorts of conditions, which were often far from favourable. *Britannia* was usually privileged to enjoy a tow from her naval escort between regatta venues. In addition the escort quite often provided the luxury of laundry and uniform-drying services for the crew of the royal cutter.

The average full race distance for the big handicap class usually measured about forty-five miles, which meant two rounds of a typical Solent course. Under near flat calm conditions, when the yachts had been involved in something of a 'drifting match', a race, at the stewards' discretion, would often be stopped at the end of one round.

In order to boost the assembly, the 153 ton ketch *Cariad*, owned by the Rt. Hon. John Gretton, CBE, and the 106 ton ketch *Valdora*, belonging to Sir William Portal, Bart, sportingly took part in a small number of events. A second prize gained by *Cariad* was the only flag shared by the two competing ketches during the week.

On Monday, August 6th, 1923, the race for the yachts of any rig exceeding 70 tons (TM) launched the proceedings of the Royal London Yacht Club Regatta, using the facilities of the RYS, with a 10 a.m. start. Two prizes were offered, these being £60 for the winner and £20 second flag. The course sailed measured 39 sea miles, starting from the squadron in a windward direction marked by the Solent Bank and North-East Middle buoys. A select fleet of cutters included HM the King's *Britannia*, Mr R.H. Lee's *Terpsichore*, Mrs E.R. Workman's *Nyria* and *Moonbeam IV*, which was sportingly entered by Mr C.P. Johnson and, although of much lower rating, acquitted herself extremely well, aided by a generous bonus from the handicappers. *Britannia* sailed scratch, giving *Nyria* 8 mins 51 secs, *Terpsichore* 8 mins 27 secs and *Moonbeam IV* 25 mins 21 secs.

Moonbeam IV made the best of the start by leading to windward some two minutes ahead of the little fleet, all of which overhauled her before rounding the western mark, beating against a foul tide. They ran back through the Roadstead with spinnakers out to starboard in light airs. *Britannia, Nyria, Terpsichore* and *Moonbeam IV* sailed close together in that order, until they made Osborne Bay, when *Nyria* caught a catspaw and overtook the royal cutter. On the beat returning from the eastward, *Nyria* succeeded in forging ahead from the fleet and actual times at the completion of first round were: *Nyria* 1 hr 13 mins 11 secs, *Britannia* 1 hr 15 mins 14 secs, *Terpsichore* 1 hr 19 mins 34 secs, *Moonbeam IV* 1 hr, 22 mins 13 secs. Positions changed yet again when *Britannia* found the freshening wind very much to her liking and worked out a fair lead from *Nyria*. Meanwhile, *Terpsichore* began a continuing series of Solent mishaps on this, the opening contest of the week, suffering a burst mainsail which forced her retirement whilst the sun smiled upon her competitors. The omen was indeed to prove one of an ill nature for *Terpsichore*'s continuing 1923 Cowes Regatta hopes.

Oddly enough, whilst *Britannia* was first to cross the finishing line, she came last on corrected time. For *Britannia* the handicappers had meanly misread their crystal ball. *Nyria* took the second flag, saving her time by just 45 seconds, but the honours were accorded to *Moonbeam IV*, which sailed a magnificent race to finish several minutes inside her handicap allowance. The corrected time results were:

Moonbeam IV (winner)	3 hrs 27 mins 10 secs
Nyria (second prize)	3 hrs 42 mins 29 secs
Britannia	3 hrs 43 mins 2 secs

His Majesty King George V was sailing aboard *Britannia* (with Prince George, Princess Victoria and the Duke of Connaught) and, whilst he did not succeed in taking the winning flag, the act of being first across the finishing line was probably a consolation prize. The majority of onlookers would have wrongly assumed the royal cutter to have won first prize in any case!

With *Terpsichore* dressed in a spare mainsail, she was entered for the King's Cup event, which took place on Tuesday, 7th August, 1923. The race was organised for vessels of 30 tons register and upwards, belonging to the RYS, to sail under handicap allowances. The 46 mile course was twice round The Queen's, plotted to the East Lepe buoy in the west, extending round the Warner Lightship, to return from the east. This was the first race of the day, with a 10 a.m. start.

Mr R.H. Lee's *Terpsichore* sailed scratch, allowing Mr C.P. Johnston's *Moonbeam IV* 19 mins 56 secs, Mr Kenneth Preston's cutter *Paula* 24 mins 22 secs, Col. J. Gretton's ketch *Cariad* 26 mins 50 secs, Sir William Portal's yawl *Valdora* 42 mins 56 secs, and Lieut. Col. A. Gage's auxiliary schooner *Amphitrite* 72 mins 50 secs.

The crowds thronging the public walkway seaward of the squadron starter's office were treated to a classic line-up. With the exception of *Paula*, which sported a jib-headed topsail, the rest of the assembly carried full canvas including jackyarders. The line was crossed in close company on the starboard tack with *Moonbeam IV* repeating the previous day's manoeuvre and taking the advantage, although *Terpsichore* and *Paula* ran her closely. Next followed *Valdora* to leeward, *Amphitrite* taking fifth position and *Cariad* sixth. When *Terpsichore* went into the lead she looked as if she might have discovered some favour of the gods, but she was finding it difficult to shake the tenacity of *Moonbeam IV*. With twenty minutes to make up and only another thirty miles to sail, the task was formidable enough if she was to have any hope of taking the cup. Following the beat from the start line to the East Lepe, *Moonbeam IV* was still hanging on to *Terpsichore* during the first run to the Warner. *Paula* came next, followed by *Valdora*, with *Amphitrite* to leeward and *Cariad* to the rear. On the long beat returning from the Warner, *Terpsichore* had only extended 6½ minutes lead over *Moonbeam IV* by the end of the first round. The times noted were *Terpsichore* 12 hrs 34 mins 56 secs, *Moonbeam IV* 12 hrs 41 mins 24 secs, *Paula* 12 hrs 59 mins 11 secs, *Valdora* 1 hr 0 mins 50 secs, *Cariad* 1 hr 9 mins 43 secs, *Amphitrite* 1 hr 58 mins 45 secs. The old schooner sailed on gamely for a while but, being hopelessly unable to progress within her time allowance, retired to reach her moorings during the second round. By this time the fleet had been well spaced out beyond the point where any dicing might have been expected. The finishing line was crossed first by *Terpsichore*, just 12 mins 21 secs ahead of *Moonbeam IV* which, of course, meant that the latter easily saved her time to take the cup. In the event it proved to be one of *Terpsichore's* more fortunate days of the week; at least she finished a race and claimed second placing.

The recorded finishing times (corrected for handicap allowances) were:

Moonbeam IV (winner)	3 hrs 18 mins 42 secs
Terpsichore	3 hrs 26 mins 7 secs
Valdora	3 hrs 29 mins 0 secs
Paula III	3 hrs 52 mins 29 secs
Cariad	4 hrs 7 mins 55 secs

The second Royal Yacht Squadron programmed event of the Week, held on Wednesday, August 8th, 1923, for yachts exceeding 100 tons TM was a rather disappointing and protracted one. There was a paucity of air to enliven any prospect of good sport at the 10 a.m. start line. During the day the wind vanished to the extent where yachts were completely becalmed for long periods, necessitating the employment of kedge anchors. The intended use of the Queen's two round forty-six mile course was judiciously reduced to half distance, finishing after one round. Prizes of £70 for the winner and £30 second were offered. Although it was a distinctly unfavourable day for yacht racing generally, the near tropical summer heat proved ideal for bathing off the shore in flat water. This was to be yet another day when *Terpsichore's* unhappy total of frustrating incidents was aggravated, although her main sparring partner suffered in sympathy, being disqualified for another reason which she scarcely deserved.

The four entries consisted of the sovereign's *Britannia*, on which he was sailing, Mr R. H. Lee's cutter *Terpsichore*, Mrs E.R. Workman's cutter *Nyria* and Col. J. Gretton's ketch *Cariad*. *Britannia* had to make a more liberal time allowance than that conceded on the Monday, giving *Nyria* 8 mins 54 secs, *Terpsichore* 9 mins 58 secs, and *Cariad* 36 mins 48 secs.

Britannia and *Nyria* were seen to be practically level in drifting over the line as the starting signal was fired, with *Terpsichore* just astern of the two and *Cariad* much later. Such breeze as could be detected came from the westward direction, but the effect of the ebbing tide almost certainly proved the main assistance in progressing around the East Lepe buoy. *Nyria* was first round, followed in order by *Terpsichore* and then *Britannia*. *Cariad*, struggling along behind, began to close towards the royal cutter, which was not enjoying the sultry air in combination with the foul tide as she headed east for the Warner Lightship. Progress at this stage proved impossible in a flat calm with hardly a detectable ripple. Nature could not have been less kind to the yachtsmen at that moment, as they were obliged to kedge and some time elapsed before they found it possible to proceed. It developed into an uninspiring and rather straggling contest, with *Nyria* giving a remarkable exhibition of her ability to progress with sails hardly filled. On the return run from the westward *Terpsichore* made a *faux pas* by passing the mark boat on the wrong side and shortly gave up. Once more, *Terpsichore* was to become discredited, not in fact due to any inherent lack of design integrity or inability to display a measure of sailing performance on par with her contemporaries. The day's jinx was seemingly related to handling but, in fairness, the lack of wind and/or a perverse current could have robbed her skipper of a preferred manoeuvre.

Britannia came in second when the race was stopped at the end of the first round, but was disqualified on a technical point, whereby the rules were infringed. It so happened that *Britannia* had left behind her kedge anchor off Gurnard early in the race, when the item had become entangled with a cross-Solent telephone cable.

Nyria finished the race without the need to call upon her time allowance and, with *Britannia's* unfortunate breach of sailing regulations, Col. Gretton's ketch *Cariad* qualified for the second prize, this being her first flag of the season. The corrected finishing times noted were:

> *Nyria* (winner)   4 hrs 14 mins 5 secs
> *Cariad* (second)   6 hrs 23 mins 43 secs

The crew of the grand old ketch displayed a most admirable degree of patience to prove worthy of her flag, arriving 2 hrs 9 mins 38 secs behind the cutter!

The race for the town prizes on the Thursday of Cowes Week 1923, in which *Terpsichore* participated in the company of *Britannia*, *Cariad* and *Nyria*, proved to be yet another experience to add to the modern cutter's catalogue of misfortunes after a brilliant start. Prizes amounting to £100 were put up by the residents of Cowes. The programmed race was for yachts in excess of 100 tons (TM) and the course to be sailed was twice round the Solent Bank, North-East Middle and South-East Middle buoys, a distance of approximately forty sea miles, starting at 10 a.m. The royal cutter sailed scratch, allowing her competitors *Nyria* 6 mins, *Terpsichore* 8 mins 40 secs and *Cariad* 37 mins 20 secs. A classic start was made with *Terpsichore* to windward, crossing the line first on the port tack, giving every indication of a masterful approach to a serious day's sport. *Britannia*, *Nyria* and the ketch *Cariad* were sailing in close company on the starboard tack. They were assisted by an ebbing tide in a beat to the western mark, which *Terpsichore* rounded first, benefiting by that close-winded capability which she so often exhibited during her later racing seasons. Second place was smartly taken by *Nyria*, followed by *Britannia* some forty seconds later. The lovely old ketch *Cariad* was gamely struggling in the rear. At the end of the first round *Britannia* had overhauled *Nyria* whilst *Terpsichore* was still in the lead. Their recorded times (uncorrected) were very much in favour of *Terpsichore*, as she was not calling on her time donation at this stage.

The figures were:

Terpsichore	12 hrs 48 mins 50 secs
Nyria	12 hrs 50 mins 57 secs
Britannia	12 hrs 51 mins 38 secs
Cariad	1 hr 21 mins 53 secs

When *Nyria* and *Britannia* were seen off Gurnard Ledge in the second round, they appeared from the shore to be at practically level pegging and, after rounding the Solent Bank mark on the run back, *Britannia* overtook *Nyria*, passing through her lee. The wind freshened to *Britannia*'s advantage and she took the lead from *Terpsichore* to sustain this position, seemingly afforded by the latter's continued string of misfortunes. *Terpsichore* was timed to be well within her limit of allowance when Nemesis intervened: she ran aground in Gurnard Bay but a mile and a half from the finish. Clearly, at this stage, *Terpsichore* had demonstrated an ability to successfully compete with yachts of her rating without a time concession once she could get away from these extraneous influences but, for the third time this week, her opportunity was denied. *Britannia*, although first home, was insufficiently ahead of *Nyria* to prevent the Bermudan from saving her time.

Corrected finishing times were:

Nyria (winner)	3 hrs 0 mins 2 secs
Britannia (second)	3 hrs 2 mins 58 secs
Cariad	3 hrs 13 mins 36 secs

Some two hours later *Terpsichore* refloated and was towed back to her moorings in the Cowes Roadstead with no apparent damage.

The 1923 RYS programme of the Week was subject to an eleventh hour adjustment, when racing fixtures for the Regatta Day were cancelled as a mark of respect following the unhappy news of the death of President Harding. The third event for the British–American six metre yachts contest was postponed until the following day (Saturday), August 11th. Racing for yachts upwards of 100 tons (TM) was also sympathetically rearranged.

This was a further occasion when the contestants were deprived of their sailing needs, only to take part in a virtual drifting match which became tedious in the extreme. The 10 a.m. start for the big handicap class was based upon two rounds of the Queen's course (approximately forty-six sea miles) for the RYS prizes of £70 first, £20 second and £10 third; the competitors were the royal cutter *Britannia* (scratch), Mrs E.R. Workman's *Nyria* (allowed 6 mins 54 secs), Mr R.H. Lee's *Terpsichore* (9 mins 58 secs), Col. J. Gretton's *Cariad* (42 mins 56 secs), Sir William Portal's *Valdora* (52 mins 54 secs). The starting gun sounded, emitting its puff of smoke as if to mock those frustrated skippers whose charges were kedged eastward of the line. Equally frustrated was the crowd on the esplanade, who were feeling cheated at the end of a week when they saw Wednesday's display almost repeated.

After a considerable delay the assembly was favoured by the turn of the tide to drift substantially westwards to the East Lepe buoy, rounded firstly by *Nyria*, which was scarcely to her advantage, as the wind died completely, utterly becalming the fleet and kedging it for five hours before making it possible to return past the club house from the first mark! The crawl to the east continued throughout the afternoon and it was well past 6 p.m. before any signs of their return from the Warner became evident. *Nyria* was first over the line when she received her gun, the race being stopped after one round. She had completed twenty-three nautical miles in approximately nine hours, an average of 2.55 knots! Meanwhile the two ketches *Cariad* and *Valdora* had retired from the contest.

Terpsichore came home some eight minutes later and *Britannia* drifted four minutes behind. After such displays of endurance, it was fitting that the three finishing cutters, at least, won prizes of some value.

The actual and corrected finishing times recorded were:

Yacht	Actual	Corrected
Nyria (winner)	6 hrs 56 mins 50	6 hrs 49 mins 6
Terpsichore	7 hrs 4 mins 57	6 hrs 54 mins 9
Britannia	7 hrs 8 mins 53	7 hrs 8 mins 53

Whilst the corrected times are quoted as a matter of convention, time allowances in such conditions were hardly meaningful.

Following the breathless end to the yachting festival at Cowes, the opening day of the racing at Ryde, under the joint auspices of the Royal Victoria and the Royal Thames Yacht Clubs, provided practically ideal sailing conditions, starting with a steady breeze which freshened after lunch. The Sailing Committee was chaired by Lieut. Col. J.E. Rhodes.

On August 13th, 1923 there were three entries for the RVYC International Gold Challenge Cup race inviting yachts of any rig in the over 100 ton (TM) class starting at 11 a.m. *Britannia* sailed scratch, allowing *Terpsichore* 9 mins 58 secs for the forty-six miles long Victoria Course and *Nyria* was allowed 6 mins 54 secs. A very light west by south-west wind was noted as the yachts anticipated the start.

Nyria crossed the line first, with *Britannia* marginally astern of her. *Terpsichore* had badly misjudged her time to cross, coming some two minutes after the leader. Mrs Workman's cutter was first to round the west middle mark with *Britannia* on her beam shortly after, overtaking as they passed through Stokes Bay. At the end of the first round the trio was still headed by *Britannia* and seen to be profiting from a stiff breeze as the race progressed.

The actual first round times were:

Britannia	2 hrs 30 mins 54 secs
Terpsichore	2 hrs 36 mins 40 secs
Nyria	2 hrs 37 mins 45 secs

Terpsichore had sailed hard in the freshening wind, making up her loss of time to pull one minute ahead of *Nyria*, and the advantage opened up until the end of the second round.

During the final leg of the course, with an easing of the wind, the lead which *Britannia* had built to distance herself from *Terpsichore* was becoming steadily eroded to the point where she was unable to save her time on Mr Lee's cutter. Whilst the former crossed the finishing line first, she had to be content with a second prize.

Yacht	Actual	Corrected
Terpsichore (winner)	4 hrs 55 mins 33	4 hrs 45 mins 35
Britannia (second)	4 hrs 47 mins 6	4 hrs 47 mins 6
Nyria	4 hrs 58 mins 46	4 hrs 51 mins 52

In addition to the honour of winning the International Gold Challenge Cup, the race winner had the option of a silver salver or £50 prize money. The second prize amounted to £20.

The race on Tuesday, organised by the Royal Victoria Yacht Club, was sailed for the Assheton–Smith Challenge Cup, starting from the headquarters of the latter on Ryde Pierhead. A prize of £50 was donated by the commodore to the winner in addition to the honour of receiving the vase.

The three entrants were the same as those on the previous day. *Britannia* sailed scratch, allowing *Nyria* 6 minutes 5 seconds and *Terpsichore* 9 minutes 58 seconds for the full course of forty-six miles. The wind was so faint that the struggle lasted into late afternoon, when only one round had been completed. *Terpsichore* retired some time before the finish, leaving *Nyria* well ahead of *Britannia*, which came second some ten minutes later.

The corrected finishing times were:

Nyria	5 hrs 29 mins 56 secs
Britannia	5 hrs 46 mins 6 secs

The Solent had exhibited yet another day of sporting disappointment.

The feeling of gloom was hardly dispelled when only *Britannia* and *Nyria* took part in the big handicap class for yachts exceeding 100 tons (TM) on Wednesday and Thursday of the Ryde Regatta.

Without *Terpsichore* making a third contestant, the regatta scenario had declined, providing little continuing interest for the thousands of spectators, many of whom had arrived to watch the King's cutter sail to victory. This was, for them, a week of disappointment, with *Terpsichore* taking the honours on Monday and *Nyria* scoring three successes in a row on Tuesday, Wednesday and Thursday, as the popularity of the class had undoubtedly waned. It was clear that *Britannia*'s handicap concession to *Nyria*, whilst not altogether disproportionate to their ratings, precluded the former's success in light airs. Clearly a class of two competitors signals a virtual stalemate.

Corrected finishing times for the last two days were:

Wednesday:

Nyria	2 hrs 31 mins 55 secs
Britannia	2 hrs 33 mins 23 secs

Thursday:

Nyria	4 hrs 18 mins 41 secs
Britannia	4 hrs 21 mins 48 secs

It seems that *Terpsichore*'s absence from these contests was on account of an examination of her keel and rudder at Southampton, following the grounding at Gurnard Bay in the week previously.

In the year 1923 Messrs Ewing McGruer and Herbert Reiach founded the McGruer Hollow Spar Company at Gosport, Hants, within a short distance of Camper & Nicholson's yacht yard. The products employing composite wooden spar construction for yacht masts, booms, gaffs, bowsprits etc., met with eventual functional and commercial success for many classes of vessels in the late Twenties. Whilst this was a new enterprise for McGruer, the principle of hollow spars had been experimented with in Edwardian days.

The original idea of using a steel 'pipe' for *Terpsichore*'s mast was far from ideal in practice and this led to McGruer's investigation into the possibility of applying his system to offer a lighter stick. In the first instance, it was decided to experiment with a column of relatively short length, bearing in mind that under gusting conditions maximum compressive loadings exceeding 120 tons were likely, with buckling tendencies relieved by crosstrees, struts and rigging stays. The initial design of mast was based upon a solid lower element with a hollow fabricated topmast portion spliced on, to finish as a 'Marconi' one piece mainmast.

In retrospect, considering all the teething troubles which the new cutter had suffered since launching, this feature seems to have been an outsize gamble. The attraction of a related reduction of ballast was undeniable, but, until such a system had been proven, the risk must have been evident. The absence of suitable waterproof wood adhesives, such as synthetic resin glues, at this time was a likely handicap to McGruer's early perfection of a composite stick.

The validity of the experiment is difficult to justify in the light of an incident recalled by John Nicholson. "Following the adoption of the McGruer topmast", he relates how

"*Terpsichore* had just finished a race, to be seen with her topmast whipping like a trout rod before fracturing, with the vessel heeling and toeing in a jumpy sea."

The price of experiment had been subsidised by further damage to *Terpsichore*'s unhappy reputation. But with perseverance in the development in successive seasons, *Terpsichore*'s competitors and also many smaller class yachts shared the perfection of McGruer's patent designs for mast and spars. It seems hardly appropriate that *Terpsichore* should have suffered the doubtful honour of acting as guinea pig.

Mr Clarence Hatry's *Westward*, the 338 ton schooner, had not fitted out for the 1923 regatta season and the future for the big cutter class, struggling with only three major entrants, looked bleak when the sad news of the death of Mr Lee towards the closing months of the programme seemed to suggest that *Terpsichore*'s string of misfortunes was finally capped. Mr Lee had invested a great deal of enthusiasm in his yawl *Wendur* in the years before the outbreak of war and had nobly persevered in overcoming the early shortcomings of *Terpsichore*. It was a very great pity that he did not live to witness the later achievements of his beautiful cutter. That his infectious enthusiasm of the immediate post-war seasons was greatly missed by his colleagues in the Royal Yacht Squadron is beyond doubt.

There was one officer of *Terpsichore*'s crew who seemed to feel the death of Mr Lee more keenly than the rest. It so happened that a certain verbal contract which Mr Lee had left behind him was destined to lapse. Tom Diaper,[2] following his epic journey to the USA in 1920 under his brother Alf in the 23 metre *Shamrock*, had for some time sought the position of master on one of the big class yachts, following his return home to the Itchen district of Southampton. In the event, he accepted the position of second mate to sail on Mr Lee's *Terpsichore* as the next best offer. In 1923 Tom was verbally promoted to the post of skipper, to start his duties as master of *Terpsichore* from the 1st January, 1924, having built up a substantial rapport with his owner. Tom relates in his log the elation which he felt at the prospect and the bitter disappointment which he suffered in consequence of Mr Lee's demise. In his jottings he says, "I am confident I should have made myself for life, but before the time came for me to do that, and before we had finished laying up, the sad news came that the owner had passed away with a stroke while out shooting and so we were all paid off."

Just to add to the further anxieties for the prospect of continuation of the big handicap class, Mrs Workman[3] met with a serious accident in a crash which would effectively preclude her bringing out the 169 ton cutter *Nyria* in the 1924 season following her yacht's brilliant performances since 1920.

The future of the big class looked to be very much in the balance as it seemed most unlikely that His Majesty King George would bring the third remaining big cutter to the racing circuit in 1924, as Mr Lee had done in 1922 to make a brave attempt at representation.

A gloomy local populace declared the end for big cutter racing, which, after so many years of valiant effort, must lead to the end of Cowes Week itself. This proved a mistaken public attitude for the twin reasons that big cutter racing continued for many years beyond this point and, of course, that Cowes Week currently enjoys greater numerical support than ever, with an increasing international attention.

Following Mr Lee's passing, his executors placed *Terpsichore* on the sale list and it was felt at the time that the possibility of finding a sufficiently wealthy buyer, able to recruit a competent crew and seriously fit out the cutter for the next season's calendar, was a slender one. In any case, there was no certainty of *Britannia*'s participation and, even counting this prospect, a big class of just two cutters would have been wholly undesirable, to say the least.

Meanwhile, His Majesty King George V announced through Sir Phillip Hunloke that he would not be racing *Britannia* during the forthcoming 1924 season, which suggested a possible flagging of interest in smaller classes of the sport as a knock-on effect.

Quite suddenly, a light was signalled at the end of a gloomy vista. *Terpsichore* found a buyer in Mr Herbert Weld–Blundell, a Dorsetshire gentleman of Lulworth Castle, and he immediately announced an intention to make a bid to save the class continuity by entering his purchase in the 1924 yachting events. His hopes were centred on the prospects of getting support from owners of other competitive vessels. In this he was quite successful.

Firstly, Sir Phillip Hunloke announced a change of mind on the part of His Majesty. Secondly, Sir Charles Allom decided to race his lovely cutter *White Heather II*, which had been out of commission since 1921. Thirdly, the millionaire grocer, Sir Thomas Lipton, endorsed Mr Weld's lead by fitting out his 23 metre *Shamrock*, of 1908 vintage, following her return from the USA.

Mr Herbert Weld was a gentleman of diverse interests, including yachting, which qualified him to be elected as Commodore of the Royal Dorset Yacht Club in the early Twenties. The opportunity to purchase a first-class cutter such as *Terpsichore* proved irresistible, even at the age of seventy-two, satisfying a long-standing desire to identify with family tradition. He was elected to the Royal Yacht Squadron in 1924 and was extremely proud of his ancestry, his family being associated with the sport of big cutter racing in the early part of the nineteenth century with yachts of outstanding performance known as *Louisa*, *Alarm* and the earlier *Lulworth*.

It was, therefore, appropriate that Mr Weld Blundell should wish to rename *Terpsichore* and adopt the name of *Lulworth*, from which point onwards she has been officially referred to as *Lulworth* (ex-*Terpsichore*) . The narrative must now continue adopting her new owner's revised designation appropriately. *Lulworth* continued to be her label until she retired from racing in 1930, and beyond.

Mr Weld–Blundell, D.Litt. was a great scholar, a very quiet and modest individual, although he invariably surprised many people who on first acquaintance thought him to be somewhat lethargic. His pursuits included natural history, archaeology and languages. He was elected an Honorary Fellow of Queen's College, Oxford for his outstanding achievements, and, on occasions when he happened to be 'drawn out', he astounded his audience by the depth of his specialist learning.

The story of Mr Weld's apparently detached attitude to the excitement of racing, if it is to be credited, has been related a number of times, but no explanation has been offered. The local newsagents at Cowes used to circulate the bigger yachts in the Roadstead with copies of the national newspapers by means of a special delivery launch, before the start of a day's racing. Mr Weld would disappear into *Lulworth*'s beautiful cabin lounge with *The Times*, seldom reappearing until racing was well underway, when he would greet the assembly on the aft end of the deck with a, "Hello!" and, taking a casual scan of the action, laconically ask, "Have we started?" to the astonishment of the company. One should not necessarily express surprise, as his world had boundaries substantially beyond *Lulworth*'s wheel and it is possible that a study of stock market values for his investments reflected his continuing ability to offer employment to his skipper and crew. Whilst a man has firstly to work hard in finding opportunities to make a fortune, it is often even harder to preserve it. Nevertheless, it would have been the norm for most people to 'switch off' any external distractions and savour the thrill of crossing the start line aboard such a magnificent possession as the cutter *Lulworth*.

[1] Cornelius Vanderbilt was commodore of the New York Yacht Club prior to 1914.

[2] The Diaper family distinguished themselves in the handling of 'crack' racing yachts, boasting a catalogue of successes which could fill many chapters. The father of the family, Captain Tom Diaper, reached the top of his profession as a one-time skipper of the American cutter *Navahoe* when she visited England to race in competition with *Britannia* for the Brenton Reef and Cape May cups in 1893. His son Tom sailed with him as an extra and later joined his cousin, Captain Ben Parker, who was skipper on the Kaiser's *Meteor II*. Tom the younger had an astonishingly successful career in sailing a number of smaller racing yachts for German owners until 1914.

[3] Mrs Workman's husband was a director with Messrs Workman Clark & Co. Ltd., of Belfast.

Mr Jack Workman, who was also formerly connected with the company, is now Admiral of the Royal North of Ireland Yacht Club at the age of ninety-one. He was responsible for the design of the 'Lake Class' yachts some seventy years ago.

PART III

1924

WHITE HEATHER II ENJOYS A REAPPEARANCE

The 1924 Cowes Regatta Week was graciously honoured by the presence of Their Majesties, King George and Queen Mary. The traditional twenty-one gun salute was fired from the RYS battery when the royal yacht *Victoria and Albert* brought the admiral of the RYS into Cowes Roads on the evening of Friday, 1st August. The pageant was reinforced with a sample of naval might by the battleship *Warspite* with its grim and grey backdrop to the festive atmosphere, the destroyer *Vampire* built locally by J. Samuel White and Company Ltd., pre-1914, and H.M.S. *Newark* escort to the sovereign's racing cutter *Britannia*.

Although the shoreside yachtsfolk had yet to be fully convinced, some confidence in the future for serious big cutter racing began to evidence itself during 1924 following the discordant series of events since the attempted re-establishment in 1920.

Mr Herbert Weld–Blundell had given *Terpsichore* the new title of *Lulworth* after his family seat at Lulworth Castle, a logical action indeed, particularly bearing in mind the memory of the exploits of his grandfather's cutter named *Lulworth* which carried off Her Majesty Queen Victoria's Cup back in 1857. As the original *Lulworth* had by 1924 long been broken up, there seemed to be no obvious need to christen his new acquisition *Lulworth II*. In the winter of 1923-24 a number of further improvements to tune the racing performance of Mr Weld's newly-acquired cutter were put in hand with Camper & Nicholson at Gosport. She displayed a distinctly new look, appearing in a white mantle this year, which enlivened her profile.

The season of 1924 saw the formation of an elite fleet of big class cutters in handicap racing events for yachts exceeding 100 tons TM. This was the first post-war appearance of the 1908 vintage 23 metre *Shamrock*, owned by Sir Thomas Lipton. She had sailed to America in 1920 to be used in tuning trials for *Shamrock IV* before the millionaire grocer's unsuccessful fourth bid for the Americas Cup. The 23 metre cutter returned to England in 1923 to be prepared for the coastal regattas at home. Sir Charles Allom's 1907 cutter *White Heather II*, which had been laid up since the 1921 season, was very successfully fitted out to rejoin the class once more. *Britannia* (the pride and joy of King George V), with a long pedigree of triumphs, was renovated during the winter of 1923-24 for continued racing. The former *Terpsichore*, renamed *Lulworth* by her new owner, was the fourth contestant yacht. These four cutters formed the nucleus of a distinguished assembly, joined later, in 1925, by the Herreshoff-designed schooner *Westward* when the fleet became known as 'The Big Five', forming the hard core of the fleet in succeeding seasons.

On the Saturday prior to Cowes Week, during the Royal Southampton Yacht Club Regatta, a tragic accident occurred when *Britannia, White Heather II* and *Shamrock* were competing. As *Shamrock* was rounding the Solent Bank buoy at the western end of these waters in a stiff breeze, First Officer W. Lewis (a native of Tollesbury, Essex) was thrown overboard. A lifebelt was immediately pitched towards him and the gig was quickly lowered as *Shamrock* came about, signalling retirement from the contest. Despite an exhaustive search, assisted by *Britannia*'s escorting minesweeper, HMS *Newark* (commander Martin de Meric), no trace of the seaman could be found. In falling from the bow of *Shamrock* he was believed to have suffered an injury, being struck by the yacht. *Shamrock* returned through the Solent with shortened sail, her flag fluttering from half-mast as she made her unhappy way to Southampton. This was destined to be a gloomy day in the annals of local events, as the flag of the Royal Yacht Squadron

Castle and those of member yachts were already flying their burgees at half-hoist on account of the passing of a respected member, Sir Hugh Drummond. Following the *Shamrock* tragedy, the King sent a sympathetic message to her owner, Sir Thomas Lipton. The RSYC prize was won by *Britannia*, which finished ahead of *White Heather II*.

On Monday, the first day of the 1924 Cowes Regatta Week, weather conditions did not appear to be at all promising, the day starting with heavy rain, which dampened the ardour of those gathered on shore to view the racing. Fortunately it had eased by the 10 o'clock start for the big cutters, but continued dull and showery throughout the day. In traditional fashion the Royal London Yacht Club had the distinction of holding the opening regatta and the RYS facilities were provided to conduct the events. Full canvas was set by the contesting yachts to take advantage of a strong westerly breeze.

Unfortunately *Lulworth* was absent from the start line because she was late making the passage from Southampton. This left only *Britannia, Shamrock* and *White Heather II* in competition. A handicap allowance of 2 mins 36 secs was accorded to *White Heather II* by the first two. With the starting signal from the RYS cannon *Shamrock* crossed the line marginally behind the royal cutter to windward, whilst *White Heather II* came a few seconds later. The long beat to the Solent Bank buoy found *Britannia* 47 seconds ahead of *White Heather II* in rounding the first mark, after battling over a foul tide. *Shamrock* was bringing up the rear. With spinnakers set and favoured by a flowing current, the three cutters made a record dash to the North-East Middle mark, only to face the westerly wind and an incoming tide on the return. Their positions remained unchanged in the course of the second round, at the end of which *Britannia* was first home, with *White Heather II* some 2 mins 7 secs astern. This meant that *White Heather II* took the first prize, saving her time by 29 secs! Sir Charles Allom's cutter was in fighting form as she made two later victories to claim the Week's top honours.

The corrected finishing times were:

White Heather II (winner)	3 hrs 1 min 16 secs
Britannia (second)	3 hrs 1 min 45 secs
Shamrock	3 hrs 7 mins 45 secs

On Tuesday, the opening day of the RYS Regatta, *Lulworth*, sailing with her new owner aboard, made her first appearance of the Week. The race for the King's Cup took the 10 a.m. slot, commencing the programme from the Castle Bastion, and the contest for the Big Four started at 10.15 a.m. Handicap allowances of 2 mins 40 secs were made by *Britannia* sailing scratch to *Lulworth*, *White Heather II* and *Shamrock*. The race was officially designated for yachts in excess of 100 tons TM over a course of forty sea miles. Prizes of £70 first and £20 second were offered. The yachts crossed the line in close formation, with *Britannia* leading, closely followed by *Shamrock, White Heather II* and *Lulworth* cautiously astern for good reason. As the cutters were getting away, a very messy situation, at least potentially so, arose with the paddle steamer *Duchess of York* backing out of Cowes Harbour and arriving at the line simultaneously with the gun announcing the start. Both *Shamrock* and *White Heather II* found themselves on a course certainly not of their preferred choice, heading for the steamer with little room to manoeuvre. A very nasty prospect was fortunately relieved when the two cutters came about, skilfully managing to avoid each other in the process.

For *Shamrock*, it seemed she was not destined to race on that day, being overtaken by a physical mishap a few seconds later. As she moved away, her throat halyards failed and her mainsail came down, precluding further participation. This was not an uncommon fault, as it had happened to most of the big cutters at some time. *Britannia* led the way to the Solent Bank buoy and on to the North-East Middle mark, working out a strong advantage over the rest of her contemporaries. *Lulworth* overtook *White Heather II* on the first leg but *Britannia* had left

both of them well astern by the end of the first round, their
times being:

Britannia	12 hrs 35 mins 30 secs
Lulworth	12 hrs 46 mins 7 secs
White Heather II	12 hrs 48 mins 25 secs

On the second round, in beating to the western mark, *White
Heather II* suffered a duplication of *Shamrock's* ill luck when
her throat halyards also failed. This put the third remaining
contestant out of the competition, leaving only *Britannia* and
Lulworth to finish. At this stage it was scarcely any contest,
with *Lulworth* so far behind the royal cutter.

The corrected finishing times were:

Britannia (winner)	2 hrs 50 mins 32 secs
Lulworth (second)	3 hrs 0 mins 53 secs

The racing on Wednesday of the Royal Yacht Squadron
Regatta for yachts exceeding 100 tons TM was something of a
farce due to the peculiarities of the weather. *Shamrock* was *en
hors de combat*, as a secondary effect of the previous day's
halyard failure. Her topmast was found to be sprung, putting
her out of participation. And so the event left only *Lulworth,
White Heather II* and *Britannia* represented, although Sir
William Portal's lovely old ketch *Valdora* had been entered
following her success on the previous day in the King's Cup
event. With a Thames Measurement of 106 tons, *Valdora* was
able to claim inclusion. Handicap allowances were allocated as
follows: *Britannia* to sail scratch, allowing *Lulworth* and *White
Heather II* 3 mins 4 secs each (penalised by 24 secs more than
the day before, which seemed a drop in the ocean considering
her ten minute advantage of the previous day). *Valdora* was to
have received 47 mins 32 secs had she completed the course.

When the gun fired and the Blue Peter came down, the four
contestants were kedged behind the line in flat calm conditions.

This situation remained, as successive classes were signalled to start racing from the same location. Utter confusion was witnessed from the shoreside, with the unbelievable sight of nearly thirty yachts ranging from the Big Four down through the 35-100 ton class, twelve metres, eight metres and six metres, mixed together, at all points of the compass, nearly stationary, some of which had been towed in position to drop their kedges! Patience was sorely tried in the long wait for a movement of air to facilitate some progress on their respective courses. The King and the Duke of Connaught were aboard *Britannia* at the outermost end of the line. Scarcely a breath of air could be detected for over half an hour when *White Heather II*, being the most sensitive of the Big Four, to murmurings of a draught, hauled up her kedge to steal slowly westward. As she crept away over a foul tide her progress became slower, and eventually the stately cutter came back to kedge once more. After a further hour's wait *White Heather II* made a second attempt and marginally succeeded this time, followed by *Britannia* making minimal headway, then came *Lulworth* with her spinnaker set to overtake *Britannia* on the 'run' to East Lepe, but such was the pace of progress that it would have been a misnomer to categorise it as racing. *Valdora* failed to leave the start line and returned to her moorings. *White Heather II* was first to round the East Lepe buoy and, having overcome the tidal obstacle, found the bonus of a strong flood tide assisting her to work out a very substantial lead over the other two, which were still struggling to clear the East Lepe Mark. *Lulworth* some time later, with *Britannia* a few seconds astern, found just enough air to make the turn and progress through the Roadstead to fetch the Warner. For those on shore the racing was distinctly lacking in interest, but, with brilliant sunshine and intense heat at times, it was an ideal day for those whose inclinations were towards sunbathing, swimming off the beach, or even a leisurely turn with the oars. In the afternoon came the suggestion of a faint breeze, but it was too late to have any serious influence on the competition and, furthermore, it was insufficient for the committee to order a second round. As the three cutters headed for the finishing line after one round had been navigated, *White Heather II* received the gun, to take first prize of £70. *Lulworth* came second to take the £20 prize some forty-two minutes after the winner and *Britannia* (sailing scratch), in conditions she must have found scarcely tolerable, was forty-seven minutes behind *White Heather II*. Whatever the outcome of such a contest there could have been little satisfaction for any of the competitors on this day. However, a race is never lost until it is won, and, whilst Captain Fred Mountifield skippered the yacht most nearly attuned to the handicaps of the day, his skill in wringing substantial profit from such a farce was, undeniably, most praiseworthy.

The corrected finishing times were:

White Heather II (winner)	3 hrs 35 mins 18 secs
Lulworth (second)	4 hrs 17 mins 50 secs
Britannia	4 hrs 22 mins 34 secs

Following the general disappointment of the previous day's less than spirited racing activities, Thursday provided ample compensation for the spectators ashore who eagerly congregated along the esplanade and the green to feast their eyes upon those tall masts and acres of canvas being amply served by some stirring breezes, their hearts tuned in to the movements of competing yachts, as the day unfolded. Whilst it was almost always possible to follow the progress of the big cutters along a substantial part of the westward course from a position allowing a survey of the start, the yachts virtually disappeared from any discernible positional alignment after passing the Castle Point buoy to sail eastwards. In consequence, there was usually a great buzz of excitement when the first sails were sighted on the return leg approaching the club house for a second round. The observer with the better telescope stole the envy of his neighbour.

The committee members on the first floor balcony of the Royal London appeared to be the main focus of envy, as glances were stolen by sightseers below, admiring the magnificent spyglass belonging to the club trained upon the returning fleet.

With the blessing of a good steady breeze and periods of bright sunshine, the elements provided all that was to be desired for a splendid day's sport. Three of the Big Four competed for the town prizes of £75 (first) and £20 (second). Sir Thomas Lipton's *Shamrock* was once again conspicuous by her absence. *Britannia* (with the admiral of the RYS aboard, with guests including the Duke of Connaught, Lady Baring and General Cornelius Vanderbilt) joined the competition with Sir Charles Allom's *White Heather II* and *Lulworth*, owned and raced by Mr Herbert Weld–Blundell.

The three cutters being sailed in the over 100 ton class were programmed to make two rounds of Tuesday's course (with the Solent Bank buoy to the westward and the North-East Middle as the eastern mark).

The fresh north-westerly breeze gave a lively impetus to the start as the competitors crossed the line under full reach canvas. *Britannia* sailing scratch (to allow *Lulworth* and *White Heather II* 2 mins 40 secs each) was first away, *White Heather II* crossing next, with *Lulworth* close behind. Reaching the Solent Bank buoy, the order changed with *White Heather II* first to round the mark, immediately followed by *Lulworth* challenging the leader's weather and *Britannia* a minute or so later. *Lulworth* was seen to be keeping closest to the island shore to avoid the effects of a strong incoming tide. On the return to the North-East Middle buoy *Lulworth* passed *White Heather II*, taking the lead, and later *Britannia* followed to overtake Lord Waring's cutter, but *Lulworth* continued to open up the distance between herself and the royal cutter.

The first round times were:

Lulworth   11 hrs 45 mins 28 secs

Britannia	11 hrs 48 mins 5 secs
White Heather II	11 hrs 49 mins 35 secs

These positions were maintained until the end of the second round when *Lulworth* took the winning gun to enjoy first prize, as she was in no need of any time allowance from *Britannia*, with three minutes to spare. *White Heather II* managed to hold on doggedly to *Britannia* but, although unable to repass her, *White Heather II* saved her time to take second prize. And so *Lulworth* avenged Tuesday's defeat by the admiral's cutter.

The corrected finished times noted were:

Lulworth	1 hr 35 mins 10 secs
White Heather II	1 hr 39 mins 4 secs
Britannia	1 hr 40 mins 48 secs

Enjoying a reaching wind over the whole distance, *Lulworth*'s time shows a substantially high average speed, covering forty miles at 11.15 knots. This was her maiden success for the new owner and provided ample evidence of her competitive potential, which shone through in the next two seasons. It seemed that the spectre of the unlucky *Terpsichore* could be fading at last!

The concluding day of the Week, or Friday the Regatta Day as it was known, saw the return of Sir Thomas Lipton's *Shamrock* to the big class, although her participation was not conspicuously rewarding. Despite some setbacks, managing only nine entries in the first of her post-war seasons, these opportunities in 'tuning up' with her contemporaries, if only briefly, were to prove of inestimable value in succeeding years.

The weather conditions on the last day of racing were ideally suited to the temperament of *White Heather II*. With her inherent talent for making optimum use of light airs, she scored yet another victory, making a total of three for the week. Her performance at Cowes made a substantial contribution to her success in topping the seasonal honours of the class (achieving seven firsts and eight seconds in nineteen starts). Once again, *Lulworth* had succeeded in giving a fair account of herself by claiming the second flag.

The corrected times for the Regatta Day big handicap class racing were:

White Heather II (winner) prize £70   4 hrs 18 mins 10
Lulworth (second)) prize £20   4 hrs 21 mins 26
Britannia   4 hrs 25 mins 10

The 1924 Royal Victoria Yacht Club Regatta opened on Saturday, August 7th in very disappointing weather conditions for sailing, with scarcely a breath of air initially. The big cutters had moored at Cowes overnight at the conclusion of the RYS Regatta, which was celebrated by the traditional display of fireworks. *Britannia* was towed to Ryde by her minesweeper escort HMS *Newark*. Mr Weld's *Lulworth* was sailed from Cowes but in the calm conditions she arrived at the start line much too late to take part in the race for the RVYC International Gold Challenge Cup Trophy. This left only *Britannia, Shamrock* and *White Heather II* to race on level terms, sailing the long Victoria Course of forty-six sea miles. The wind picked up as the three yachts headed for the Nab End Gas buoy; a beat to windward with the tide under them. *Britannia* held a slight lead with *Shamrock* and *White Heather II* in close company as the yachts ran past Ryde Pier to the western mark. *Shamrock* was assisted by the full force of an ebbing tide as she stood over to the mainland shore and forged well into the lead. *Britannia* lost ground as the vessels made their second beat eastwards in a fluky wind. On the run back during the second round *White Heather II* suffered a split spinnaker which precluded her from challenging the green cutter's dominating stance. *Britannia* was not finding the wind she needed and sailed back to her mooring at Cowes after passing the western buoy.

Shamrock and *White Heather II* finished some twenty-one minutes apart to take first and second places respectively. Starting at 10.15 a.m., it had been a long, uninspiring day with *White Heather II* suffering the price of her spinnaker failure.

Finishing times were:

Shamrock (cup)	6 hrs 26 mins 53
White Heather II (second)	6 hrs 47 mins 27

Racing on the following Monday enjoyed brilliant sunshine with a light south-westerly breeze. The event was sailed over the long Victoria Course for the Assheton-Smith Challenge Cup. The four big cutters, *Britannia, Shamrock, White Heather II* and *Lulworth*, took part "competing on level terms". At the 10.15 a.m. start *Lulworth* was first to cross the line, nosing ahead of the royal cutter, with *Shamrock* and *White Heather II* in procession. *Britannia* was trailing behind the little fleet as it fetched the Nab End buoy.

Spinnakers were set to port on the run from the Nab End to the Outer Spit buoys with *Lulworth* firmly in the lead, pacing in order *Shamrock, White Heather II* and *Britannia*. Reaching back past Ryde Pier, *Lulworth* had a lead of some forty secs ahead of *Shamrock*, two minutes over *White Heather II* and five minutes over *Britannia*. The recorded first round times indicate that *Lulworth* was substantially extending her advantage, these being noted thus:

Lulworth	1 hr 46 mins 15
Shamrock	1 hr 56 mins 22
White Heather II	2 hrs 1 mins 10
Britannia	2 hrs 3 mins 9

Mr Weld's cutter was leading Sir Thomas Lipton's *Shamrock* by some twelve minutes on the second leg to the Nab when the latter suffered the repeat misfortune of a sprung topmast, forcing an early retirement. *White Heather II* was a minute or so behind *Shamrock* at this juncture.

With sailing conditions matching her character, *Lulworth* exhibited a competitive edge which developed during the two following seasons' sailing on level terms. During this day the result was never in doubt from an early stage.

The finishing times noted were:

Lulworth (cup + £50 prize)	4 hrs 6 mins 27 secs
White Heather II	4 hrs 18 mins 34 secs
Britannia	4 hrs 22 mins 32 secs

The cash prize of £50 for the cup winner was donated by the Commodore, Sir William P. Burton, KBE.

Tuesday's event, under the flag of the Royal Thames Yacht Club for yachts in excess of 100 tons TM, was over the thirty-five mile Short Victoria course, with an 11 a.m. start, and was entered by *White Heather II, Britannia* and *Lulworth*, which again competed without handicap adjustments. Unfortunately, *Shamrock*, although entered, was unable to take part owing to her need for a new topmast; this was being effected at Southampton. At 11 a.m. *White Heather II* was first to follow the starting signals and then *Lulworth* took the lead, maintaining the position during a reach eastward to the Warner Lightship. *White Heather II and Britannia* followed closely in order. On the return reach to the Outer Spit buoy the 'procession' scarcely varied; it could still have been a winning gun for any one of them. Following the turn to windward as they made for the western mark, *Britannia* overhauled *White Heather II* and established a fifteen second advantage. Meanwhile, *Lulworth* was pointing high into the wind with the lee rail awash, demonstrating a weatherly quality to lead the royal cutter by approximately ninety seconds as the breeze freshened.

The times recorded at the end of round one were:

Lulworth	12 hrs 47 mins 30 secs

Britannia	12 hrs 49 mins 3 secs
White Heather II	12 hrs 49 mins 31 secs

The order through the second round remained unchanged, *Lulworth* managing to hold off a strong challenge from *Britannia* whilst *White Heather II* was not appreciating the freshening blow and fell further behind the others. The final gap of ninety-seven seconds between the royal cutter and *Lulworth* spelled out the evenness of the battle between the two yachts, with the conclusions of the first and second rounds showing how conditions were suited to their mutual preference.

The results were:

Lulworth (winner + £80)	2 hrs 25 mins 8
Britannia (second + £40)	2 hrs 26 mins 45
White Heather II (third + £20)	2 hrs 30 mins 30

With first flags on two consecutive days, it seemed that *Lulworth* (ex-*Terpsichore*) must be emerging from the frustrations of extended ill luck which had dogged her progress hitherto. It suggested that Charles Nicholson's influence was at long last beginning to show dividends.

The second day of the Royal Thames Yacht Club Regatta (Wednesday of Ryde Week) did not produce any sparkling entertainment for the shoreside crowds. The programme was based upon the lines of Tuesday's event and in the calm conditions the sport proved most disappointing for crews and spectators alike. The race was defined as a handicap contest for yachts exceeding 100 tons TM but the Big Three entrants sailed again on level terms. The starters were the King's *Britannia* (221 tons), Sir Charles Allom's *White Heather II* (179 tons) and Mr Herbert Weld–Blundell's *Lulworth* (186 tons). Conditions at the 11 a.m. start produced a scarcely detectable breeze. For the first hour the three competitors were just able to hold position against a west flowing tide, with spinnakers set. Fluky airs contributed later to some erratic movements. *White*

Heather II showed to slight advantage by taking an early move ahead and was subsequently overhauled by *Lulworth*. Towards the end of the beat to the Warner with the tide favourable, *White Heather II* regained her leading role over *Lulworth*, which was nearly two minutes ahead of *Britannia*.

White Heather II maintained her reputation as a light weather vessel, receiving the winning gun after a mediocre contest which was stopped on the completion of one round.

The noted finishing times were:

White Heather II (winner + £80) 2 hrs 55 mins 44
Lulworth (second + £40)   2 hrs 59 mins 8
Britannia (Third + £20)   3 hrs 1 mins 34

For *Lulworth* (ex-*Terpsichore*) the 1924 Solent season proved what might be considered a transitional success, where she managed to distance herself from her earlier tribulations to establish a claim of indisputable competitive status. Whilst she gained only one first flag from four entries during Cowes Week, she came second in the three other contests. Her performance in the Ryde events, sailing without handicap time concessions to gain two first and one second flag in three starts, consolidated the claim. The portents suggested that *Lulworth* was earning a happier reputation under her new ownership. Certainly her overall 1924 performance was inferior to that of *White Heather* and *Britannia*, but with consideration of the fewer races in which she participated and the belated class revival, it seemed that Mr Weld had acquired a really formidable challenger, particularly if she raced for an extended calendar. She was, at last, beginning to show her mettle after such an extraordinary catalogue of ill fortune, reaching a long-delayed maturity.

On the 13th August, 1924 whilst racing in the Royal Albert Yacht Club Regatta off Southsea, Major Hunloke lodged a protest on behalf of the King's *Britannia* against *Lulworth* for an alleged infringement of the rules.

In its Notices to Mariners, the Admiralty had advised that a designated area described by marker buoys to the east of the Sturbridge Shoal was nominated a 'Prohibited Area'. This directive was almost ordered certainly in connection with mine-laying exercises.

Major Hunloke interpreted the instruction to mean that yachts should keep out of the 'Prohibited Area'; bearing in mind his responsibility as skipper of the King's yacht, the Major could scarcely have dared to defy the authority of the Royal Navy.

Lulworth's skipper took the attitude that a race was a race and there was nothing in the Yacht Club's rules to award control of such an event to the Admiralty and he therefore continued to sail through the area. Whilst we have no evidence to the contrary, it is possible that *Lulworth*'s action was taken with tongue in cheek. One supposes that, if *Lulworth*'s skipper had time to ponder his options at all, he judged the infringement of such a naval directive to be of scarcely any importance to the defence of the realm. On the other hand, *Lulworth*'s owner, as a member of the Royal Yacht Squadron, was entitled to fly the white ensign, a privilege restored by the Admiralty in 1920, whereas all other vessels outside the Navy and the RYS were limited to displaying the 'Red Duster'. The question could be asked: 'Does a concession from the Admiralty to fly its ensign automatically commit a yacht owner to accept naval disciplines?'

Oddly enough *Lulworth* was destined to find herself substantially in debt to the Admiralty some years later whilst in differing ownership and circumstances, when the minesweeper HMS *Selkirk* (escort of the King's *Britannia*) rendered yeoman service to the stranded white cutter as related in the 1928 reminiscences.

At the time of the Royal Albert incident *Lulworth* was just astern of the royal cutter and, by ignoring the Admiralty directive, was able to overtake the latter.

Major Hunloke duly lodged a protest declaring that *Lulworth* had taken unfair advantage, further claiming that *Britannia*'s subsequent tactics were hampered by his immediate opponent's action.

The Royal Albert Yacht Club Committee took the view that the Admiralty marker was not intended as a definition of the club's course, there being no mention of it in the day's sailing instructions.

After due consideration, taking into account the fact that *Lulworth* maintained her position ahead of *Britannia* to win the race by a fair margin, the Royal Albert Yacht Club Committee disallowed Major Hunloke's protest.

The case put forward on behalf of *Britannia* was that the Admiralty had statutory authority over the Spithead Roadstead and, further, that the committee "cannot have intended, or connived at, competitors sailing their races in defiance of that authority. Least of all should the King's yacht be expected to do so".

The Council of the YRA found itself in a quandary over the incident, especially Major Hunloke.[1] In its view *Lulworth* had not infringed the sailing instructions. The upshot of the case was that the Royal Albert "have taken the only course possible in the circumstances, i.e. that of sending to the *Britannia* a sum equivalent to the second prize in the race".

Honour appeared to have been satisfied on this particular occasion, but obviously my Lords of the Admiralty had no wish to find themselves in conflict with civilian sporting activities, more especially where the sovereign or his representative might become embarrassed. In 1925 the YRA received a letter from the Admiralty inviting the former to indicate which mined areas needed to be cleared for racing in that year. Accordingly, the YRA sent the appropriate charts to the lords commissioners of the Admiralty in the manner directed.

Major Hunloke appeared to have taken his annoyance to extremes, displaying a rather immature 'I'm not going to play' attitude by withdrawing *Britannia* from racing the next day.

Major Hunloke was said to have very little sense of humour and, being a dedicated skipper, was apparently unable to stand back and acknowledge a funny side to his embarrassment.

---

[1] Major Hunloke was not only the master of *Britannia* at this time, but also vice-president of the RYA. To fairly act the part of plaintiff and foreman of the jury simultaneously was hardly enviable.

1925

LULWORTH ESTABLISHES A SEASONAL SUPREMACY

Cowes Week of 1925 made a muted start after the festivities were threatened by a national crisis associated with the historic coal dispute. Many local folk had toiled selflessly since the close of the 1924 event to produce a programme and organise a recurrent regatta. It was felt that the normal visit of the King and Queen must be in jeopardy, but happily an eleventh hour settlement prevented such a disruption. The arrival of Their Majesties was celebrated in a restrained atmosphere, presumably in deference to the gravity of the moods of John Citizen (?). The *V & A* entered its customary mooring location, in line with the Victoria Pier on the esplanade, without the normal cannonade. The RYS guns and those of the battleship HMS *Royal Oak* (the guardship) remained silent. The destroyer HMS *Valorous* and the minesweeper HMS *Newark* also quietly attended. The royal party was joined by Captain Sir Charles Cust, Bart, RN, (equerry-in-waiting), Col. Clive Wigram, the Hon. Sir Derek Keppel (master of the royal household), the Hon. Sir Sidney Greville, Admiral the Hon. Sir Stanley Colville, Admiral Henry Campbell, Major Phillip Hunloke (groom-in-waiting); in attendance on the Queen were Mr Harry and Lady Joan Verney; and on the Duke of Connaught, Lieut. Col. Douglas Gordon.

The sober introduction to the 1925 Regatta was quickly forgotten and the celebrations peaked, to be declared a post-war record. This was the year of a long-awaited triumph for *Lulworth*. Her potential was demonstrated this season in no uncertain terms, although her Solent successes were fairly modest. Not only did she head the honours for the big cutter assembly, but she carried off the coveted King's Cup in addition. The big class competition had been stepped up to include the two schooners, namely *Westward* of 338 tons designed by Herreshoff in the USA before the war and now owned by Mr F.T.B. Davis, a self-made contestant who had prospered in South Africa as a stevedore, and the other being the much smaller 154 ton *Susanne*, again of pre-war vintage, in the new ownership of Mr Robert McAlpine. *Westward* was formerly owned by Mr Clarence Hatry and *Susanne* by Mr Warwick Brookes.

Following her seasonal triumph of 1924, *White Heather II* also found a new owner. She became the object of Lord Waring's affections, who entered her with fair success until the end of September 1930. Racing was no longer programmed for the over 70 ton handicap class, but for yachts of any rig exceeding 100 tons. The big cutters, *Lulworth, Britannia, Shamrock* and *White Heather II*, sailed on level terms without handicap adjustments, as they had done towards the close of the 1924 season. This proved to be a more wholesome arrangement than hitherto. A concession was made, however, in deference to Mr McAlpine's sporting entries in Cowes Week, whereby *Susanne* received a time concession, and Mr Davis's *Westward* conceded a few seconds per mile to the cutters.

One of the most exciting tussles for the over 100 Tons TM handicap class was sailed on the opening day of Cowes Week in 1925, the progress of which I was privileged to watch from the proximity of the RYS.

The first race on Monday, August 3rd started at 10 a.m., for a first prize of £60 and a second of £20. The course was twice round the Solent Bank and North-East Middle buoys, a total distance of thirty-nine miles. The assembly consisted of the cutters *Lulworth, White Heather II, Shamrock, Britannia* and the schooners *Westward and Susanne*. A time allowance of 33 mins 48 secs was received by *Susanne* from each of her rivals.

In the eyes of a very junior observer, the starting spectacle was truly magnificent, with an approach to the line being made on the starboard tack and then the whole fleet was seen to come about with a rattle of canvas, to cross the line as the gun fired. There were no recalls. This was a sight which remains for ever in the memory. There was a light westerly breeze which freshened as the race progressed and tapered off towards the end. *White Heather II* was first over the line to leeward, being soon passed by *Shamrock* to windward. *Britannia* was close to *White Heather II*, with *Lulworth* and *Westward* following. *Susanne*, conspicuously late for her appointment, trailed well astern of the rest.

On the beat to the Solent Bank buoy, *White Heather II* forged ahead with an early advantage compounded by the assistance of an ebbing tide, but the four cutters with all light weather canvas set, were well matched and continued to take and retake each other.

Their positions were frequently changing. *Britannia*, with a spinnaker set, led the run back from the westward, only to be overtaken by *Shamrock* whilst passing through the Roadstead. *White Heather II* later claimed second position with *Lulworth* and *Westward* challenging. *Shamrock* strengthened her lead and *Lulworth* worked her way up to take second place. After the beat back from the North-East Middle buoy *Shamrock* led *Lulworth* by one and a half minutes, with *White Heather II* gamely hanging on just half a minute later, whilst *Britannia* came fourth, marginally ahead of *Westward*. The first round times were:

Shamrock	12 hrs 33 mins 55 secs
Lulworth	12 hrs 35 mins 34 secs
White Heather II	12 hrs 36 mins 4 secs
Britannia	12 hrs 38 mins 6 secs
Westward	12 hrs 38 mins 21 secs
Susanne	1 hr 3 mins 23 secs

When the yachts returned from the westward on the second round, their positions had changed yet again as they sailed past the club house.

Westward carried her spinnaker further than the others, closing on *White Heather* and *Britannia*. Meanwhile *Lulworth* had overtaken *Shamrock* to lead the fleet. But the struggle which had entailed so many changes in progress was not yet concluded. During the second round *Lulworth* was battling hard with a locally foul tide,[1] although enjoying a fair breeze. It seemed that victory must be within Hogarth's grasp and then Dame Nature took control when the fickle character of Solent airs deprived *Lulworth* of her wind. Meanwhile the wily Captain Mountifield in *White Heather II*, stealing an inshore course with a slackening current, found a gusting breeze to close the gap and edge ahead of the leader. And so *White Heather II* took the first gun with just fourteen seconds to spare, whilst *Lulworth* drifted over the finishing line with her sails scarcely filled, to take second prize. The day had seen big class yacht racing sport at its finest, with many changes of leadership almost until the winning gun was fired. Dame Nature had played her trump card to pick a winner. The corrected finishing times were as follows:

White Heather II (winner)	2 hrs 42 mins 49
Lulworth (second)	2 hrs 43 mins 3
Shamrock	2 hrs 43 mins 37 secs
Britannia	2 hrs 45 mins 5 secs
Westward	2 hrs 46 mins 37 secs
Susanne	3 hrs 30 mins 22 secs

A protest by *Westward* against *Lulworth* was not sustained. (The former claimed that she had been given insufficient room by the latter at the start.)

With the exception of the performance of *Susanne*, reference to the table of results of this race provides a clear and indisputable indication of the relative capabilities of the cutters in particular, showing how closely matched they were in competing without time allowances. Of the first four, only 2 mins 16 secs separated *White Heather II* from *Britannia*.

The fickle nature of the Solent tidal and eddying movements was so often apparent following the start of the big handicap class yachts in heading westward for the East Lepe or Solent Bank marks. There were occasions when those vessels drawing a lesser depth of water would seek an inshore course, sufficiently clear of the treacherous reef of rocks which edged the esplanade and the green, to take advantage of a one to two knot ebbing inshore tide. The crowds of spectators lining the shore enjoyed the thrill of the luffing tactics by opponent skippers, as a master could often be heard from the beach to hail through his megaphone for "water". At mid-distance between the island and the mainland, competing yachts might at the same time be struggling against a one knot current, or perhaps sailing in slack water. Alternatively one or two of the class might be seen crossing the Solent to seek advantage of the ebb following the Hampshire coast. There were so many odd competitive situations mastered by wily Solent skippers and crews to take tactical tidal profits – indeed, such information might have offered the basis of a valuable literary work – but, to the best of my knowledge, these gems were not for publication, remaining secrets of the sport.

It was usually considered that the King's Cup race was the event of the Week from a yachting point of view and it was most disappointing to find the weather conditions on King's Cup Tuesday so unfavourable. In contrast to those of the previous day there seemed to be an almost total absence of that ingredient so essential to yacht racing. The breeze was so slight that great difficulty was experienced in crossing the starting line and, when the yachts finally succeeded, they substantially relied upon the ebb tide to progress in a westward direction. In Beaufort Notation, readings between 0 and 1 obtained throughout the long day.

Whilst a spectacle of this kind is boring in the extreme to the crowds on shore, a great deal of skilful seamanship is demanded of the helmsman and crew to extract the maximum advantage over competitors in such conditions. The qualities of extreme patience and continuing tactical practices are demanded to replace the more satisfying thrills of heeling to a breeze, which does not appear obvious to the spectator on shore.

The race organised by the Royal Yacht Squadron for the King's Cup was a handicap event for squadron yachts exclusively, of 30 tons and upwards. The starters were Mr Weld's cutter *Lulworth*, Mr F. Chaplin's yawl *Coral*, Sir F.G.P. Preston's ketch *Genesta*, Mr Oswald Sanderson's yawl *Julnar*, Sir William Portal's ketch *Valdora* and Col. John Gretton's ketch *Cariad*. The course known as the Queen's was programmed over a total distance of forty-six miles.

Lulworth sailed 'scratch', allowing *Cariad* 42 minutes 10 seconds, *Valdora* 46 minutes, *Julnar* 52 minutes 54 seconds, *Genesta* 110 minutes 24 seconds and *Coral* 111 minutes 10 seconds for the full course.

When the starting gun fired all of the competing vessels appeared to be completely becalmed. *Coral*, with an inshore berth, crossed the starting line first, assisted by an ebb tide, followed by *Lulworth* (1½ minutes late) and *Valdora* (16½ minutes behind). *Genesta, Cariad* and *Julnar* trailed at intervals, the last named being forty minutes late! They made their way at a crab's pace along to the westward mark and were out of view for some hours. Only *Lulworth* and *Genesta* continued the leg to the Warner Lightship after returning to view, the rest of the competitors were completely frustrated and gave up. Both *Lulworth* and *Genesta* were out of sight for a very long period and all other racing in the smaller classes had long since finished when *Lulworth* took the winning gun after just over 9½ hours of endurance. *Lulworth* received the gun at the end of the first round, averaging 2.42 knots for the course. Enough was enough!

Her competitors, realising that they had no chance to win the Cup, gave up the struggle earlier. It was, however, considered a great honour for Mr Weld to win the King's Cup and his victory was very popular with his contemporaries, following his election to the Royal Yacht Squadron in 1924. Here was an instance of a yacht designed with heavy weather capability completing a contest with almost no air to assist her. A great deal of credit had to be accorded to the yacht's company, in all fairness, by making such successful and patient use of the Solent tides!

Although the race for the King's Cup had endured until just after 7.30 p.m. in the evening, the event had just finished before His Majesty was due to dine at the squadron, where he landed at 8.15 p.m. with the Duke of Connaught, accompanied by the Hon. Sir Derek Keppel, Capt. Sir Charles Cust, RN, and the Earl of Mount Edgcumbe, to be greeted by the commodore and a deputation of squadron members. Mr Weld was amongst the many dinner guests, and received the trophy presented by the King after the loyal toast.

Following the flat conditions for the King's Cup race, Wednesday August 5th offered a most decided improvement in sailing conditions. The race opened with a light breeze, the sky dull and threatening with rain, but soon after the start the sun appeared and shone throughout the day, with the breeze steadily freshening.

The programme opened with a race for yachts exceeding 105 tons for prizes of £70, £20, £10, sailing the Queen's forty-six nautical mile course. *Westward* was the scratch vessel, allowing *Lulworth*, *White Heather II*, *Shamrock* and *Britannia* 3 minutes 50 seconds each (5 seconds/mile), the schooner *Susanne* 36 minutes 3 seconds, and the ketch *Valdora* 46 minutes. The start with a following wind to the eastward was later helped by an ebbing tide, affording a beautiful sight of the yachts with spinnakers set. The yachts were spread well apart, there being some 2½ minutes between *White Heather II* in first position and *Westward*, which was last to cross the line. The 'procession' to the Warner as the fleet passed Osborne Bay was noted as *White Heather II*, *Valdora*, *Susanne*, *Shamrock*, *Lulworth* and *Britannia*, with *Westward* separated from the rest. On the beat back from the eastward to make the East Lepe mark, *Shamrock* and *Lulworth* had made masterly impressions on the fleet, assisted by a substantial improvement in wind forces. *Britannia*, finding the elements more to her liking, had overtaken *Valdora*, *Susanne* and *White Heather II*, coming into third place at the end of the first round. The times recorded were:

Shamrock	1 hr 44 mins 29
Lulworth	1 hr 46 mins 6
Britannia	1 hr 49 mins 52
White Heather II	1 hr 52 mins 20
Westward	1 hr 52 mins 26
Valdora	2 hrs 16 mins 27

Susanne retired from the contest.

On the second round *Shamrock* maintained her lead and *Britannia* overtook *Lulworth* to finish in second place. As the third gun thundered, *Lulworth* and *Westward* appeared from the shore to be practically 'neck and neck' but the former had the latter's time donation in hand. *Valdora* was only 63 seconds behind *Lulworth* on corrected time! The results were:

Shamrock (winner)	4 hrs 15 mins 35 secs
Britannia (second)	4 hrs 17 mins 55 secs
Lulworth (third)	4 hrs 19 mins 40 secs
Valdora	4 hrs 20 mins 43 secs
White Heather II	4 hrs 21 mins 24 secs
Westward	4 hrs 23 mins 31 secs

Thursday of the Week proved disappointing in the extreme, with rain pouring down from the early morning until the conclusion of racing, thus depriving the yachtsmen and spectators of their normal enjoyment. The shoreside was practically deserted at the 10 a.m. start, and, for the few who enthusiastically turned out, visibility was obscured by a thick haze enveloping the Solent, a humid by-product of the rain. It was not always easy to follow the Solent events from the shoreside and such conditions served to exaggerate the difficulty. With water oozing into one's coat collar, only to discover that *Lulworth* was not preparing for the start, the day was obviously destined to offer a negative prospect for the lad. There was yet another factor in play; that being the probable effect of a stiff southerly breeze, which, if it persisted, could only predetermine the winner as a reward for a soaking! And so it was proven.

The race for yachts exceeding 105 tons, some forty sea miles, was sailed for Cowes town prizes of £70 first and £20 second, over the course sailing eastwards to the South-East Middle, North-East Middle and Solent Bank buoys, twice round. The schooner *Westward* allowed the three cutters *Britannia*, *Shamrock* and *White Heather II* 3 minutes 20 seconds each (5 seconds/mile).

The published corrected finishing times were:

Westward (winner)	2 hrs 12 mins 16
White Heather II (2nd)	2 hrs 15 mins 32
Britannia	2 hrs 18 mins 16
Shamrock	2 hrs 19 mins 28

The termination of the 1925 Cowes Regatta Week was celebrated in customary fashion, reaching a crescendo of jubilation with a memorable display of fireworks. Throughout the day, which was mainly dull with occasional interruptions of dazzling sunshine, the vessels lying in the Roadstead contributed to the carnival atmosphere, lavishly decorated with multi-coloured bunting as a backdrop to the revelry enjoyed on shore.

The main racing attraction of the day was the handicap event for yachts exceeding 105 tons for prizes of £70, £20, and £10, sailed over the forty-six mile Queen's Course. The Big Five, with the schooner *Westward* sailing scratch, were to be seen jockeying for positions ahead of the 10 a.m. starting signal; the cutters each received an allowance of 3 minutes 50 seconds for the full course. A brisk southerly breeze favoured the schooner, to allow reaching conditions for the greater distance.

White Heather II was first away to windward of the fleet with an in-shore position, very closely followed by *Shamrock*, *Westward* and *Britannia*, whilst *Lulworth* trailed some thirty seconds behind. The King was aboard *Britannia* with the Hon. George Colville as a guest and Mr Davies entertained the Earl Jellicoe and his daughter on the Herreshoff schooner.

On the reach to the Warner, *Lulworth* made her way through the fleet, overhauling *White Heather II, Shamrock* and *Britannia* to indulge in a desperate struggle with *Westward* for first position. With her great spread of canvas set to take advantage of the southerly wind, the schooner edged ahead, leaving the cutter in second place. *Britannia* meanwhile, proudly responding to the stiff breeze, overtook *White Heather II* and *Shamrock*, which was left marginally astern. On the return leg to the East Lepe mark *White Heather II* regained her former advantage over *Britannia* and, as the fleet passed the club house to make a second round, the times noted were:

Westward	12 hrs 14 mins 58
Lulworth	12 hrs 16 mins 42
White Heather II	12 hrs 17 mins 24
Britannia	12 hrs 18 mins 25
Shamrock	12 hrs 19 mins 51

At this stage *Westward* was just 1 minute 44 seconds ahead of *Lulworth* and the four cutters were separated by only 3 minutes 9 seconds. On the second round the wind eased slightly to become fluky as the yachts rounded the Warner to race back to the line. Both *Lulworth* and *Britannia* were overtaken on the final reach, *White Heather II* moving into second place with *Shamrock* finishing fourth.

Westward stretched her lead to take the first flag some 3½ minutes ahead of *White Heather II* on corrected time. *Lulworth* had to be content with third prize after her valiant earlier battle against the schooner.

Corrected finishing times taken:

Westward (winner)	2 hrs 20 mins 14
White Heather II (second)	2 hrs 23 mins 44
Lulworth (third)	2 hrs 24 mins 42
Shamrock	2 hrs 25 mins 37
Britannia	2 hrs 27 mins 1

The 1925 Royal Victoria Yacht Club's Regatta opened on Saturday, August 8th. Grey skies in the early morning cleared to provide brilliant sunshine which was accompanied by a light sou'west'r to allow very desirable sailing conditions for the Big Five. Sir William Burton was commodore of the RVYC and, with Major B. Heckstall-Smith, presided over the Race Committee. (The former was skipper of *Shamrock IV* when she raced for the Americas Cup in 1920.)

Racing started at 11 a.m. for the RVYC International Gold Challenge Cup, programmed for yachts exceeding 100 tons (TM) The course of forty-six miles took the yachts eastward to the Nab End Gas buoy, Outer Spit buoy and the Ryde West Middle marks, working twice round. *Westward* sailed scratch, allowing the four cutters 3 mins 50 secs each (5 secs per mile).

Sir Thomas Lipton's *Shamrock* took the weather berth over the start line, which extended from Ryde Pier. She was escorted in order by *White Heather II*, *Lulworth*, *Britannia* and *Westward*. It was fairly obvious from the start that the south-westerly breeze favoured the fastest contestant in reaching peak performance on this particular course, and, unless a major change of wind direction occurred, the schooner would inevitably qualify for the first flag. *Shamrock* took the lead, passing to windward of *Lulworth* and *White Heather II*. The giant schooner, as usual, started behind the cutters to avoid the embarrassment of a possible recall, but quickly passed through the lee of her competitors to establish a leading role by the time Bembridge Ledge was fetched. With the benefit of reaching winds, *Westward* had the race in hand by saving her time allowance at the end of the first round and, barring accidents, the result became a foregone conclusion, which led the spectators on shore to concentrate their interests on the rest of the fleet. With only three minutes separating the four cutters, the times at the end of the first round were:

Westward	1 hr 4 mins 39
Shamrock	1 hr 10 mins 15
Lulworth	1 hr 11 mins 8
White Heather II	1 hr 11 mins 26
Britannia	1 hr 13 mins 19

During the second round *Westward* continued to distance herself still further from the cutters, which were sailing closely together in a tremendous battle for supremacy.

There was a fitful breeze blowing most of the day and as the wind eased *White Heather II* benefited, overtaking *Lulworth* and further threatening *Shamrock's* position, but she could do no better than to make the finishing line some nineteen seconds behind her green-hulled contemporary.

However, *Lulworth* was awarded the second prize, because of cross protests from *White Heather II* and *Shamrock* on the alleged grounds of sailing dangerously and the fact that *White Heather II* had touched *Shamrock* during the contest. Both protests were upheld by the race committee.

The corrected finishing times were:

Westward (cup)	3 hrs 12 mins 4
Lulworth (second)	3 hrs 22 mins
Shamrock	3 hrs 20 mins 47
White Heather II	3 hrs 21 mins 6
Britannia	3 hrs 27 mins 8

The racing results for the Big Five noted from the 1925 Royal Victoria Yacht Club Regatta produced some sharp contrasts in performance 'presided over' by the changing intensity and direction of the wind forces. A classic example of *Lulworth*'s fortunes on two consecutive days of competition can be instanced beginning with the Monday event for the Assheton–Smith Challenge Cup, a valuable trophy which might be retained by an owner who won the race three times. It had earlier been won once by *Britannia* in 1920 and by *Lulworth* in 1924.

Sport was marred initially by a deluge of rain and this persisted almost until the winning gun was fired. There seemed to be virtually a complete absence of wind, whilst the rain was at its worst and the ensemble disappeared into a misty vision for some time, scarcely drifting to advantage, eventually becoming lost from sight. The wind was fluky at all points south on the compass, when the downpour eased and later developed into a moderate force 4 on the Beaufort scale.

With the cup came cash prizes of £50 from the commodore and a second of £20 for the following flag. The vessels were sent over a reversed course, round the Ryde West Middle, the Outer Spit and the Nab End Gas buoys. The competitors were *Lulworth*, *Britannia*, *Shamrock*, *White Heather II* and the schooner *Westward* sailing scratch, allowing the four cutters each 3 mins 50 secs. The cutters sailed on level terms. With an 11 a.m. start the yachts crossed the line led by *Britannia* and in order were *White Heather II*, *Shamrock* and *Westward* with *Lulworth* bringing up the rear.

The schooner, using her usual tactics, was careful to avoid a recall, but reached through the lee of her competitors to take the lead, enjoying the advantage of a southerly light air by half the distance of the first round. Whilst *Britannia* had made a brilliant start, the relative calm did not suit her and *White Heather II* forged ahead. *Lulworth* and *Shamrock* in close company were dicing on the first stretch to the West Middle. *Lulworth* was seen to make a short board on the starboard tack and *Shamrock* naughtily crossed *Lulworth*'s bows on the port tack, forcing her to bear up slightly rather than come about under *Shamrock*'s lee. As a result of an infringement of the rule by *Shamrock*, a protest flag was hoisted by *Lulworth* and in consequence *Shamrock* retired, returning to her moorings a few minutes after starting. The reaching conditions would normally have favoured *Westward* but *White Heather II* was lucky enough to pick up a catspaw and on the reach back from the Nab End led the schooner by nearly five minutes, leaving no doubt of the white cutter's inherent superiority in light conditions. The first round times were:

White Heather II	2 hr 3 mins 17
Westward	2 hr 8 mins 10
Lulworth	2 hr 17 mins 51
Britannia	2 hr 22 mins 9

Assisted by a slightly improving breeze, *Westward* was rapidly closing on *White Heather II* and the former took the lead at the western mark and subsequently left the cutters behind on the long reach eastwards. Following such a wet start and a paucity of air, *Britannia*'s crew must have been relieved when she retired to Cowes, leaving the western mark astern.

White Heather II was seen to be losing her advantage and found *Lulworth* close on her heels during the second round, but, with the fluky conditions, Captain Mountifield found sufficient wind to ignore Hogarth's challenge.

The finishing times (corrected) were:

Westward (cup)	4 hr 40 mins 9
White Heather II	4 hr 42 mins 7
Lulworth	4 hr 45 mins 33

The Royal Thames Yacht Club Regatta started on Tuesday,[2] the next day. Conditions were slightly improved, suffering but a few showers with variable winds shifting from south to west, varying in intensity between force 2 and 4 on the Beaufort scale. For the one day of the whole meeting, the yachts had later to include a beat to the westward and so the schooner's chances of a second runaway win were lessened. The race for yachts of 105 tons upwards for prizes of £80, £40 and £20 was sailed twice round the Ryde West Middle, and the Nab End Gas buoys, some forty-two sea miles. *Shamrock* was the only absentee from the Big Five on this day. It is unlikely that this had any connection with the protest by *Lulworth* on the previous day.

The order across the line at the 10 a.m. start was led by *White Heather II* followed by *Lulworth, Britannia* and *Westward*. The schooner was well to the leeward of the cutters once again, passing behind the fleet with a directionally favourable reaching breeze to establish the lead. It seemed that she might be about to repeat yesterday's triumph, as an initial reaching wind to make the western mark permitted a similar course of action around the eastern mark on the first round. This put her well ahead of the cutters by some 4 minutes, against a time allowance of 3 mins 30 secs for the two complete rounds. Meanwhile *Lulworth* and *White Heather II* were engaged in a closely-fought duel whilst *Britannia* had insufficient wind for her ultimate capability and trailed a few minutes behind. *Lulworth* was able to show *White Heather II* an ability to point higher on the beat back as the wind veered to meet them. Accordingly *Westward* began to suffer at *Lulworth*'s hands as she stole some minutes from the advantage earlier built up by the schooner. At the end of the first round the times, with *Westward* seemingly still comfortably in the lead, were:

Westward	12 hr 40 mins 5
Lulworth	2 hr 45 mins 45
White Heather	12 hr 48 mins 10
Britannia	12 hr 56 mins 10

The foregoing times are actual (uncorrected) and, although *Lulworth* had eaten into *Westward*'s lead, the former could scarcely anticipate any hope of a first flag at this stage. Continuing a beat to the western mark, *Lulworth* sailed superbly, reducing her deficit completely and overtook the schooner; meanwhile both *Britannia* and *White Heather II* were getting ominously close to *Westward*'s station. *Lulworth* rounded the western mark well ahead of *Westward* and, with spinnaker set to starboard, made the pace for a near record easterly run, assisted by a flowing tide. Some minutes later *White Heather II*, profiting from a fluky breeze, overhauled *Westward*. *Britannia* was rapidly closing the gap, but missed saving her time by a mere two minutes. Their positions were held to the winning gun, with *Lulworth* avenging her defeat by *Westward* on the previous day, the victory being entirely without need of the 3 mins 30 secs time allowance which the schooner was required to donate to each of the cutters. The windward leg of the course had presented the two white cutters with an opportunity to demonstrate an inherent mastery over the schooner.

Finishing times (corrected) read:

Lulworth	3 hr 48 mins 40
White Heather	3 hr 50 mins 31
Westward	3 hr 55 mins 44
Britannia	3 hr 57 mins 7

The race around the Isle of Wight over a distance of fifty-four nautical miles, programmed for Wednesday of the RTYC 1925 Regatta, was the major event of the day. The cup, to be presented by HM King George V, was the coveted prize for competing yachts of 35 tons TM upwards. With such a wide tolerance of tonnage and rig, the event was to test the wisdom of the handicappers in the extreme.

Of the seventeen entries, there were twelve contestants which actually crossed the starting line, including Mr Weld's

Lulworth, Mr F.T.B. Davis's schooner *Westward*, Lord Waring's *White Heather II,* Mr R. McAlpine's schooner *Susanne*, Mr R. Clark Neile's schooner *Adventuress*, Mr C.E. Newbiggin's yawl *Palmosa*, Mr H.K. Andreae's cutter *Corona*, Sir Howard Frank's cutter *June*, Sir E. Iliffe's and Mr A. Messer's cutter, the 15 metre *Mariquita*, Mr J.S. Highfield's cutter *Dorina*, Mr J.W. Cooke's cutter *Thanet* and Mr W. Brooke's cutter *Hispania*.

Westward sailed scratch to allow *Lulworth* and *White Heather II* 4 mins 30 secs, *Mariquita* 27 mins, *Corona* 28 mins 48 secs, *Susanne* 48 mins 48 secs, *June* 56 mins 42 secs, *Hispania* 57 mins 36 secs, *Dorina* 62 mins, *Thanet* 72 mins, *Adventuress* 100 mins 48 secs, and *Palmosa* 118 mins 43 secs.

For those spectators who had forsaken their beds at an unsocial hour to witness an early start, the sacrifice was amply compensated by a bonus of rare and rather mysterious entertainment at Mr Weld's expense.

A classic exhibition of jockeying for the start line from Ryde Pierhead was seen as a preliminary. Next *Lulworth* breached the line a couple of seconds before the Blue Peter came down and sailed on. *White Heather II* followed immediately after the signal, heading, in order, *Hispania, June, Thanet, Mariquita, Westward, Palmosa, Dorina, Corona, Adventuress* and the beautiful Fife schooner *Susanne*, which was a long way astern of the others. The schooners were sailing substantially to leeward of the fleet. Jackyarders were hoisted boldly by *White Heather II* and *Corona*, but caution was exercised by *Lulworth* and the smaller vessels in setting jib headers, deferring to the elements anticipated in the open waters of the Channel. No explanation was made for *Lulworth*'s subsequent behaviour. The usual recall gun was fired on the heels of the starting signal and No.2 was run up from the club house flagstaff. *Lulworth* sailed on. The siren was then sounded to reinforce the committee's directive. *Lulworth* sailed on. After she had progressed for about half a mile of the course, a further effort was made to attract the errant yacht's attention by the firing of a two gun salvo. At long last, the coin dropped. A self-inflicted additional penalty of at least five to six mins was earned by *Lulworth* in returning to recross the line. However, undaunted *Lulworth* cheerfully continued to play her part. At this stage it must have been obvious that she had scarcely any hope of winning against the scheduled heavy loadings of handicap allowances benefiting the smaller vessels. Whilst the behaviour of *Lulworth* might ordinarily have been considered as somewhat bizarre, delay in obeying the recall might have resulted from either the interests of safety, or good sportsmanship extended to minimise any embarrassment for the large fleet of competing yachts.

The fleet reached away in the fresh breeze to the westward, led by *White Heather II* which was still in the van as they passed Old Castle Point and beyond through Cowes Roads. Early in the contest the schooner *Adventuress* retired. The south-west wind increased in volume as the yachts were seen to approach The Needles and conditions were severely aggravated by a heavy downpour of rain, to the extreme discomfort of the participating crews. It was, therefore, not altogether surprising that *Dorina, Palmosa and Hispania* gave up before rounding the lighthouse, with such disenchanting prospects ahead. Mr Davis's hopes with *Westward* were frustrated as the big Herreshoff schooner suffered the indignity of grounding and sticking fast on one of the shingle banks off Totland Bay, not to be refloated until the afternoon. She sailed back to her moorings with no apparent damage.

Meanwhile, *Lulworth* had progressed remarkably well to overhaul the fleet with the exception of *White Heather II*, which was enjoying a five minute advantage as the Needles Lighthouse was rounded. Discounting the former's apparent display of nonsense at the start, the two old rivals might otherwise have provided an exciting exhibition of dicing, as this margin persisted until the finish.

Just before midday *White Heather II* was sighted through the misting rain with *Lulworth* trailing at the eastern end of the

Garden Isle. The two big class cutters were followed by *Corona* (which had incidentally been handicapped by the loss of her topmast) and *Mariquita*, which was stealing the advantage.

Then came Mr Robert McAlpine's schooner *Susanne*, which had greatly benefited from the reaching breeze for most of the distance. Next showed Sir Howard Frank's *June* and the little 42 ton cutter *Thanet*, owned by Mr J.W. Cook, which eventually saved her time into third place.

White Heather II was first to cross the finishing line, having covered the course in 4 hours 45 mins 1 sec. *Lulworth* came just 4 mins 50 secs later, separated from her class rival by less than the time initially lost.

The royal trophy was won very decisively by Mr Robert McAlpine's *Susanne*, which finished nearly half an hour later than *White Heather II*, the little white schooner having saved her time with fifteen minutes in hand.

To fix fair and reasonable handicap allowances for yachts of differing rigs and tonnages between 42 and 323 TM was no easy task. A study of the first six places shows the yachts within a twelve minute span over the fifty-four nautical mile course. Indeed, the crystal ball reflected some imaginative criteria!

Susanne acquitted herself remarkably well, ending in a very decisive result. Although *Lulworth* was placed by handicap last of seven finishers, her average speed of 11.36 knots (taken from her absurd restart time) was no mean performance.

The results were as follows, with both actual and corrected times:

	Actual	Corrected
Susanne	12 hrs 45 mins 10	11 hrs 58 mins 51
June	12 hrs 58 mins 45	12 hrs 2 mins 3
Thanet	1 hr 19 mins 38	12 hrs 7 mins 38
Mariquita	12 hrs 37 mins 37	12 hrs 10 mins 27
White Heather II	12 hrs 15 mins 1	12 hrs 10 mins 31

| *Corona* | 12 hrs 39 mins 22 | 12 hrs 10 mins 34 |
| *Lulworth* | 12 hrs 19 mins 51 | 12 hrs 15 mins 21 |

In 1925 the yacht owners or owners' representatives came together to agree upon a common wage structure for yacht hands. Whilst the attitude was not intended to encourage the formation of a union, there appeared to be a wide scale of individual rewards which had arisen, quite naturally, by the owners preserving freedom of wage negotiation. It was pointed out that a very unfair advantage could almost certainly arise whereby an owner would, as the highest bidder, assemble the finest crew to the detriment of competitors. (In a discussion held three years earlier the consensus was that no action should be taken.)

This later meeting to discuss a common wage structure was attended by Mr H. Weld (*Lulworth*), Major Hunloke (*Britannia*), Mr T.B. Davis (*Westward*), Sir Thomas Lipton (*Shamrock*) and Lord Waring (*White Heather II*). The meeting decided that mates should receive £5 per week while the other members of the crew, such as the head bowsprit man, would receive £2 17s 6d per week. Prize money of £1 for a win, 10/- for a second and 5/- for a third placing would be paid out at the end of the season. The captain would take 5% of all winnings and the mate £2 per race. All hands would be given two shillings and sixpence as 'grub' money on race days and a clothes issue for crews was drawn up.

There were doubtless a number of repercussions as a result of this schedule because some crew members suffered a wage cut, whilst others enjoyed the benefit of an increase. At least the seamen had no complaints about unequal treatment from this point onwards.

Lulworth's outstanding success in the first class during 1925 is emphasised on page 237 of Douglas Dixon's book *The King's Sailing Master* with a most informative tribute. I quote: 'It was *Lulworth*'s year. She had been bought by Sir Mortimer Singer.[3] She made twenty-seven starts[4] and flew twenty-seven prize flags when she came home to pay off – eight firsts, eleven seconds, and eight third prizes.' Whilst Dixon's comment is in itself a very substantial testimony to the achievements of *Lulworth* in the 1925 season, her victory in the King's Cup contest for a wider class of yachts affords a further increase in the totals.

In his mammoth work entitled *The King's* Britannia, John Irving comments of the year 1925: 'This was a *Lulworth* year; her change of ownership[3] seemed to have given her an entirely new lease of life and the hitherto unlucky ship rose to a crest of form which she rode for three seasons. She had a stern battle with *Shamrock* for the coveted head of class and *White Heather II* was not very far behind them.

'*Britannia*, however, was nowhere this year...'

---

[1] Solent tidal behaviour is complex in the extreme. It is usual for the flood to enter the Channel past The Needles and Hurst Castle some one to two hours in advance of entry from the eastern end, between Bembridge and Lee-on-Solent. The obvious result allows movement of the water flooding and ebbing in an area between Calshot and Cowes Harbour at the same time.

[2] The race on Tuesday, August 11th, 1925 marked the one hundred and fiftieth anniversary of the foundation of the Royal Thames Yacht Club and, to commemorate the occasion, a silver medal was given to the owner of each competing yacht, and a bronze medal to the skipper or one of the crew, if an amateur.

[3] Whilst the claims for Lulworth's class leadership are not in dispute for the year 1925, mention of Sir Mortimer Singer's commencement of ownership should have been accorded to the year 1926. Mr Herbert Weld–Blundell raced Lulworth for the 1924 and 1925 seasons.

[4] Dixon might appear to have overlooked or intentionally disregarded the result of the race around the Isle of Wight in the RTYC Regatta, which was sailed on 12th August, 1925 when Lulworth came last, although her placing was doubtless due to an unusually late start and, furthermore, she was not competing in her class on that day.

1926

LULWORTH STAGES A VICTORIOUS ENCORE

Royal interest in the 1926 Cowes Yachting festival stimulated ever-increasing enthusiasm for the sport from yachtsmen, society patrons and spectators in general, who gathered with the conviction that Cowes, as ever, was a "must". Their Majesties arrived in the royal steam yacht, popularly known as the *V & A,* its dark blue and gold lines sporting two jauntily raked funnels, artistically flared at their tops. The magnificent floating palace was anchored in its customary location at the centre of the scene from the Cowes parade. This year's guardship, HMS *Ramillies*, yet another resplendent example of Britain's naval power of the times, was commanded by Captain E. Wigram CMG, DSO, RN, supported by the destroyer HMS *Windsor* (Commander H.P. Boxer RN) and the minesweeper HMS *Sherborne* (Lieut. Commander W. Harris RN), which performed the duty of escort to the Admiral's racing cutter *Britannia*. Literally dozens of the most opulent steam and motor yachts were tiered across the immediate waterway, leaving a deep channel for the ocean-bound liners between the yachting rendezvous and the Brambles Shoal.

In the new ownership of Sir Mortimer Singer, 1926 was the year when *Lulworth* consolidated the rise to the top of her class established in the previous season's regattas. Her performance figure for this year was substantially better than that of the year 1925, creating a record of thirteen firsts for the Big Five in 29 starts, still substantially racing on level terms with her contemporaries. The 1926 seasonal results conclusively demonstrated an edge over her competitors: truly *Lulworth* had shown a mastery in two successive years which remained unbeaten. It is, of course, accepted that *Shamrock* achieved an equivalent record of thirteen firsts in the year 1928, but with a greater number of starts, thereby diluting her resultant overall performance figure.

Understandably it must have been discouraging for Sir Philip Hunloke to find the sovereign's *Britannia* dropping behind in the league table from seven seasonal firsts in 1924 to just four firsts in 1926, and suggested improvements to the royal cutter were ordered in the winter following.

However, *Lulworth*'s two successive seasonal achievements were attributable in no small measure to the latent genius of Charles Nicholson, whose fatherly influence brought about changes to establish a giant capable of producing a series of results to lead the flotilla on level terms racing without time allowances.

The 1926 Regatta Week at Cowes began on August Bank Holiday Monday, with the sunniest of weather conditions; the absence of a lively sailing breeze, however, dampened the enthusiasm of the yachtsmen as well as the longshore sporting fraternity.

The Royal London Yacht Club opened the Week using the facilities of the Royal Yacht Squadron as usual to provide signals and firing of cannon. The first race for yachts in excess of 100 tons TM over a course of some forty miles starting from the squadron club house, twice round the Solent Bank and North-East Middle buoys was joined by the Big Five: *Lulworth, Britannia, Shamrock, White Heather II* and *Westward*. Whereas the cutters had for some time been racing on level terms, *White Heather II* was inexplicably donated a time allowance of 1 min 57 secs on this day by the others for the two rounds. A striking picture was posed as the assembly sailed close-hauled to the start line with all canvas set. *Shamrock* was first over the line followed by *Britannia, Lulworth, White Heather II* and the schooner *Westward*, which came three minutes later. The beat to the western mark, although assisted by an ebbing tide, was painfully slow owing to the light airs. *Britannia* was the first to round the Solent Bank buoy (belying her reputation as essentially needing a blow to take the lead) with *White Heather II* next, *Shamrock* third, *Lulworth* fourth and *Westward* a long distance astern. Very slow progress was observed with the fleet running free against a foul tide to the easterly mark after the yachts had been detained at the western end of the course for a long time. Meanwhile the crowds on shore sought alternative entertainments. Long before the yachts passed the squadron sailing eastwards, the 'S flag[1] signal was flown to advise that only one round would be sailed. In the event the decision was to prove a wise one as the time had stretched to nearly six hours to cover one round of twenty nautical miles by the finish.

With a slightly improving breeze, there was some lively tactical manoeuvring on the final beat to the finish line between *Britannia*, *Lulworth* and *Shamrock* for second place. The time allowance of less than a minute for one round was not required by *White Heather II* for she had beaten the royal cutter by eighty-five seconds.

The corrected finishing times noted were:

White Heather II (winner)	3 hrs 53 mins 53
Britannia (second)	3 hrs 55 mins 27
Lulworth (third)	3 hrs 58 mins 47
Shamrock	3 hrs 59 mins 26
Westward	4 hrs 21 mins 7

The Royal Yacht Squadron Regatta opened on Tuesday, August 3rd, 1926, the first event being the King's Cup, a handicap event for yachts of 15 tons TM upwards belonging to the RYS. The trophy had been won by *Lulworth* in the 1925 event with calm weather conditions, and in 1926 the winner was Mr Frank Chaplin's yawl *Coral*. *Lulworth* was sailing on this day with her four contemporaries of the Big Five, leaving the King's Cup competition to the smaller yachts.

The second event was for yachts exceeding 110 tons register for prizes of £80 first, £20 second and £10 third. The course sailed was twice round the Solent Bank, North-East Middle and South-East Middle buoys (approximately forty sea miles). Sailing on level terms were HM the King's cutter *Britannia*, Sir Mortimer Singer's *Lulworth*, Sir Thomas Lipton's *Shamrock*, Lord Waring's cutter *White Heather II* and Mr F.T.B. Davis's schooner *Westward*. The winner of the contest could have been almost predicted from the start. With a southerly breeze, the race was sailed at a near record pace since reaching conditions prevailed throughout.

Shamrock was first to cross the line with *Lulworth* following to windward, shadowed by *White Heather II, Britannia* and *Westward* on her beam. The schooner was quickly in her stride to pass through the lee of the cutters and reach the Solent Bank buoy well in advance of the others, a position which she characteristically maintained throughout the event. With a good steady breeze persisting, *Lulworth* overtook *Shamrock* to lead the cutters round the western mark, but *Westward* was steadily increasing the margin between them. *White Heather II* was the third yacht round, leading *Shamrock* and *Britannia*, which was threatening to overtake the green cutter. As the fleet passed through the roads to fetch the North-East Middle buoy, *Britannia* left *Shamrock* behind. The schooner, enjoying a day with the wind in her favour, had things perfectly suited to her temperament, gaining four minutes ahead of *Lulworth* (still leading the cutters) at the end of the first round. The times recorded were:

Westward	12 hrs 1 min 54
Lulworth	12 hrs 5 mins 36
White Heather II	12 hrs 6 mins 31
Britannia	12 hrs 7 mins 10
Shamrock	12 hrs 8 mins 9

The main interest in the race was concentrated on the four giant cutters at half distance, these having less than three minutes' difference between them.

There was no change of position during the second round and the times noted indicate how remarkably well matched the four cutters were, all originating from different periods but sailing under relatively steady conditions, reaching near ultimate speeds. A glance at the finishing times shows a band of 4 minutes and 15 seconds between the first and last cutter to finish. This indicated a reasonably consistent performance for the first and second rounds of the course.

The finishing results were:

		Average speed (knots)
Westward	1 hr 45 min 51	11.39
Lulworth	1 hr 54 mins 55	10.91
White Heather II	1 hr 55 mins 45	10.86
Britannia	1 hr 57 mins 26	10.78
Shamrock	1 hr 59 mins 10	10.69

The boy had thoroughly enjoyed the day's racing, not that his favourite yacht was the winner, but because under practically 'laboratory' conditions of a steady breeze on the beam, *Lulworth* had outpaced her rival cutters and robbed *White Heather II* of second place, if only by a small margin.

Wednesday's contest for yachts of 110 tons upwards was sailed over two rounds of the Queen's course, encompassing the East Lepe buoy and the Warner Lightship. The wind direction was similar to that of the previous day but lower in weight. The indications from the start were that nature had arranged things to ensure a repeat victory for the schooner as a reaching breeze persisted for the duration of the race.

All of the Big Five yachts crossed the 10 a.m. start line, although *White Heather II* suffered cruel luck when she had to retire shortly afterwards with a failure of her port runner block anchorage.

The overall pattern of the day's racing was not unlike that of Tuesday's event, with *Westward* proving an easy winner by a margin of twelve minutes over *Shamrock* on a longer course and in a lighter breeze. The three cutters had sailed to closer finishing limits than those recorded for the day before, with only 2 mins 55 secs separating *Shamrock* and *Lulworth*. *Britannia* had maintained a claim to third flag whilst the other two cutters had exchanged positions of merit.

The finishing times noted read:

		Average speed (knots)
Westward	2 hrs 26 min 1	10.37
Shamrock	2 hrs 38 mins 55	9.89
Britannia	2 hrs 40 mins 4	9.85
Lulworth	2 hrs 41 mins 50	9.80

The average speeds confirm the effect of a lighter breeze than that prevailing on the previous day. Racing for the Cowes town prizes of £80 first, £20 second and £10 third took place on Thursday August 5th, 1926 by yachts exceeding 110 tons TM. The entrants competing on level terms were *Lulworth*, *White Heather II*, *Shamrock* and *Britannia*. The course programmed was twice round the Solent Bank, North-East Middle and South-East Middle buoys (approximately forty miles). The day was one of uninterrupted sunshine with a very light breeze. The wind was so muted at times that it became difficult to establish any progress against the strong current, which was ebbing when the fleet made to return from the western mark, although the wind piped up later in the day.

Guests sailing with HM the King on *Britannia* included the Duke of Connaught, Earl Jellicoe and Sir John Ward.

The start was an extremely cautious one for a good reason: a recall would, in all probability, have been extremely costly timewise. The competing yachts were well behind the line when the starting cannon boomed with a west flowing tide to assist them. *Lulworth* passed through the lee of *Britannia*, with *White Heather II* and *Shamrock* crossing the start line in that order. The schooner *Westward* came nearly 5½ minutes later, making sure of avoiding a recall in such light airs. Conditions did not augur well for the sport initially, as 4½ hours elapsed before Lord Waring's *White Heather II* was the first to round the Solent Bank buoy. It was a grand picture as the ensemble sailed back past the club house in close formation, but, with spinnakers set and filling with an increasing movement of air, they appeared well separated offshore. *White Heather II*, which so often hugged the coast, was farthest from it on this day, with *Shamrock* inshore slowly heading to capture the lead. Closely following astern in order came *Britannia*, *Lulworth* and *Westward*, which was struggling with her early deficit. A moderate breeze piped up to offer improved sailing conditions, although tending to be fluky.

Meanwhile shoreside excitement built up as the cutters made several positional changes on the eastern run, with *Lulworth* first to round the South-East Middle. On the beat back to the club house, Sir Mortimer Singer's cutter held her advantage, despite a spirited challenge from Sir Thomas Lipton's *Shamrock*. Not far distant, the King's *Britannia* was engaged in a desperate struggle for third place with Lord Waring's *White Heather II*, which passed the royal cutter off Old Castle Point, a mile from the finish, the race being stopped after one round had been sailed. Mr Davis's *Westward* was outsailed by the cutters to cross the line nearly ten minutes behind *Britannia*, which finished in fourth place. *Lulworth* received the winning gun, which was her first victory of the week, just 1 min 27 secs ahead of *Shamrock*.

The finishing times (confirming a slow pace for the contest in the day's light airs) read:

Lulworth (winner)	3 hrs 53 mins 20
Shamrock (second)	3 hrs 54 mins 47
White Heather II (third)	3 hrs 56 mins 47
Britannia	3 hrs 57 mins 23
Westward	4 hrs 6 mins 35

On Friday, the final day of the 1926 Cowes Regatta, the shoreside atmosphere was charged with its customary excitement. The day started with a glimpse of hazy sunshine offering the promise of a fine day. A steady breeze came piping from the west, but the omen was not fulfilled as the afternoon was marred by a heavy downfall of rain which seriously disadvantaged the onshore events planned for the seafront. At this stage, some anxiety was generally felt by the revellers about the prospect of the evening firework finale, which, happily, was not jeopardised as the weather improved in good time, and celebrations reached their traditional zenith. The Royal Yacht Squadron's event for the Big Five first class yachts was sailed for vessels exceeding 110 tons, twice round the Queen's course for prizes of £80 first, £20 second and £10 third. The cutters *Britannia*, *Shamrock*, *White Heather II* and *Lulworth* sailed on level terms with No.5, the schooner *Westward*, conspicuous by her absence from the start.

As the yachts came to the line, a classic line-up formed, with *Britannia* nosing ahead of *Shamrock*, followed by Lord Waring's *White Heather II* and *Lulworth* striking to windward immediately behind her.

The tide was in their favour as they made the beat to the East Lepe buoy which was rounded closely bunched, substantially in the order from the start.

With spinnakers set to port for the run to the Warner, the order on passing through the Roads had changed, with *Shamrock* now in the lead and *White Heather II* approximately thirty seconds astern of the green cutter.

Britannia had lost her pace-setting position, and was seen level with *Lulworth* as they passed the Royal Yacht Squadron. On the return beat from the Warner *Britannia* and *Lulworth* had both overtaken *White Heather II*, now some ten minutes distant. The first round times were Sir Thomas Lipton's *Shamrock* 12 hrs 54 mins 19 secs, the King's *Britannia* 12 hrs 56 mins 45 secs, Sir Mortimer Singer's *Lulworth* 12 hrs 59 mins 40 secs and Lord Waring's *White Heather II* 1 hr 0 mins 4 secs.

Lulworth and *Britannia* closed up, having a hard tussle on the heels of *Shamrock* as they approached the East Lepe Mark when the wind strengthened. The rain spoiled visibility from the shoreside as *Shamrock* was overtaken by the first two on the free run to the Warner. Making the final leg on beating back to the finish, *Britannia* was enjoying the fresh breeze, stealing ahead of *Lulworth* to win by a margin of seventy-nine seconds; so Sir Mortimer's white cutter had proven a worthy competitor to take the second flag.

The actual finishing times noted without need of correction on this day read:

Britannia (winner)	3 hrs 33 mins 18
Lulworth (second)	3 hrs 34 mins 37
Shamrock (third)	3 hrs 34 mins 55
White Heather II	3 hrs 36 mins 5

A great cheer arose from the loyal subjects along the esplanade, sheltering under their umbrellas, praising the royal cutter's victory. This was *Britannia's* first win of the Week and the last of her 1926 season.

The crews of *Lulworth*, *Shamrock* and *White Heather II* raised their voices in unison to salute the admiral's victory.

Lulworth featured brilliantly in a truly thrilling race to delight the crowds on Saturday, the opening day of the 1926 combined Royal Thames and Royal Victoria Yacht Club Regattas, sailed from the Ryde headquarters of the latter. The principal event was programmed for a handicap race to include yachts exceeding 110 tons TM to circuit the Isle of Wight for prizes of £80 first, £40 second and £20 third. The competing

---

[1] The international code flag letter 'S' shows a blue rectangular inset centred upon a basic white ground.

yachts comprised the royal cutter *Britannia*, Sir Mortimer Singer's cutter *Lulworth*, Lord Waring's cutter *White Heather II*, Mr F.T.B. Davis's schooner *Westward* and Mr Robert McAlpine's schooner *Susanne*. The weather for this occasion was almost 'out of a book' with brilliant sunshine and an ideal breeze enabling jackyarders to be just comfortably accommodated as the fleet sailed from their moorings at Cowes early in the morning, to join sport at Ryde. The King arrived aboard the *Victoria and Albert* to take the RVYC salute of twenty-one guns and later boarded his cutter for the day's event. Sir Thomas Lipton's *Shamrock* did not take part owing to damage sustained by her spinnaker boom on the closing day of the Cowes Regatta. The yachts sailed on level terms with the exception of the schooner *Susanne*; she was given forty-five minutes for the course. This was in an easterly starting direction, keeping north of the Norman Fort and Sand Head buoy, leaving Bembridge Ledge, Bridge and Warren Ledge buoys to starboard. The windward berth was occupied by *Britannia*, which was first over the line, followed by *Westward* with *Susanne* immediately to windward of her. Lord Waring's *White Heather II* came next, just ahead of Sir Mortimer Singer's *Lulworth*, cautiously proceeding in deference to her 1925 island circuit preliminary! Spinnakers were worn for a mile or two, until the wind veered to set reaching conditions for the remaining part of the leg to the Warner Lightship. As the fleet rounded the eastern mark, it became a reach along the southern shores of the Wight in the direction of St Catherine's Point. With conditions ideally in her favour, *Westward* led the fleet through Sandown Bay and the approximate times taken at Shanklin were:

Westward	1 hr 13 mins 31
White Heather II	1 hr 14 mins 58
Britannia	1 hr 15 mins 21
Lulworth	1 hr 15 mins 48
Susanne	1 hr 23 mins 36

The big cutters and the larger schooner were battling in relatively close company, with only 2 mins 17 secs between them at this stage, whilst *Susanne*, the smaller schooner, had trailed by only ten of her forty-five minutes' allowance for the complete round. After passing St Catherine's Point with a change of direction towards the north-west, the cutters were able to win back *Westward*'s advantage, as the single stickers made the beat towards The Needles Mark. With the fleet heading into the wind, *Lulworth* gave yet another display of her windward mastery by sailing through the opposition and heading the race, making Freshwater Bay to starboard. Meanwhile the schooner *Westward* was outsailed by *Britannia* and *White Heather*, with *Susanne* in position at the rear, gradually easing behind. This order was not to persist after The Needles had been cleared and the fleet made the run home through the Solent. *Westward* had the bit between her teeth and, with every available stitch of canvas hoisted, was straining to catch the leader, having taken *Britannia* and *White Heather II* in her advance as she threatened *Lulworth*'s hard-fought position. It appeared to the onlookers viewing the Cowes Roadstead that, as *Westward* came into focus, she must prove a certain winner when she sailed past *Lulworth* some three miles from the RVYC Committee HQ. There could be no margin of time allowance for the leading cutter on this occasion, as any deserved donations from the schooner, however small they might have been, were just not scheduled. Despite the doggedness of *Lulworth* in closely trailing the schooner, the effects of *Westward*'s greater sail area in combination with a seventeen per cent excess of waterline length, whilst running free, spelled the loading of the dice against the cutter, short of some unforeseen prospect. The indications were that *Westward* must surely take the first gun as she drew forward only two or three hundred yards from the line. To the amazement of the spectators, Skipper Hogarth pulled an old trick out of his bag, issuing the lusty directive, "In spinnaker and stand by to gybe."

Lulworth responded, and was observed to immediately reset her mainsail/topsail, temporarily stealing the wind on *Westward*'s quarter, sending her sails helplessly flapping with an accompanying rattle of gear and canvas.

Remembering Mr Davis's capacity for violent and colourful exclamation, the scene might have appropriately been enshrouded in blue smoke. From that moment onwards, *Lulworth* drew level, passing under *Westward*'s lee to cross the line less than a bowsprit length ahead of her, separated by a mere two seconds, providing a rare but truly classic example of an epic finish!

The corrected finishing times were:

Lulworth (winner)	3 hrs 55 mins 9
Westward (second)	3 hrs 55 mins 11
White Heather II (third)	4 hrs 3 mins 57
Susanne	4 hrs 6 mins 21
Britannia	4 hrs 7 mins 7

Oddly enough, neither of the first two yachts' skippers, although patently aware of the drama, was strictly sure of the official result of the race. The handicaps in communication of the period were such that, in order to obtain confirmation, it was necessary for a dinghy to be rowed ashore from *Lulworth*, making a personal visit to the headquarters of the RVYC. As her oarsmen approached their cutter on the return, with blades pointing skywards, a prospective supping of the local Mew Langton brew automatically suggested the impeccable means of an evening celebration in the taproom of Ryde's Squadron Hotel.

The annual dinner of the Royal Victoria Yacht Club fitted neatly into Sir Mortimer Singer's social diary on the same evening, when the trophy was presented to him. The Commodore, Sir William Burton, KBE, presided, supported by a member of a prominent Isle of Wight family, namely Major

General the Rt. Hon. Jack Seely, CB, CMG, DSO, the club's vice-commodore.

Weather conditions for racing on Monday, the concluding day of the 1926 Royal Thames Yacht Club Regatta, were more suited to the smaller classes of yachts since only a very moderate west-sou'-west'r prevailed. It quickly became obvious, as the big handicap yachts got underway, that unless the wind piped up, *White Heather II* and *Shamrock* must lead the more weatherly *Westward*, *Britannia* and *Lulworth* to victory. With a murky sky at the start of a forty-two mile course, the Big Five sailing without time allowances competed for prizes of £80 first, £40 second and £20 third.

White Heather II was first to cross the line at the 10 a.m. start, there being no recalls. *Shamrock* followed in her lee, with *Lulworth* coming a close third. *Britannia* came next, heading into wind and scarcely heeling to show her contempt for the ration of air. *Westward*, taking her usual follow-up from the rear, looked equally dispirited. Lord Waring's cutter maintained her advantage and was first round the middle mark, shadowed by *Shamrock*. The order of the pentagon was unchanged as the fleet passed the Royal Victoria Yacht Club HQ with spinnakers set to starboard, heading for the Nab End buoy. As they progressed at a moderate pace past the old forts, spinnakers were hauled in to reach the remaining easterly distance. On the return leg to complete the first round, *White Heather II* and *Shamrock* (about two minutes later) had worked out a fair advantage from the rest of the class. After the Nab mark was rounded, *Westward*, appreciating the return reach, made a half-spirited effort to overtake firstly *Britannia* and secondly *Lulworth*, which established the schooner in third position just twelve seconds ahead of Sir Mortimer's cutter at the end of the first round. However, *Lulworth* passed *Westward* again on the 'windward' leg, only to lose the position later. And so, as the race progressed, the two passed and repassed each other when the conditions of the course favoured their inherent merits. *White Heather II* and *Shamrock* pulled ahead to become substantially distanced from the rest of the contestant vessels and *Britannia* gamely struggled on in the rear without her essential motivation. As the yachts left the Nab astern on the final leg of the second round, *Westward* clinched her bid for third place by overhauling *Lulworth* once more during the reach for Ryde Pier, just six seconds ahead, to receive the third gun. *White Heather II* made a comfortable win over *Shamrock* in second place, some three minutes distant. It was hardly a lively day's racing, which extended to nearly five hours to complete the course, with the winner averaging only 8.60 knots.

The finishing times were:

White Heather II (winner)	2 hrs 53 mins 35
Shamrock (second)	2 hrs 56 mins 10
Westward (third)	3 hrs 3 mins 14
Lulworth	3 hrs 3 mins 20
Britannia	3 hrs 6 mins 25

It seemed that *Westward* had avenged her defeat of Saturday by marginally beating *Lulworth* into third place!

The programme for Tuesday did not include a competition for the over 110 ton class, as in previous years, much to the disappointment of the crowds gathered along the Ryde seafront. They were, however, rewarded to find a muster for Wednesday morning with nature providing thrilling ingredients to make the day's racing truly sensational. The yachts taking part were the King's *Britannia*, Sir Mortimer Singer's *Lulworth*, Lord Waring's *White Heather II*, Sir Thomas Lipton's *Shamrock* and Mr F. Davis's *Westward*, all racing on level terms. A fresh sou'-west wind at the start worked up to gale force later in the day, the event becoming tattooed by heavy rain squalls, much to the discomfort of crews and onlookers alike, since the former must have been well and truly soaked by the froth and spindrift of the Spithead chop.

In addition to competing for the cup, prizes of £80 (first) and £20 (second) were offered. The course to be sailed was the Long Victoria, twice round, totalling approximately forty-six nautical miles.

As the signals were given for a 10.30 a.m. start in a westerly direction, *Shamrock* was first over the line with *Lulworth* on her weather, followed by *White Heather II* and *Westward* together, whilst *Britannia* was a trifle late but with the windward position to her advantage. They made a long reach to the West-Middle buoy, with *Lulworth* enjoying the lead, circling the mark just over a minute ahead of *White Heather II*, whilst *Shamrock* followed some eight seconds later. *Britannia* shadowed *Shamrock* very closely and the schooner *Westward*, most surprisingly, with her normal tendency to profit from a reach, was timed two minutes behind *Lulworth*. Running back with spinnakers out to starboard, the fleet rounded the Outer Spit buoy in the same order. The boisterous weather showed no easing of intensity as *Lulworth* led the beat back from the Nab End Gas buoy, followed by *Britannia* in second place, now marginally leading *Shamrock*.

I vividly remember the events of the afternoon of this race when I was catching prawns in Osborne Bay. My interests were sharply divided between fishing and observation of the giant cutters on the return leg from the Nab End mark. The event had started with a stiffish breeze, but not sufficient to require any shortening of sail. Attention became focused upon *Lulworth, Britannia* and *Shamrock* battling in that order, as they met the lively westerly. A distinctly ominous cloud lurked over the mainland when, quite suddenly, the breeze developed in intensity, becoming a dark shadowy ripple romping across the Solent and then a chilly squall in a matter of seconds, triggering a most awesome vision. Like model yachts on a pond catching a sudden gust, the competing vessels heeled to an incredible angle, with the exception of *Shamrock*, whose mast failed with a resounding crack like amplified rifle fire above a collective din of flapping sails and rigging.

Fortunately there were no injuries to the crew or guests aboard *Shamrock*. Sir Thomas Lipton was sailing with Major B. Heckstall–Smith (the RYA secretary) and other friends. The mast snapped off close to the deck and the green hull was seen tossing around on the stormy waters in a state of utter confusion. (Help was promptly rendered by *Britannia's* escorting minesweeper HMS *Sherborne* and eventually the yacht received a tow to Camper & Nicholson's Gosport yard, whose manager had engaged a tug for this service.)

Both *Lulworth* and *Britannia* had decks awash and were in a temporary sympathetic state of confusion, exposing a substantial area of keel, their sails virtually disappearing from my view for a second or two. They were quickly righted, as they immediately pointed into the wind, tossing around, with all gear furiously flapping and rattling whilst the respective crews struggled to down salt-sprayed topsails. Little time seemed to have been lost in getting either of these giant yachts under sheeted control to continue sailing.

YRA rule 29 (when accidents occur, competing yachts must help to save life) was readily and instinctively complied with. *Lulworth* and *Britannia* put about to go to the assistance of *Shamrock* but this subsequently proved unnecessary, as HMS *Sherborne* had lost no time in steaming to the scene.

Had the race been abandoned at this juncture, one would scarcely have been surprised, for, if there was sufficient strength in the elements to cause *Shamrock's* mast and rigging 'structure' to tease its ultimate load capacity, then it follows that the margin of safety for the other contestants (*Lulworth*, *Britannia* and *White Heather II*) was practically infinitesimal under common conditions. However, it had happened to all of them on different occasions, sometimes twice or three times in a season.

The two first-class cutters, with drastically shortened sail, resumed the contest. It was, indeed, a very strange sight to witness *Lulworth* and *Britannia* both exercising the maximum of prudence by finishing a Solent Regatta duel 'cruising' home in a continuing stormy breeze, under jib and mainsail only.

On the same day, Sir Howard Frank's Bermudan 19 metre cutter *Norada*,[1] sailing in the 35 to 110 ton class for the Fourth Earl of Desart's Challenge Cup, suffered a fate similar to *Shamrock*'s, when her tall mast went over the side. One of her ABs was swept overboard, happily being rescued uninjured by the swift action of the yacht's company. The yacht lay helpless, close to the West-Middle mark for some time, before a tow was rendered by Camper & Nicholsons, with subsequent repairs to be executed at Gosport.

However, to continue with the story of *Lulworth*'s contemporaries, Lord Waring's *White Heather II* was seen to be in difficulty when her jib halyards gave way, which inevitably led to the yacht's retirement. The three remaining contesting yachts of the Big Five ensemble battled on, undoubtedly with some temerity, for the wind was gusting in the order of Beaufort Force 5-6 and the unusually stormy Spithead seas were making conditions distinctly uncomfortable for the intrepid sportsmen.

At the end of the first round *Lulworth* had clearly demonstrated a commanding lead as a distinctly hard weather vessel, four minutes ahead of *Westward* and eleven minutes in front of *Britannia*. The noted times for the three were:

Lulworth	12 hrs 45 mins 43
Westward	12 hrs 49 mins 26
Britannia	12 hrs 56 mins 41

Skipper Archie Hogarth, not wishing to tempt fate too far and having had a sharp reminder of *Shamrock*'s ill luck not far astern, had wisely ordered *Lulworth*'s topsail and jib topsail to remain on deck. The hope of maintaining leadership was quite obviously paramount. *Lulworth* appeared to find little difficulty in holding her position till the conclusion of the day's sailing; one to be remembered. As the gun was fired for Sir Mortimer

Singer's most weatherly yacht, there was evidenced a more conclusive defeat of Mr Davis's schooner than the semi-bowsprit measurement on the Saturday before!

Oddly enough, during the second round, Major Hunloke (gallantly?) rehoisted *Britannia*'s topsail for part of the distance, succeeding in reducing the royal cutter's deficit by some four minutes from her first round timings. This action seemed strangely inconsistent with the royal cutter's later policy.

The finishing times were:

Lulworth (cup)	3 hrs 15 mins 57
Westward (second)	3 hrs 19 mins 37
Britannia	3 hrs 23 mins 1

Never were prawns more greatly enjoyed for the evening's repast. Apart from the fruits of the catch, the lad had been happy to share, however distantly, the achievements of Sir Mortimer's magnificent toy which boasted six flags from eight 1926 Solent Regatta entries: three firsts, two seconds and one third. It had been a particularly rewarding day - reported with some eloquence by a local journalist:

'...altogether it was a sensational day's racing, the like of which is seldom seen at Solent regattas.'

This was not, in fact, the conclusion of nature's sudden wrath. Sir Phillip Hunloke's enthusiasm appeared to have been blunted by the day's experience, which, uncomfortable in the extreme as it had almost certainly proven, led to a rather drastic decision. No doubt his sovereign must have been advised or influenced by a lurid Press, prior to taking such action. In the middle of the South Coast regattas *Britannia* was withdrawn from any further racing, all entry fixtures being cancelled for the season at the West Country events. The royal cutter was towed to Marvin's East Cowes boatyard, stripped of her gear and berthed in the usual place for the winter, just inside the Clarence Road entrance. The official statement issued for Press consumption was to the effect "that alterations made in the previous lay-up had not proved to be as successful as was hoped. Whilst in light winds *Britannia* was sailing much better, in a stiff breeze her handling suggested the advisability of cancelling further racing engagements." One is tempted to speculate upon the possibility that at least three of the big cutters ran temporarily out of control when the freak squall struck. A decision such as *Britannia*'s would hardly have been taken without fear of a potential catastrophe. Life aboard the big cutters was not all plain sailing. There was a substantial element of risk for the crews and owners alike.

Occasionally a member might suffer quite serious injury, or even lose his life in being washed overboard to be drowned in a heavy sea before he could be rescued; such was a Captain's responsibility over and above the handling of a valuable ship.

Britannia had already suffered some damage to her spars earlier in the season, whilst racing in the Clyde Regatta, which precluded her appearance at Belfast Lough for the Royal Ulster Yacht Club events, and it seems that the decision to opt out of the remaining South Coast regattas for the season was, at this juncture, not unwise. Her change of rig suggested that she might have become overcanvased, although the Solent squall had taken a greater toll of *Shamrock*.

The owners of the big cutters subsequently volunteered to reduce the heights of sail plans by some four feet during the following season.

With the successive seasonal victories of 1925-1926, *Lulworth* had clearly demonstrated a mature superiority in performance, which led the YRA to take a decision to redress the situation, but the remedy of juggling with time allowances for the next two seasons, although not unreasonable in principle, lacked a great deal of discretion in its eventual application.

---

[1] The nineteen metre *Norada* eventually shared a mud berth on the Hamble riverbank with Lulworth, as neighbouring houseboats, in their eventual retirements after World War II.

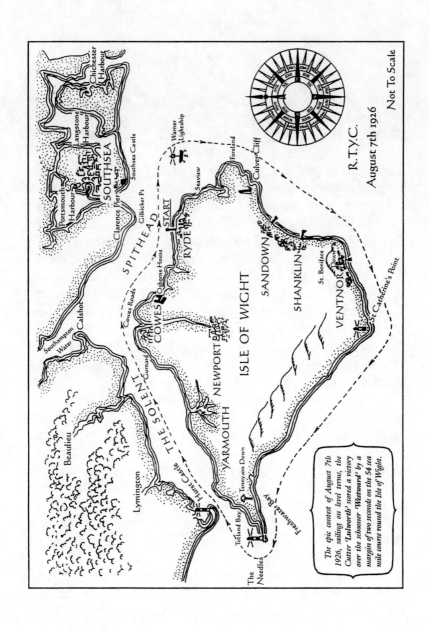

The epic contest of August 7th 1926, sailing on level terms, the Cutter 'Lulworth' scored a victory over the schooner 'Westward' by a margin of two seconds on the 54 sea mile course round the Isle of Wight.

R.T.Y.C.
August 7th 1926

Not To Scale

Chichester Harbour

Langstone Harbour

SOUTHSEA

Southsea Castle

Portsmouth Harbour

Clarence Pier

Gilkicker Pt

Warner Lightship

Foreland

Seaview

Culver Cliff

SPITHEAD

START

RYDE

Osborne House

SANDOWN

St. Boniface

SHANKLIN

Down

VENTNOR

St. Catherine's Point

Cowes Roads

COWES

Gurnard

NEWPORT

ISLE OF WIGHT

YARMOUTH

Tennyson Down

Calshot

Southampton Water

THE SOLENT

Beaulieu

Lymington

Hurst Castle

Totland Bay

The Needles

Freshwater Bay

1927

BRITANNIA RULES THE WAVES

The royal visitors made an early arrival at Cowes for the 1927 Regatta Week. The picturesque royal yacht *Victoria and Albert* brought the King and Queen to the Yachtsman's Festival on Friday July 30th, taking up the customary mooring off the esplanade, virtually centre stage. The imposing guardship HMS *Ramillies*, seen at Cowes in 1926, was once again in attendance, accompanied by the destroyer HMS *Westminster* and also the minesweeper HMS *Tiverton*. The Roadstead, from Gurnard to Osborne Bay, was lined with an extravagant fleet of steam, motor and sailing vessels, the owners of which came to participate in the festivities and proclaim an allegiance to the 'Sailor King'. The familiar big sailing yachts used for cruising, such as Mr W.G. Jameson's lovely black schooner, *Magdalene II* (which regularly moored off the green during the Week) and the auxiliary barque *Fantôme II*, which belonged to the Hon. Ernest Guinness, were joined this year by Mme Heriot's schooner *Ailée* flying the Tricolore, thus adding a nostalgic touch appreciated by those whose memories of the regatta were pre-1914.[1] The French six and eight metre yachts belonging to Mme Heriot took part in their class events with conspicuous success.

Following *Lulworth*'s enjoyment of the limelight in the 1925 and 1926 coastal regattas when she had established a supremacy in her class, putting the unfortunate struggles as *Terpsichore* well and truly behind her, the authorities came to a decision whereby her domination was to be curtailed; somewhat indelicately as it proved.

With the premature adoption of the 1928 rule in the 1927 season of the big class, the opportunity was taken to penalise *Lulworth* by the introduction of some generous time allowances to benefit *Britannia*, *Shamrock* and *White Heather II*. (The scope of these penalties was further exaggerated in the 1928 season.)

The official attitude was claimed to be one of establishing a formula for rating and time scale to produce time allowances for differing ships, so that their chances of winning should be fair and equal. This was indisputably laudable in principle, but to start with a pseudo-scientific comparison of a vessel's contributory performance characteristics and subsequently allot some arbitrary loading of the dice to determine fair time allowances required the absentee wisdom of Solomon. Whilst no one would have denied the success of the grand old cutter *Britannia* in being top-class for the 1927 season, this being a most spectacular not to mention popular result, it has to be acknowledged that she was assisted to a degree by *Lulworth*'s having to virtually 'stand down' to the tune of a 4.0 secs/mile allowance to an old sparring partner.

Whilst *White Heather II* tied with *Britannia* to claim eight first flags, the latter made five fewer starts, resulting in seasonal performance figure analyses of 1.69 and 1.91 respectively.

My memories of the 1927 Cowes Regatta are of a rather dull week with mostly light airs and extensive calm patches which lent little excitement to the Big Five events, with the exception of a sparkling breeze on the Thursday.

The weather on Monday for the 1927 RLYC Regatta was most depressing, with continuous heavy rain throughout the day, whilst oilskins found favour with all but the dedicated crewmen, who suffered a soaking to be remembered. Accompanying the rain was a light northerly wind lending reaching favour to Mr Davis. His schooner *Westward* and the cutter *Lulworth* were tied scratch, allowing *Britannia*, *White Heather II* and *Shamrock* each 2 minutes 36 seconds over a thirty-nine nautical mile course, circling the Solent Bank and North-East Middle marks twice round. A very light northerly wind was blowing as the yachts crossed the start line in the order of *Shamrock*, *Lulworth*, *Westward*, *White Heather II* and *Britannia*, all setting yarded topsails and balloon jibs as they reached for the Solent Bank buoy against a foul tide. *Lulworth* and *Shamrock* were in close company when they made a turn of the first mark, but, as seemed inevitable, *Westward* forged into the lead on the long reach to the North-East Middle buoy. Profiting from a faint breeze which suited her, judging on past form, *White Heather II* overtook *Shamrock* and *Lulworth* to make second place which she held until the finish.

The finishing times were:

	Actual	Corrected
Westward (first)	2 hrs 58 mins 32	2 hrs 58 mins 32
White Heather II	3 hrs 7 mins 23	3 hrs 4 mins 47
Shamrock	3 hrs 9 mins 3	3 hrs 6 mins 27
Lulworth	3 hrs 10 mins 36	3 hrs 10 mins 36
Britannia	3 hrs 14 mins 50	3 hrs 12 mins 14

The King's Cup race was programmed for a 10.00 a.m. start from the castle club house on Tuesday, August 2nd 1927. The day opened with brilliant sunshine, but with scarcely a movement of air initially. Only one round of the Queen's course, just twenty-three nautical miles was circuited. None of the Big Five yachts was represented, but entries consisted of fourteen smaller vessels of 15 tons register upwards, owned exclusively by RYS members. Eleven contestants made the start line, all of which completed the distance. The little yawl *Rona*, of 1895 vintage, owned by Mr Wyndhay Damer Clark, MA, won the coveted trophy after 6 hrs 36 mins 26 secs endurance, averaging approximately 3½ knots!

The Big Five were entered for the RYS Regatta on Tuesday, starting at 10.15 a.m., to sail for prizes of £80 (first), £20 (second), £10 (third) over a forty mile course circuiting the Solent Bank, North-East Middle and South-East Middle buoys. *Westward* sailed scratch, allowing *Lulworth* 1 min 20 secs, and

Britannia, Shamrock and *White Heather II* 4 mins each. (In consequence the other three cutters enjoyed a 2 minute 40 second time allowance from *Lulworth*.) The fleet was scattered behind the start line, motivated substantially by the tide as there was a dearth of air, the nearest the Solent has ever experienced in all probability to a flat calm. The conditions were such that the majority hovered around off the squadron for nearly two hours before any forward progress was possible. Just to add to the confusion, *Lulworth, White Heather II* and *Westward* were recalled at the start, the trio being over the line as the starting signal fired. There was no scarcity of time to restart, obviously, but the motive power was absent! Kedges were in fashion. *Shamrock* was first to find a catspaw, followed slowly by *Lulworth* and *Britannia*, with *White Heather II* coming approximately half an hour later. As they made for the Solent Bank mark, Sir Thomas Lipton's cutter *Shamrock* distinguished herself by running aground off Lepe, although she was well ahead at that moment. Commander Kenneth Mitchell brought up the minesweeper HMS *Tiverton* (*Britannia*'s escort) to proffer assistance, which was politely declined, as it was considered better to wait and float off on a rising tide. Eventually, as *Shamrock* refloated, fortunately undamaged, she was towed back to her Cowes moorings by a picket boat from the royal guardship HMS *Ramillies*.

Meanwhile *Lulworth* set the 'crawl', followed by *White Heather II* and *Britannia*, which were in close company. *Westward* was struggling in the rear, well behind the rest, as if to protest that she was no light weather fairy! Conversely, *Lulworth* was making some headway with the minimum of wind whilst on other days she showed a quality of conspicuous ability in the roughest Solent weather. Expectations for this day were centred upon a win by *White Heather II*, these being the conditions nearest suited to her. The wind, such as it was, freshened a little, but was extremely fickle, with changing calms and flukes in differing areas. Nature was intent upon playing a roguish role in an uninspiring drama. There was only a minute or two separating the three cutters at the end of the first round whilst *Lulworth*, although still in the lead, had insufficient margins over progressive time concessions to her contemporaries. The actual times noted for the first round were:

Lulworth	3 hrs 9 mins 26
White Heather II	3 hrs 10 mins 16
Britannia	3 hrs 10 mins 34
Westward	3 hrs 23 mins 44

The tide was ebbing to assist the beat to the Solent bank on the second round, and, contrary to all tradition, *Britannia* had found enough wind on this balmy day to overtake *White Heather II* and *Lulworth* despite the royal cutter's reputation for needing a gale to get her moving. Major Hunloke's experience in making the optimum use of Solent tides dated from Queen Victoria's reign!

Britannia gradually increased her lead over *White Heather II* and finished late in the afternoon as the winner, with approximately 1½ minutes in hand.

The corrected times were:

Britannia	5 hrs 15 mins 39
White Heather II	5 hrs 17 mins 17
Lulworth	5 hrs 21 mins
Westward	5 hrs 29 mins 3 secs

Racing on Wednesday of the 1927 week at Cowes saw the retirement of *Lulworth* during the first round. With a burden of time concessions there was unlikely to be any profit from a drifting match on this day. Starting with a slight easterly breeze, the other competitors made first round times as noted:

White Heather II	1 hr 51 mins 49
Shamrock	1 hr 55 mins 49

| *Britannia* | 2 hrs 1 min 39 |
| *Westward* | 2 hrs 4 mins 55 |

During the afternoon the fleet was becalmed off Ryde esplanade and, as there was no expectation of an improvement in conditions, both *Britannia* and *Westward* confessed their frustrations by retiring early in the evening. It was not until 10 p.m. that *White Heather II* drifted into Cowes Roads to drop her kedge once more. Over an hour later *White Heather II* found either a catspaw or a welcome current to take her to the RYS castle finish line, becoming the winner long after dark, having averaged 3.40 knots. *Shamrock* nobly persisted in waiting to secure the second prize, well after midnight, to establish a course average of 2.96 knots!

The corrected finishing times were:

| *White Heather II* (winner) | 11 hrs 25 mins 2 secs |
| *Shamrock* (second) | 1 hr 24 mins 12 secs |

Following such nocturnal adventures, it was an example of their sportsmanship to make an appearance at the Thursday fixture, if only to be recalled for their seeming mutual impatience on this occasion. On Thursday of the Week the Big Five competed for the Cowes Town Cup, with associated prizes of £80 for the winner, £20 second and £10 third prize, in conditions which were locally pronounced as ideal. It was a brilliantly sunny occasion with a strong and refreshing east wind, resulting in some first-rate competition. Once again, the big schooner sailed scratch, allowing Sir Mortimer Singer's *Lulworth* 4 minutes, Sir Thomas Lipton's *Shamrock* 5 mins 20 secs, Lord Waring's *White Heather II* 5 mins 20 secs, and HM the King's *Britannia* 6 mins 40 secs. In consequence, *Lulworth* had to allow *White Heather II* and *Shamrock* each 1 min 20 secs and *Britannia* 2 mins 40 secs. The course of forty nautical miles was identical to that sailed on Tuesday.

Starting to the eastward, *Shamrock* and *White Heather II* were carried forward of the line on a flood tide when the Blue Peter came down, suffering the indignity of a recall signal which cost each of them some four minutes' delay. *White Heather II* was seen to be last away. Meanwhile *Lulworth* led the fleet with *Britannia* to leeward of her, whilst *Westward* was on the leeside of the royal cutter.

For *Lulworth* there was all to sail for, having made a comfortable start heading to windward over a fair tide, as the fleet worked eastward on a choppy sea to the first Mark. It seemed that the recalls might have reduced the competition to some extent, but *Lulworth* would have a hard tussle to overcome her handicap penalty of 2 mins 40 secs due to *Britannia* on such a day. The odds in favour of the American schooner were for ever present in a stiff breeze, and greater with a possible shift in wind direction.

Lulworth, with *Britannia* marginally astern, left *Westward* well behind on the first leg. As *Lulworth* showed to advantage by pointing higher into the wind, her tacks became fewer and the gap between Sir Mortimer's and the King's cutters opened up. When the trio rounded the South-East Middle buoy the order was unchanged. On the return leg, running to the Solent Bank mark, *Lulworth*'s mastery was stolen by the schooner travelling with her acres of billowing canvas at a probable thirteen knots plus. Although *Westward*'s superiority in speed running free had enabled her to take first place in rounding the Solent Bank mark, *Lulworth* made up her deficit to lead the schooner on the beat back to the start line; *Britannia* showing a close third position just within her time allowance from both the leaders.

The times noted at the end of the first round were:

Lulworth	12 hrs 22 mins 15
Westward	12 hrs 23 mins 4
Britannia	12 hrs 23 mins 31
Shamrock	12 hrs 30 mins 4

White Heather II   12 hrs 32 mins 40

The final result of the race was still open for the three most weatherly yachts in leading order. The cutters *Lulworth* and *Britannia* were separated by only 1 minute and 16 seconds after covering twenty miles of the course and, with *Lulworth*'s handicap allowance of 2 mins 40 secs to her nearest rival, the former had less than a margin. It seemed that the two cutters must be anticipating a grand contest unless the wind veered south, allowing the schooner to steal an advantage.

However, *Lulworth* managed to improve her position to take the first gun, finishing 2 minutes 37 seconds ahead of *Westward* clear of any time allowance. *Britannia* crossed the line in third place, saving her time on *Westward* to take the second prize, but was 3 minutes 32 seconds behind *Lulworth*; the royal cutter failed to save her time on the winner by just fifty-two seconds. On this day, nature had generously proffered a stiff breeze to afford the two most weatherly cutters a most exciting tussle.

The finishing times were:

Actual

Lulworth	2 hrs 30 mins 18
Westward	2 hrs 32 mins 55
Britannia	2 hrs 33 mins 50
Shamrock	2 hrs 44 mins 55
White Heather II not timed	

Corrected

Lulworth (winner)	2 hrs 26 mins 18
Britannia (second)	2 hrs 27 mins 10
Westward (third)	2 hrs 32 mins 55
Shamrock	2 hrs 39 mins 35

The racing on Friday (Regatta Day) was once more a painfully slow affair as the weather reverted to the calms experienced earlier in the week. The yachts were stopped after one round of the Queen's course, some twenty-three sea miles.

Lulworth, following her success of the day before, distinguished herself by unfortunately running aground near Ryde. She was towed off by HMS minesweeper *Tiverton* (commanded by Kenneth Mitchell), which had offered similar assistance to *Shamrock* on the previous Tuesday. No damage was reported and *Lulworth* returned to her moorings under headsails. The order of the finish was *White Heather II* first prize £80, *Shamrock* second prize £20, *Westward* third prize £10, *Britannia* fourth. The winner came comfortably ahead of Sir Thomas Lipton's cutter with over ten minutes to spare.

The shoreside Regatta Day festivities were concluded with a vastly swollen attendance of visitors to the port, who came to indulge in the customary rituals as they became increasingly sandwiched, tinned sardine-fashion, in the limited area of the West Cowes promenade. These spectators had made their several ways by every available means of transport in order to witness the traditional grand finale with a display of *feu d'artifice*. Promptly at 9.30 p.m. a jumbo-sized example of the Messrs Pain's sky rockets signalled the start, with its ample decibel rating, as the twilight obligingly faded. For the following half hour, the skies over Britain's premier yachting centre (arguably the world's) were intermittently sprayed with multi-coloured giant sparks which scattered their visual largesse, delighting the yachtsfolk and their island hosts alike.

Immediately following the events at Cowes, the first class cutters took part in the Royal Thames Yacht Club Regatta which commenced on Monday August 8th with a handicap race for yachts in excess of 110 tons (TM). The Big Five were represented in total in this race around the Isle of Wight for prizes of £80 first, £40 second and £20 third. The mixture of changing climatic circumstances through the duration of the race was quite extraordinary. The day started with threatening clouds, whilst drenching showers gave way to conditions of a flat calm. Spithead imitated a mill pond for a while with scarcely enough air to fill competing canvases. As the yachts disappeared from sight, a steady breeze sprang up, coming from a south-westerly direction. The wind gradually increased in strength to allow some fine sport until the end of the contest.

The schooner *Westward* sailed scratch, allowing *Lulworth* 3 mins 36 secs, with *Britannia*, *Shamrock* and *White Heather II* having a concession of 7 mins 13 secs. This meant that *Lulworth* had, of course, to allow her contemporary cutters 3 mins 37 secs. The official total distance was stated to be fifty-four nautical miles. The start was hardly spectacular since the fleet drifted down to the line assisted by a fair tide in a westerly direction. *Britannia* led with *White Heather II* on her lee, then came *Shamrock*, with *Lulworth* to windward of her and *Westward* came last, which she frequently did to avoid a recall signal. They all crept away with spinnakers set to port to catch any suspicion of air coming from the east. The wind veered round to the south, increasing slightly when spinnakers were shipped and the fleet settled down to a reach through the Cowes Roads. Sailing the western channel of the Solent a fast broad reach was enjoyed to The Needles where *White Heather II* led *Shamrock* by 4 mins 45 secs, with *Lulworth* a further three minutes astern. *Britannia* was not far behind the leading cutters but, as was the case with *Westward*, the wind was insufficient for her to perform to advantage. Following the turn at The Needles lighthouse pointing to windward along the Channel coast to St Catherine's, *White Heather II*'s lead was shown to be somewhat eroded, with *Shamrock* just 2 mins 45 secs behind her. In turn, *Lulworth* was timed only forty-eight seconds behind *Shamrock*, followed by *Britannia* 6 mins 17 secs astern, and *Westward* 9 mins 50 secs distant from the royal cutter. With the wind now in the south-west, spinnakers were bent for the run across Shanklin–Sandown Bay to make the turn at Bembridge. *Lulworth* had caught and overtaken *Shamrock* on this leg to establish a slight lead over the latter, whilst *White*

Heather II, still well ahead, took the first gun.   Although *Lulworth* was the second arrival, Sir Mortimer Singer's yacht had to concede the position to *Shamrock* on time allowance.

The actual finishing times for the island circuit were:

White Heather II	3 hrs 33 mins 58
Lulworth	3 hrs 37 mins 3
Shamrock	3 hrs 37 mins 59
Britannia	3 hrs 46 mins 46
Westward	3 hrs 58 mins 37

and corrected finishing times adjusted for time concessions read:

White Heather II (winner)	3 hrs 26 mins 45 secs
Shamrock (second)	3 hrs 30 mins 46 secs
Lulworth (third)	3 hrs 33 mins 27 secs
Britannia	3 hrs 39 mins 33 secs
Westward	3 hrs 58 mins 37 secs

The Tuesday of the RVYC 1927 Regatta did not include an event for the big handicap class, but the racing on the day following was vitalised by the rustle of a good stiff breeze. The chosen course, known as the Long Victoria, measured forty-six sea miles, comprising two rounds of the Ryde West-Middle, Outer Spit and Nab End Gas buoys. The Big Five came to the Royal Victoria Yacht Club start line, located by the club house at the end of the long Ryde Pier for the 10.30 a.m. start. *Westward* sailed scratch, allowing *Lulworth* 4 mins 36 secs, *Shamrock* and *White Heather II* each 6 mins 8 secs and *Britannia* 7 mins 40 secs. Both *Lulworth* and *Shamrock* boldly hoisted full canvas. *White Heather II* and *Britannia* cautiously set their jib headers, the former being reefed as well. The schooner was modestly rigged with her jib header, which proved just adequate for the day's competition.

It was a truly magnificent sight to watch the five take the starting gun, all within fifteen seconds of each other, reaching at top speed with a strong sou'west'r and heading west. The order across the line was led by *Shamrock*, followed by *White Heather II*, *Lulworth*, *Westward* and *Britannia* making for the West-Middle buoy. As they rounded the first mark *Lulworth* had taken the lead, but the race was still wide open, with only a minute separating the first and last vessels, leaving much left to sail for.

The schooner was just twelve seconds astern of the leader as the first mark buoy was rounded. Reaching in such favourable breezy conditions, *Westward* showed to some advantage, having taken *Lulworth* to work out a lead of half a minute when the two returned past Ryde pier head. By the time the yachts had fetched the Nab End buoy, *Westward* had increased her lead by approximately two minutes over Sir Mortimer Singer's cutter, whilst *Britannia*, approving of the blow, occupied third place. At this juncture *Shamrock* was finding conditions approaching the unmanageable, probably regretting the choice of a jackyard topsail from the beginning. (The 23 metre *Shamrock* was, of course, a substantially weatherly vessel, having sailed the Atlantic seven years ago, returning four years later rigged as a yawl with greatly reduced canvas.)

Both *Britannia* and *White Heather II* were feeling the extremes of the elements and decided to make a hitch. At the end of the first round the latter retired from the race.

The first round actual times were:

Westward	12 hrs 28 mins 55
Lulworth	12 hrs 32 mins 5
Britannia	12 hrs 34 mins 54
White Heather II	12 hrs 37 mins 50

The two cutters continued to battle with near storm conditions during the second round and *Westward* finished 5 mins 40 secs ahead of *Lulworth*, which came second, beating *Britannia* by 5 mins 19 secs.

Mr Davis's schooner won the RVYC International Gold Cup, added to the honour of which was a monetary award of £80.

The corrected finishing times were:

Westward (cup winner)	2 hrs 27 mins 9
Lulworth (second)	2 hrs 28 mins 13
Britannia (third)	2 hrs 30 mins 28

Bearing in mind the acknowledged superiority of the giant schooner's reaching performance over the smaller cutters, *Lulworth* sailed remarkably well on this day, finishing 1 min 4 seconds outside her time concession over the forty-six mile distance. The result testified to her most weatherly character when she carried a topsail in defiance of such stormy odds. Her complete sailing time of 4 hrs 2 mins 49 secs shows an average of 11.37 knots against *Westward*'s 11.64 knots (actual, without handicap adjustment). Although *Britannia* was given a time allowance of 3 mins 4 secs by *Lulworth*, the royal cutter failed to save her time by a small margin.

When it is considered that *Lulworth* had been excluded from any reasonable opportunity to remain at the top of the class performance table in 1927, she nevertheless acquitted herself remarkably well in meeting of the burden loaded upon her by the handicappers. Her record of five first flags in twenty-seven starts, which might ordinarily have been discounted as no great achievement, shines above *Shamrock*'s tally, for instance, of five firsts for thirty-three starts, aided by the substantial advantage of a 2 secs/mile concession from *Lulworth*.

The typical 'grandstand' appreciation of the yacht racing scene from Cowes esplanade was inevitably linked to the thrill of the start, with intermittent glimpses of the competing yachts as they appeared in and disappeared from view, extending to the observation of their dispositions when the smoke billowed from a booming cannon announcing the finish. Interest thereafter was almost wholly concentrated in clocking and adjusting handicap allowances to establish placings as the opposing vessels crossed the finishing line.

In order for a juvenile to acquire an informed anchorage for the study of regatta events scheduled for the big handicap class, in particular, it was a necessary preliminary for him to acquire a RYS programme. This often involved the sacrifice of a modicum of pocket money for some weeks in advance. The outlay of one shilling for this considered extravagance was, somewhat reluctantly, exchanged with a peddler who occupied a pitch near the club house slipway. There was little difficulty in locating this entrepreneur, whose raucous voice hollered an entreaty to purchase one of these master documents, with the reiterated call of, "Squadron programme!" at five second intervals throughout each race morning. If the youthful purchaser had the supreme good fortune to be the proud possessor of an American five shilling Ingersoll pocket watch, matched by an adequate mathematical intelligence, he had practically 'arrived' in the front rank of observers. The loan of a parental telescope or a pair of binoculars often served to confirm his status. The elusive qualification of patience, however, was undeniably the crowning asset!

A contrasting and more relaxed aspect of the proceedings could be enjoyed on occasions from the vantage point of a dinghy anchored in shallow water such as that which 'wetted' the Shrape shoal, well clear of the regatta courses. In such an environment one had an impression of literally 'being in the picture'. The mind was concentrated upon the boyish feast of glistening idealised profiles swiftly propelled by the unseen hand of nature acting upon some 10,000 square feet of white canvas rigged from a towering 170 foot mast, crowned by a racing burgee struggling to part from its halyards. The blissful impression upon the inward eye had scarcely any immediate affinity with the more purposeful intended competition between these works of art in motion; to the point where the order of procession became of negligible or indeed zero consequence. No matter – the lad was sharing the Solent with these treasures. This was, in itself, a patent experience of life's most fulfilling moments.

The holiday atmosphere ashore was utterly divorced from the ecstatic captivation of such sightings from a point just a few feet above the water line at relatively close quarters, whilst the observer was pleasantly lulled by the movement of a dinghy responding to the motion of a Solent swell.

At the close of the 1927 season *Lulworth* found herself being offered on the sale lists when Sir Mortimer Singer contracted Charles Nicholson for the building of *Astra*.

---

[1] The classic schooner bearing the name of *Ailée* in 1927 was, in fact, the original property of the former Kaiser Wilhelm, designed by Max Oerst and built in the Kiel shipyard of Krupps in 1909, christened *Meteor IV*. She raced at the Cowes and Kiel Regattas in competition with giant schooners such as the Herreshoff *Westward* and *Elena*, the Nicholson *Margherita* and the Krupp *Germania* before 1914.

In 1928 *Ailée*'s owner, Mme Virginie Hériot, one of an elite company of French yachtswomen, engaged Charles Nicholson to design and build a three-masted successor of 496 tons, with staysail rig, to be known as *Ailée II*.

The original *Ailée* was sailed from her home port of Le Havre to Gosport to be re-registered under the name of Charles Nicholson (Lloyds 1928), seemingly a token of part-exchange in return for her replacement.

Plate (12)
The famous ketch Cariad *built for the Earl of Dunraven and later owned by Col. Gretton; six times winner of the King's Cup in 1905, 1910, 1912, 1921 and 1929.*

Plate (13)

Sir William Portal's Valdora *in her original yawl rig, later to be changed to ketch configuration. She won the King's Cup under handicap rating in 1922 and 1924.*

Plate (14)

A fine study of King George V's cutter Britannia *enjoying a 'blow' to demonstrate her best behaviour.*

Plate (15)
An imposing glimpse of Lord Waring's lovely cutter White Heather II
with her lee rail uncomfortably awash.

Plate (16)
Lulworth *sailing close-hauled past Ryde Pier with her vast spread of*
sail set to perfection heading for the Warner Mark.

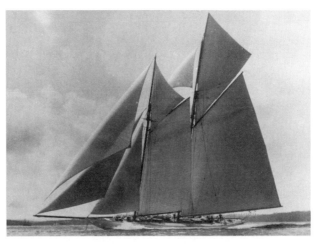

Plate (17)

The giant schooner Westward *owned by Mr. F. T. B. Davis from 1925 onwards. Without her pre-1914 contemporaries she raced under handicap with the big cutters, displaying a mastery in reaching winds.*

Plate (18)

The picturesque schooner Susanne *of 154 tons (TM) which occasionally joined the Big Class in the twenties.*

Plate (19)

The ex Kaiser's 400 ton schooner Meteor IV *seen with Dr Krupp von Bohlen's contemporary yacht* Germania. *Both built in Germany. The earlier Meteors were from either British or American yards.*

Plate (20)

Sir Thomas Lipton's 23 metre Shamrock *of 1908 vintage with her distinctive green topsides prettily posed for a classic photographic record.*

Plate (21)
The Bermudian cutter Astra *designed and built by Charles Nicholson
for Sir Mortimer Singer in 1928*

Plate (22)
The Fife designed Bermudian cutter Cambria *of 1928 with a hitch in
her mainsail.*

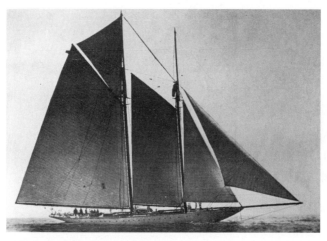

Plate (23)
The Herreschoff schooner Elena *of 1911 vintage which appeared in the
Solent in 1928 to sail with its pre-1914 rival double sticker* Westward

Plate (24)
The Nicholson cutter Candida *built for Mr. H. K. Andreae to compete
in the Big Class with handicap allowance in 1929.*

Plate (25)
The Great Cutter Lulworth showing a great cloud of canvas leading her rivals whilst running through the Solent.

1928

SIR THOMAS LIPTON'S 23 METRE *SHAMROCK* REACHES HER ZENITH

Cowes was once more favoured by the presence of King George and Queen Mary arriving for the Week on the stately royal yacht *Victoria and Albert*, accompanied this season by the 35,000 ton guardship *Rodney* and her escorts, consisting of the destroyer *Vortigern* with the minesweeper *Selkirk*. The last named had the primary duty of escorting the royal cutter *Britannia*, but in so many emergencies her various escorts performed many sympathetic services to the competing yachts. Local humorists claimed the function of *Britannia*'s escort was to rescue the sovereign should he have the misfortune to fall overboard!

On Monday of the 1928 Regatta Week *Lulworth*'s former owner, Sir Mortimer Singer, had the honour of dining with the King and Queen on the royal yacht *Victoria and Albert*. Other guests included Lord and Lady Waring, whose *White Heather II* had also provided a great deal of sporting competition for His Majesty's cutter. Sir Godfrey and Lady Baring were also included in the party.

The entertaining of other competitors from the exclusive over 110 tons big class by Their Majesties on the royal yacht took place on Wednesday, August 8th 1928. The dinner party included such illustrious personages as the Marquess and Marchioness of Camden, Lady Hermione Buller and Admiral Sir Francis Bridgeman, together with Mr Davis (*Westward*'s owner), accompanied by his wife. Mr Alexander Paton also had the honour of being included in the royal party. His recent acquisition of *Lulworth* brought the Liverpool banker into contact with the pinnacles of society, through the shared interests of a sport enthusiastically patronised by his sovereign.

Sailing with such severe handicap penalties drastically reduced *Lulworth*'s prospects in the 1928 'points for flags tables' and her seasonal record was not enhanced by her disappointing performance at Cowes where *Shamrock*, *Astra* and *Westward* shared the first flags. However, the Solent weather on the first day of the Royal Victoria Yacht Club Regatta at Ryde provided an opportunity to demonstrate *Lulworth*'s ability to withstand the 'heat of the battle' when her contemporary cutters suffered the fatigue of being battered by a gusting Beaufort force 5-6. A third flag was collected on the following day.

Oddly enough, a rumour was circulated during Cowes Week to the effect that Mr Paton had placed an order with Alfred Mylne for a new 23 metre Bermudan cutter similar to *Cambria* and *Astra*; also that Mr H.K. Andreae (owner of the 19 metre *Corona*) had placed a contract with Charles Nicholson for another new yacht to compete in the big handicap class.

With fears for the resultant fate of *Lulworth*, it subsequently proved a relief to find the first either untrue or later the subject of a cancellation. (Dame Rumour ever was a lying jade.) But the second disclosure was fulfilled by the appearance in 1929 of the Bermudan *Candida*.

After such a brief experience with *Lulworth* it seemed unlikely that Mr Paton would have contracted to build a replacement cutter at this stage. Although he may have been discouraged by her performance at Cowes and the revised handicap assessment, her potential had been demonstrated earlier and the ordering of a new replacement offered no guarantee of greater success. The fulfilment of such a fancy might more reasonably have been expected to belong to an entry of the class.

This was the year when Sir Mortimer brought the new Nicholson-designed Bermudan cutter *Astra* to join the big handicap class and Sir William Berry[1] entered with the Fife-designed 23 metre *Cambria*.

In retrospect, one might not unreasonably ponder why Sir Mortimer Singer took the decision to order a brand-new cutter in 1927-28. He had, of course, no economic restriction even though an outlay for such an extravagance must have been little short of colossal for those times. Balanced against this action, he could have had no quarrel with the performance of *Lulworth* from the time he had purchased her, two years previously. One might suggest that he was swayed firstly, to become involved in a new project to stimulate an interest and secondly, as the future prospects for *Lulworth* were influenced by overreaction to her domination of the class by the handicappers, he was not prepared to suffer such discrimination. However, *Astra*'s debut had its share of anxieties, including the loss of a mast.

Astra's showing in the 1928 racing season was inferior to *Lulworth*'s in the 1927 season despite the latter's handicap restrictions.

During the 1928 Cowes Regatta, Sir Mortimer invited his friend Mr R.G. Penny (a member of the Royal Victoria Yacht Club and a one-time owner of the twelve metre yacht *Noresca*) to share a demonstration of his new toy. Unhappily, Mr Penny suffered a severe mishap: he was struck on the head by *Astra*'s boom as she gybed, resulting in his skull and jawbone being fractured. Fortunately, the victim, who was taken to a mainland hospital, fully recovered, doubtless to the great relief of Sir Mortimer and his captain.

The 1928 Clyde fortnight proved to be, weather-wise, one of the most unmanageable Scottish regattas on record. Bearing in mind the reputation for foul elements in the West of Scotland generally, with furious south-westerly gales, wicked squalls and torrential rain, the conditions of this historic meeting of the big cutters were so abnormal to be described by a usually sober observer as "quite fiendish".

The first regatta scheduled for the opening day, June 30th, by the Royal Clyde Yacht Club, was abandoned. On the second day the conditions proved even worse, when the big class flew their burgees to indicate an intention to abstain from sailing once again.

The major event of the fortnight was the race for the King's Cup, this being the first time since 1914 that the Clyde had enjoyed the honour and so there were naturally great expectations of a brilliant series. The King's Cup race was postponed until Monday, July 3rd in the light of Saturday's conditions. Only two yachts, Sir William Berry's *Cambria* and Mr T.B.F. Davis's schooner *Westward* showed a readiness to start. But with the persistence of stormy weather conditions, it was deemed inadvisable to proceed.

On the following three days there was little sign of improvement and it was not until Friday, July 7th that the weather had moderated sufficiently for the race committee at Hunter's Quay to raise the starting flags (with some temerity) and open fire with the guns.

All the big handicap class yachts were entered, including *Lulworth, White Heather II, Shamrock, Westward* and perhaps, rather oddly, the King's own *Britannia*. The new Bermudan cutters *Astra* and *Cambria* made up the complement of starters. Whilst the weather conditions were noticeably better, all of the entrants started with shortened sail to some degree. Even with these concessions to nature, the yachts were sailing very close to the ultimate capacities of their spars and riggings, this being amply demonstrated when *Astra*, early in her first year, was dismasted by a severe gust. In addition, seven smaller class vessels suffered similarly and minor mishaps were legion.

Bearing in mind *Britannia*'s reputation as a heavy weather yacht, there was a great deal of shoreside speculation in anticipation of her winning for His Majesty his own cup. There was, in fact, a precedent for such an irregularity, when in 1894 the Prince of Wales had won the Royal Cup with *Britannia*. However, it was not an anomaly to be repeated on this day.

Whilst there persisted one of the heaviest of 'blows' on July 7th, 1928 when the 'Big Seven' crossed the starting line, *Lulworth* and *Shamrock* were quickly dicing in the van with the rest of the field strung out astern. It has to be borne in mind that *Lulworth* was penalised under the revised rating rule of 1928 whereby she sailed as scratch yacht on the same terms, incidentally, as the schooner *Westward*. The 1928 seasonal time allowances were as follows:

Lulworth	Scratch
Westward	Scratch
Astra	14 seconds per mile
Cambria	12.8 seconds per mile
White Heather II	9 seconds per mile
Shamrock	9 seconds per mile
Britannia	7.5 seconds per mile

As she led the fleet over the start line with shortened canvas, Mr Paton's *Lulworth* quickly worked out a substantial lead, making good use of her weatherly and close-winded qualities and, whilst *Shamrock* fought hard to gain the advantage, she was unable to save her time on *Lulworth*, which won the King's Cup with a margin of thirty-three seconds (corrected time) over Sir Thomas Lipton's cutter.

A greater contrast of racing conditions between *Lulworth*'s first King's Cup victory, in the 1925 RYS event in a near flat calm and her Royal Clyde Yacht Club success in almost tempestuous circumstances, could not have been more adequately demonstrated and brings to mind John Nicholson's recorded observation of *Lulworth*'s versatility in his book *Great Years in Yachting*, although not especially in connection with these two races.

On the Saturday prior to Cowes Week the Royal Southampton Yacht Club held its regatta using the starting facilities of the Royal Yacht Squadron for yachts of the big handicap class. The scene was drenched with pouring rain to the accompaniment of a strong northerly breeze as *Lulworth*, *Britannia*, *Westward*, *Astra* and *Cambria* got away on a forty mile reaching course. The sea was throwing up a lively chop and, whilst *Lulworth* was seen to get underway, she returned to her moorings before the Blue Peter came down.

It seemed from the outset that none of the cutters would have the chance to score a victory in such conditions and although the schooner, quite expectedly, drew well to the fore in the early stages of the first round, for some inexplicable reason she took the wrong course and had no option but to retire from the match. This left only *Britannia*, *Astra* and *Cambria* in the competition and although *Britannia* was first to finish, both *Astra* and *Cambria* (each enjoying a handicap allowance of 3 minutes 32 seconds from the royal cutter) took first and second prizes respectively, having saved their times by over a minute each, leaving *Britannia* with the consolation of a third prize, as the wind moderated and the sun appeared!

On Monday, the opening day of the 1928 Cowes Regatta Week, the Royal London Yacht Club staged its usual event for the big handicap class yachts of any rig exceeding twenty-one metres rating from the RYS castle headquarters. The wind had abated over the weekend to some degree, but was freshening at times and playing havoc by changing direction unexpectedly. The starters were *Westward* and *Lulworth* tied scratch, each allowing *Britannia* 4 minutes 53 seconds, *Shamrock* and *White Heather* 5 minutes 51 seconds each, and *Astra* and *Cambria* 8 minutes 19 seconds each. The course of thirty-nine nautical miles was sailed twice round the North-East Middle and Solent Bank buoys. As the fleet started eastward on a strong flowing tide, *Astra*, *Lulworth* and *Shamrock* were carried over the line, to be recalled. *Westward* made an unusually good start, followed by *White Heather II*, *Cambria* and *Britannia*. In muted airs *Astra* was last to recross, some seven minutes late. Spinnakers were worn on the first leg just beyond Old Castle Point, when the wind freshened, veering sou'east as sails were adjusted for a reach to the first mark.

Beating close-hauled on the return leg when the wind had shifted sou'west, the order was noted as *Westward* 3½ minutes ahead of *Britannia*, then came *Shamrock* just under a ½ minute later, closely shadowed by *Cambria*, *Astra* and *Lulworth*, together with *White Heather II*, in last position. On the beat back to the Solent Bank buoy for the second round, the order had changed, with *Shamrock* now in the lead followed by *Britannia* and *Westward*, whilst *White Heather II* mounted a strong challenge. *Cambria* fouled the Solent Bank mark and gave up.

Lulworth was suffering from her deficit at the start with insufficient wind to compensate. At the end of the first round the positions noted were:

Shamrock	12 hrs 43 mins
White Heather II	12 hrs 47 mins 6
Britannia	12 hrs 50 mins 22
Westward	12 hrs 52 mins 48
Astra	12 hrs 54 mins 34
Lulworth	12 hrs 57 mins 23

This was *Shamrock*'s day, for she doubled her lead in the second round to win very comfortably from *White Heather II*. The corrected finishing times were:

Shamrock (winner)	3 hrs 22 mins 17
White Heather II (second)	3 hrs 30 mins 29
Britannia (third)	3 hrs 38 mins 15
Westward	3 hrs 39 mins 45
Astra	3 hrs 46 mins 3
Lulworth	3 hrs 48 mins 25

Tuesday, August 8th 1928 saw the opening of the Royal Yacht Squadron Regatta, the premier event being the contest for His Majesty's Cup, which received a record number of eighteen entries. The muster of yachts from fifteen tons upward, with a wide variety of rigs, made a grand pageant, capturing the main interest of the shoreside spectators crowded around the castle club house and others thronging the esplanade for the 10 o'clock start. As the first leg of the course led eastwards, the green became practically deserted.

The Queen's course of forty-six nautical miles encompassed the Warner Lightship and the East Lepe buoy, twice around. There were just two non-starters from the original entries, these being the yawl *Valdora* (Sir William Portal) and the ketch *Gannet* (Capt. J.C. Carter–Leigh). However, with sixteen yachts making the start line comprising cutters, yawls, ketches and a schooner, the event was a virtual classic, including the more familiar *Moonbeam IV* (Mr H.C. Sutton) and *Cariad* (Col. Gretton), both of which had shone in earlier King's Cup races. Although the remainder were less well-known, they contributed a rich atmosphere to the ensemble.

The starters included the 37 ton yawl *Amaryllis* (property of the Royal Naval College, Dartmouth), favoured by an alteration to the rules to permit her inclusion. She was commanded by Rear Admiral Martin E. Dunbar, VC, CB (an honorary member of the RYS) and manned by naval cadets. Also taking part were Mr Frank Chaplin's 63 ton yawl *Coral*, Mr W.D. Clark's 44 ton yawl *Rona*, Col. John Gretton's 153 ton ketch *Cariad*, Capt. Cecil Slade's 107 ton ketch *Merrymaid*, Col. E.J. Hollway's 27 ton yawl *Cyra*, Mr H.C. Sutton's 93 ton cutter *Moonbeam IV*, Capt. E.T. Sotherton–Estcourt's 50 ton cutter *Gelasma*, Major A.W. Foster's 152 ton ketch *Brynhild*, Sir W.H. Dyke–Acland's 50 ton yawl *Polynome*, Lord Wolverson's grand old schooner *Maid Marion*, Wing Cmdr. Louis's tiny 15 ton yawl *Audrey*, Major W.T. Towers–Clark's 28 ton cutter *Varuna*, the Marquess of Northampton's 38 ton yawl *Véronique*, Col. the Earl of Dunraven's ketch *Moyana* and Lt. Col. Guest's cutter *Maharana*.

The handicap time concessions were necessarily generous with consideration to the varying characteristics of the competing yachts, and the allowances were scheduled as follows:

Moonbeam IV sailing scratch

Giving	Cariad	16 minutes	6 seconds
	Maid Marion	16 "	6 "
	Brynhild	19 "	10 "
	Merrymaid	29 "	50 "
	Gelasma	30 "	40 "
	Moyana	42 "	10 "
	Maharana	54 "	26 "
	Polynome	67 "	26 "
	Coral	78 "	12 "
	Cyra	82 "	00 "
	Varuna	88 "	56 "
	Véronique	104 "	18 "
	Rona	107 "	20 "
	Amaryllis	138 "	00 "
	Audrey	167 "	8 "

None of the big handicap class yachts was entered this year for the King's Cup race at Cowes, as these had earlier sailed in July to compete for another royal trophy in the Clyde Regatta, when *Lulworth* had defeated *Shamrock* by a few seconds under near tempestuous conditions, to take the vase for Mr Paton in his first year of ownership. However, their absence proved of little consequence, for the day's most prestigious event was supported by a unique assembly of racing and cruising vessels, with measurements between 15 and 226 tons (TM) These were manned by the most enthusiastic of crews, whose talents were not all boosted by racing experience.

When the Blue Peter came down to the accompaniment of the starting gun from the castle battery, the galaxy of ships exhibited an inevitably ragged approach to the line as they reached away to the Warner with a southerly breeze, assisted by a flowing tide. The fleet was led by *Maharana*, closely followed by *Moonbeam IV* and *Cyra* just astern. There were no recalls, as caution was the order of the day, with the schooner *Maid Marion* last to cross, some five minutes late. *Moonbeam IV* quickly overhauled *Maharana*, as also did *Cariad*. In rounding the Warner, third place was taken by *Merrymaid* and *Gelasma* stole fourth position a minute or so later.

Distances between the four leading yachts had stretched to some twenty minutes as they completed the East Lepe turn, then making for the line at the castle HQ to commence a second round. *Moonbeam IV* was noted to be just outside of her handicap donation to *Cariad*, only seven minutes astern and still occupying second place. By the end of the first round *Merrymaid* was sixteen minutes behind the leader. A little yawl was sighted from the club house making for its moorings at this juncture under staysail and mizzen and it transpired that the Marquess of Northampton's *Véronique* had suffered a bobstay failure, which in turn aggravated a sprung bowsprit.

The actual times noted at the conclusion of the first round read:

Moonbeam IV	12 hrs		24 minutes		25 seconds	
Cariad	12	"	31	"	19	"
Merrymaid	12	"	40	"	14	"
Gelasma	12	"	43	"	41	"
Coral	12	"	53	"	55	"
Brynhild	12	"	56	"	14	"
Polynome	1	"	3	"	32	"
Moyana	1	"	5	"	23	"
Maharana	1	"	7	"	30	"
Cyra	1	"	17	"	51	"
Maid Marion	1	"	19	"	51	"
Rona	1	"	23	"	50	"
Varuna	1	"	24	"	32	"
Amaryllis	1	"	44	"	30	"
Audrey	2	"	17	"	35	"

Shortly after Sir W.H. Dyke–Acland's yawl *Polynome* started on her second round, but she was forced into retirement when the rising wind carried away her topmast.

Meanwhile, as the fourteen remaining contestants made for a second reach to the light vessel, the favourite *Moonbeam IV* held the lead, but was not demonstrating an ability to stretch her earlier advantage, which was essential if she had any hopes of victory. The Roadstead was dotted with odd entrant yachts, widely separated, both in distance and handicap allowances. *Amaryllis* came last to begin the second round, gamely struggling on, with the comfort of a generous time allowance in the final scoring.

The competition remained wide open with the Spithead throwing up an ever-increasing chop, to cause the smaller competitors a mounting embarrassment. The conditions exacted a further toll from the list of aspirants for the trophy. Returning around Old Castle Point, having quickly circuited the Warner, were seen Lord Wolverton's schooner *Maid Marion*, the largest, and Wing Cmdr. Louis's *Audrey*, the smallest of the fleet, making for their respective moorings, having put about off Osborne Bay. Some minutes later Major Towers–Clark's little 28 ton cutter *Varuna* was withdrawn from the contest and so a 'hard core' of eleven gallant crews was left to eventually cross the finish line.

After 4 hours, 40 minutes and 42 seconds sailing, *Moonbeam IV* crossed the line first, having averaged a very creditable 9.84 knots for the distance, but she had managed only two minutes' extended advantage over *Cariad* during the second round. In the event, neither of the first or second yachts to arrive qualified for a place. *Cariad* finished fourth and *Moonbeam IV* came seventh on corrected timings. The honour of winning the coveted royal trophy came to Frank Chaplin's 63 ton yawl *Coral* (averaging 8.47 knots), thus repeating her success of 1926. The 37 ton yawl entered by the Royal Naval College was last to finish and, on corrected time, placed second, nearly five minutes behind the winner. Mr W.D. Clark's 44 ton yawl *Rona* qualified for a third placing, some seven minutes behind the victor; her 1927 triumph was not repeated but she had proven a worthy challenger.

The actual and corrected times were:

	Actual	Corrected
Coral	3 hrs 25 mins 49	2 hrs 07 mins 37
Amaryllis	4 hrs 30 mins 32	2 hrs 12 mins 32
Rona	4 hrs 01 mins 35	2 hrs 14 mins 15
Cariad	2 hrs 49 mins 43	2 hrs 33 mins 37
Merrymaid	3 hrs 06 mins 30	2 hrs 36 mins 40
Cyra	4 hrs 01 mins 55	2 hrs 39 mins 55
Moonbeam IV	2 hrs 40 mins 42	2 hrs 40 mins 42
Gelasma	3 hrs 13 mins 15	2 hrs 42 mins 35
Maharana	3 hrs 39 mins 59	2 hrs 45 mins 33
Moyana	3 hrs 35 mins 30	2 hrs 53 mins 20
Brynhild	3 hrs 27 mins 17	3 hrs 08 mins 07

At 8.20 p.m. the King came ashore from the *V & A* to dine at the RYS castle, where he presided over some seventy guests. Following the royal toast, His Majesty presented Frank Chaplin with the massive silver-gilt vase and a silver model of his cutter *Britannia*, extending royal congratulations to the winner on his victory. It had been a great day, to be long remembered.

Racing in the big handicap class on Tuesday, *Lulworth*'s placing again proved most disappointing as she carried an impossible handicap, but her showing was not without inspiration, finishing behind *Westward*, just thirty-two seconds ahead of the royal cutter on actual terms.

Westward and *Lulworth* were tied scratch to allow *Britannia* 5 minutes, *White Heather II* and *Shamrock* 6 minutes each, with *Astra* and *Cambria* enjoying 8 minutes 32 seconds each for a forty nautical mile course, twice round the South-East Middle, North-East Middle and Solent Bank buoys.

Lulworth came home second to *Westward* but her handicap penalties dropped her into fifth place. The finishing times were:

	Actual	Corrected
	Actual	Corrected
Westward	2 hrs 24 mins 42	2 hrs 24 mins 42

Shamrock	2 hrs 37 mins 16	2 hrs 31 mins 16
Britannia	2 hrs 36 mins 33	2 hrs 31 mins 33
Astra	2 hrs 42 mins 42	2 hrs 34 mins 11
Lulworth	2 hrs 36 mins 01	2 hrs 36 mins 01
White Heather II	2 hrs 42 mins 59	2 hrs 36 mins 59
Cambria	2 hrs 51 mins 11	2 hrs 42 mins 39

On Wednesday the handicap race for yachts exceeding twenty-one metres rating was sailed over the Queen's course, twice round. *Westward* and *Lulworth* allowed *Britannia* 5 mins 45 secs, *White Heather II* and *Shamrock* 6 mins 54 secs each, *Astra* and *Cambria* 9 mins 49 secs each. Prizes of £80 (first) £20 (second) and £10 (third) were offered. The initial omens for a good day's racing with a stiff westerly breeze at the 10 a.m. start were belied, as the wind quickly eased, resulting in slow progress for the fleet, which finished late in the afternoon. Each of the finishing competitors toiled for more than six hours to complete the distance. With the gaffers all sporting full canvas, the yachts made for the west'ard, crossing the start line on the starboard tack with the exception of *Lulworth*, which got away on the opposite tack, trailing her contemporaries. The Bermudan *Cambria* was first to cross followed in order by *Westward*, *Shamrock*, *Astra*, *Britannia* and *White Heather II*. With a reach to the East Lepe mark the crowds on shore enjoyed a wonderfully close sighting of the schooner as she hugged the island shores way beyond Gurnard Bay. The cutters had chosen to make for the north shore, which paid dividends for *Shamrock*, since she rounded the East Lepe buoy some ninety seconds in front of *White Heather II* whilst *Westward* came later, behind *Astra* and *Britannia*. *Lulworth* was still showing a distinct loss of sparkle, which became patently evident in the final analysis. *Cambria* retired from the match at an early stage as she unfortunately fouled *Astra* in rounding the first mark. The yachts made a broad reach returning through Cowes Roads and after passing Osborne Bay set their spinnakers for a run to the Warner Lightship. *Shamrock* held the lead, completing the first round nearly three minutes ahead of *White Heather II*, with *Britannia* in third position coming eight minutes behind the leader. First round times noted were:

Shamrock	1 hr 33 mins 13 secs
White Heather II	1 hr 35 mins 59 secs
Britannia	1 hr 41 mins 50 secs
Westward	1 hr 49 mins 40 secs
Astra	1 hr 50 mins 35 secs
Lulworth	1 hr 51 mins 55 secs

Towards the completion of the second round, the flat conditions gave way to a stirring of air and as the wind freshened *Shamrock* took the first flag to maintain a two minute advantage over *White Heather II*. *Britannia*, still in third place, managed to reduce the gap between herself and the white cutter, but the conditions were not lively enough to make up the deficit. Unhappily Wednesday had, for *Lulworth*, proven yet another day of utter frustration, when she finished with a last placing. Clearly she was the same yacht which had performed so successfully on the Clyde in July against a uniform opposition, certainly under differing weather conditions and she was, of course, no stranger to the vagaries of the Solent – her less than meritorious placings for the first three days seemed agonising to the boy.

The corrected finishing times read:

Shamrock (winner)	4 hrs 3 mins 24
White Heather II (second)	4 hrs 05 mins 39
Britannia (third)	4 hrs 08 mins 22
Astra	4 hrs 15 mins 23
Westward	4 hrs 23 mins 35
Lulworth	4 hrs 29 mins 48

The average speed of 7.43 knots made by *Shamrock* was an indication of nature's retardation of sailpower.

The Royal Yacht Squadron's opening event on Thursday for the big handicap class, including yachts exceeding a rating of twenty-one metres, was sailed for Cowes town prizes of £80 first, £20 second, £10 third. The Big Five plus the two new Bermudan cutters incidentally constituted the largest assembly of the class ever seen taking part at Cowes. The course started in a westward direction, encompassed the Solent Bank, North-East Middle and South-East Middle buoys, to be rounded twice, a distance of some forty sea miles. The handicap allowances from *Lulworth* and *Westward* tied scratch gave *Britannia* 5 minutes, *White Heather II* and *Shamrock* 6 minutes each, *Cambria* and *Astra* 8 minutes 32 seconds each. As the fleet obeyed the starting signals sporting full canvas on the starboard tack, Major Hunloke received a recall gun for *Britannia* just ahead of the starting line. Oddly enough, Fred Mountifield saw the royal cutter putting about, not realising that *White Heather II* had also transgressed. She responded to a second recall gun. *Shamrock* took the lead with *Lulworth* on her weather followed by *Westward*, *Cambria*, *Astra* and *Britannia*, which trailed 3 minutes 45 seconds later. *White Heather II* lost 10 minutes 30 seconds in making a restart. The first leg was a beat to the Solent Bank mark, suffering a foul tide. *Lulworth* appeared to be exhibiting some determination to redeem her tired regatta showings of the past three days and was first to round the first buoy, but, whatever her exertions, disaster awaited at a later stage. However, with *Astra* only twenty seconds astern and *Shamrock* three minutes later, there was ample sport to be appreciated meanwhile. It was a sunny day with a steady westerly sailing breeze as the leaders set spinnakers for an easterly run through the Roadstead. With fairly favourable conditions, *Britannia* was making up her initial time deficit occupying fourth place, just ahead of the schooner *Westward* on the return run, whilst *Cambria* and *White Heather II* struggled in the rear. *Lulworth* was still in the lead as the trio passed the castle club house heading for the North-East Middle mark and then with the "in spinnaker" order, sails were sheeted for a reach to the South-East Middle. *Lulworth, Astra* and *Shamrock* were seen to be dicing with seconds separating them, as they set off on a second round. *Westward* and *Britannia* were revelling in a tremendous scrap, the former having an eleven second advantage over the royal cutter. *Cambria* came later as *White Heather II* sailed well to drastically reduce her restart loss.

When the leading trio in the formation of *Lulworth, Astra* and *Shamrock* crossed the club house line to start the second round, only nine seconds separated them. *Lulworth* was seen to bear away to leeward, temporarily relinquishing the lead to seek a bonus from the ebbing tide of Southampton Water as it raced over Calshot Spit. With the gathering of the tidal impetus flowing along the northern Solent shores, sheets were hauled in, to point higher, as the lead was regained by the great white cutter. In parallel with the manoeuvres described, the scene was interrupted by the sighting of *Westward* running aground just to the west of Egypt Point, close to the island shore. The event concentrated the attention of the shoreside onlookers as they surged in the direction of Gurnard to investigate. *Westward* subsequently managed to refloat without external assistance and, although she suffered an agonising delay, losing fourth place, the contest was sportingly resumed.

Meanwhile, *Lulworth* appeared to be settling into a advantageous position as she continued to distance herself from *Astra* and *Shamrock*. Her mastery proved to be short-lived, however, to recall a traditional adage relating to the best laid schemes of mice and men. Such must be of negligible value pitted against the spectre of the former *Terpsichore*. With everything seemingly in her favour after seizing a hard-won advantage, *Lulworth*'s prospects were ruthlessly stolen, as she sympathetically imitated her scratch partner, except that she ran well and truly aground, on the opposite shore at Needsoare Point, which lies west of the Beaulieu River estuary. Her exaggerated depth of keel had not for the first time exhibited a punishing disadvantage in combination with a piloting jinx, as she held fast to the shoal. The order was given to down sails and the prospect of waiting for more water added to the frustration of her predicament. Happily, Captain Griffiths of the minesweeper *Selkirk* which escorted *Britannia*, gallantly rendered assistance and towed *Lulworth* off, returning the unfortunate cutter to her moorings.

Shamrock was left to continue in the lead, being first to round the Solent Bank and *Britannia* overhauled *Astra* to occupy second place. The order remained unchanged to the boom of the finishing guns with *Shamrock* first home, followed by *Britannia* and *Astra*, which had sailed remarkably well to hold close to the two gaffers. The new Bermudan just managed to save her time by seven seconds from *Shamrock*.

The corrected times noted were:

Astra (winner)	2 hrs 39 mins 38
Shamrock (second)	2 hrs 39 mins 45
Britannia (third)	3 hrs 02 mins 01
Cambria	3 hrs 06 mins 06
White Heather II	3 hrs 07 mins 32
Westward	3 hrs 20 mins 37

The final day of the Royal Yacht Squadron Regatta coincided in traditional fashion with the Cowes Town Regatta on Friday of the Week. Although the yachts moored in the Solent and the naval contingent exhibited a lavish display of multi-coloured bunting in a collective effort to provide a nautical carnival touch, the hand of nature offered a grudging contribution, with light showers delivered from persistently dull skies.

The lad had found the appearances of *Lulworth* on four consecutive days completely bewildering and even an indulgence of Micawberesque philosophy was hardly to be entertained in hoping for a reversal of fortune on this day with such a paucity of air. There was none of the usual excitement of the start for the big handicap class when record crowds had assembled for a 10 a.m. getaway. The opening event was staged for yachts in excess of twenty-one metres rating sailing for prizes of £80 first, £20 second and £10 third.

With the slightest movement of easterly breeze, the yachts were all kedged behind the start line awaiting the gun, following which, the tide drifted them westwards towards the East Lepe mark, rounded in order by *Shamrock, Lulworth, Britannia, White Heather II* with *Cambria* and *Westward* later. (*Astra* was entered but failed to join the contest.)

This order was maintained as the fleet reached eastwards through the Roads for the Warner and several hours passed before *Shamrock* was sighted to take the first gun late in the afternoon, having completed one round of the course at an average speed of 3.73 knots! Whilst the conditions hardly provided an opportunity for any truly serious racing, it was perhaps something of a consolation for *Lulworth* to take a third flag after four successive 'ducks'. Despite her generous time concessions, *Cambria*'s Cowes debut was disappointingly fruitless. Her new Bermudan contemporary *Astra* was more fortunate to have taken just one first flag by a small margin. *Britannia* had three third flags to her credit, although the flat conditions generally robbed her of any limelight. *White Heather II* acquitted herself very well to boast three second flags. The schooner *Westward* claimed one first flag on Tuesday, but, like *Britannia* and *Lulworth,* would have established greater success in more stirring elements.

The corrected finishing times for Friday were as follows:

Shamrock (winner)	4 hrs 6 mins 57
White Heather II (second)	4 hrs 26 mins 20
Lulworth (third)	4 hrs 33 mins 10
Astra	4 hrs 41 mins 14
Britannia	4 hrs 41 mins 24
Westward	4 hrs 54 mins 21

It had proven a week of supreme success for Sir Thomas Lipton with his twenty year old *Shamrock*, which, despite the muted airs, stole the show with three wins and two second places.

Quite apart from *Lulworth*'s punitive handicap burden, her change of ownership (though scarcely evident at that time) was indirectly responsible this season for the lessening of the yacht's competitive prospects in the Solent and other class events around the coast. Undoubtedly, Mr Paton had acquired a modern vessel of the most enviable racing potential, but the contract of purchase came far too late for him to recruit the services, in continuity, of Captain Hogarth. He had earlier accepted an appointment as skipper of Sir William Berry's new Bermudan cutter *Cambria* for the 1928 season, as there was no prospect for Hogarth's future with *Lulworth* whilst she remained on the sale lists. And so, in the absence of a virtuoso, the Stradivarius was destined to bitterly disappoint a certain youthful member in the audience.

The Week ended with a record gathering of revellers who came from far and wide to enjoy the sights and sounds of Messrs Pain's pyrotechnic display. A further delight was provided by the sight of the *Victoria and Albert* dressed with red, white and blue lamps.

The 1928 regattas included the company of the American-built schooner Elena [2] in the over twenty-one metre contests on some occasions, one of which was on August 13th 1928, the opening day of the Royal Thames Yacht Club's Regatta, sailed from Ryde. Notes of this particular event, over a course of forty-five sea miles, i.e. twice round the Ryde West-Middle buoy and the Nab End Gas buoy, bring *Elena* to the start of the contest, although Dame Fortune later interfered with her chance of completing the race. Prizes offered were £80 for a first, £40 for a second and £20 for a third flag.

The entries consisted of *Lulworth* and *Westward* sailing scratch at 25.70 metres rating; *Britannia* arbitrarily at 24.2 metres was allowed 6 mins 45 secs, *Shamrock* and *White Heather II*, equally rated at 23.9 metres, were given 8 mins 6 secs, *Astra* and *Cambria*, similarly rated at 23.20 metres, with times of 11 mins 31 secs apiece. The schooner *Elena*, which was owned by Mr W.B. Bell, enjoyed an allowance of 1 min 7½ secs but the determination of this concession remains enigmatic, the more so when one considers that *Lulworth* made a time allowance to the big schooner!

The wind was gusting up to Beaufort scale 5-6 on this day and the Spithead chop looked anything but inviting from the Ryde esplanade. Such were the conditions that *Shamrock* and *White Heather II* did not leave their moorings as the weight of wind was generally considered to be tempting the fates beyond an acceptable degree of prudence. The other topsailed cutters, *Lulworth* and *Britannia*, set only their reefed mainsails and the Bermudans, *Astra* and *Cambria*, were also reefed. The schooners *Westward* and *Elena* carried full mainsails but their topsails remained bare. With the ferocity of the breeze at 10 a.m. it was hardly possible for any of the contesting yachts to make an orderly start and when *Westward* crossed the line first, she was then twenty seconds ahead of *Lulworth* which occupied the weather berth, whilst *Britannia* followed ten seconds later.

Astra was 1 min 25 secs behind the gun with *Cambria* bringing up the rear just 2 mins 14 secs after the leader, but the seas soon proved to be too severe for each of the new Bermudans and they retired at an early stage. When the remainder of the field reached the Nab Tower, *Westward* held the lead, just twenty-two seconds ahead of *Britannia*, followed by *Lulworth* four minutes astern, whilst *Elena* was hanging on a few seconds behind *Lulworth*. It was on the reach back to the westward that *Elena* had the misfortune to have two hands washed overboard, which obviously put her out of the contest by delay in their rescue.

Westward had gained slightly over *Britannia* and *Lulworth* on the reach to complete the first round, with a difference of 1 min 32 secs over the former and with 5 mins 17 secs lead over the latter. Under such conditions it would have been scarcely surprising if the race committee had stopped the event on the completion of the first round, particularly in view of the demonstration of danger from the elements experienced by *Elena*'s crew that day. However, as *Britannia* was so doggedly hanging on to the schooner well within her time allowance, it might have been unfairly seen as handing the first prize to His Majesty the King, whilst depriving Mr Davis of prospects over the full circuit. In the event, any such considerations became irrelevant as *Britannia* was withdrawn following her completion of a drenching first round.

The issue was then left to be fought out between *Westward* and *Lulworth* and it became clear that *Lulworth*, with a drastically reduced area of sail, was unlikely to draw level and overhaul her larger and more heavily canvased opponent on this occasion, which amply demonstrated the unfairness of sharing an equal rating. From my memories of Solent regattas, none of the cutters ever proved a match for the schooner on a reaching course and, with the prevailing summer breezes from a southerly direction, the Solent–Spithead courses so often favoured *Westward*. On the other hand, *Lulworth* consistently showed a clean pair of heels to the schooner in beating to windward when such conditions were met on the course. In the second round, following *Britannia*'s exit from the struggle, there was obviously no need for the remaining contestants to drive their charges too hard. But a race was a race and there was no easing. *Westward* took the winning gun, covering the forty-five miles in 3 hrs 42 mins 9 secs averaging 12.15 knots, with *Lulworth* in second place, timed at 3 hrs 54 mins 15 secs, averaging 11.53^3 knots. Taking into account the difference in theoretical maximum speeds of 13.23 knots for *Westward* and 12.24 knots as projected for *Lulworth*, the latter's performance was no mean achievement when considering estimated speed differentials. Whilst *Westward* had a calculated potential of sailing one knot faster, *Lulworth* was, in fact, only 0.62 knots slower over the distance. This dismal year was not to be denied some latent claims to an undecorated distinction, but, as with most sports, there is no medal for trying!

On Tuesday of the RTYC Regatta, August 14th 1928, the wind had lightened to some degree after the stormy conditions of the day before, although the committee was exercising caution by cancelling the scheduled Round the Island race. The course sailed and prizes offered were the same as for Monday's match. The American schooner *Elena* was entered, but was withdrawn from the start suffering from a broken boom. Sir Thomas Lipton's *Shamrock* and Lord Waring's *White Heather II* joined those which had competed on the previous day.

For reasons known only to the sailing committee, the time allowances were slightly lower than those of the previous day, even though it was the same course. *Lulworth* tied scratch with *Westward* to allow *Britannia* 5 minutes 37 seconds, *Shamrock* and *White Heather II* 6 minutes 45 seconds each, *Astra* and *Cambria* 9 minutes 36 seconds each.

Cambria was first over the start line with *Lulworth* on her weather, the order following being *Shamrock*, *Westward*, *Britannia*, *White Heather II* and *Astra*, each being separated by a few seconds; literally another classic getaway.

Shamrock was seen to be overcanvased and she shortly gave up. *Westward* moved into the lead, having overtaken *Cambria* and *Lulworth* somewhat earlier.

At the conclusion of the first round *Westward* had a fifty second advantage over *Lulworth*, which was challenging in second place. *Cambria* followed, leading *Britannia* by twenty-nine seconds whilst *White Heather II* and *Astra* came in sequence. After passing the pier head at the end of the first round *White Heather II* retired; it seemed that she was not enjoying the chop. Shortly afterwards both *Cambria* and *Astra* followed suit, in all probability for the same reasons.

With the reaching breeze in her favour, *Westward* was undoubtedly in her element once again and drew well ahead during the second circuit. *Britannia* arrived approximately thirty-nine seconds behind *Lulworth* at the finish and so managed to save her time from both *Westward* and *Lulworth* to take first prize. This was *Britannia's* first success of the 1928

Solent season, in which she was privileged to capitalise from the adjusted re-rating.

The actual and corrected finishing times were:

	Actual	Corrected
Britannia (winner)	1 hr 56 mins 57	1 hr 51 mins 20
Westward (second)	1 hr 52 mins 17	1 hr 52 mins 17
Lulworth	1 hr 56 mins 18	1 hr 56 mins 18

The racing on Wednesday of the Ryde Regatta did not include the big handicap class in its calendar.

Thursday was the concluding day of the Royal Victoria Yacht Club Regatta, when the big handicap class commenced the proceedings by competing for the International Gold Challenge Cup, a trophy which was open to yachts which belonged to clubs affiliated to the International Yacht Racing Union (IYRU). The schooner *Elena* was the only foreign entry, but, as her boom had been damaged some days earlier, she was a non-starter. *Britannia* had been expected to participate, but was withdrawn from the contest. From eight entries, only six made the line.

In addition to winning the cup, a first prize of £80 was offered, the second being £25 and third £15. The forty-six mile long Victoria course was sailed in a moderate nor'west'r which eased as the race proceeded and resulted in a long drawn-out competition, extending for almost seven hours from a 10.30 a.m. start. The handicap donations from both *Westward* and *Lulworth* sailing scratch gave *White Heather II* and *Shamrock* 6 minutes 54 seconds, *Cambria* and *Astra* 9 minutes 49 seconds. The start was quite spectacular, as the sextet crossed the line with full canvas sheeted in for a beat towards the Ryde West-Middle buoy. *Lulworth* was first to cross in the weather berth, closely trailed by *Westward*, *Shamrock*, *Cambria* and *White Heather II,* in that order whilst *Astra* made the line almost one minute later. When the yachts rounded the first mark *Lulworth* was leading *White Heather II*, which had *Shamrock* almost abeam. As the fleet made the turn for the Nab, with spinnakers mutually set to port, *Shamrock* ran into trouble when she fouled *White Heather II*. The white cutter flew a protest flag and the emerald green offender made an apology by retiring from the contest. The fleet was seen to be dispersing over the course and *White Heather II* made profit from the faint airs to overtake *Lulworth*, which was visibly suffering from such a dearth of motive power. The Bermudans *Cambria* and *Astra* were both extracting the maximum benefit from the drifting tide in combination with the scarcely detectable movement of air, to the humiliation of both *Lulworth* and *Westward*, unable to muster sufficient spirit to stem the arrears. Sensing the futility of continuing, *Westward* retired in the second round, leaving a quartet of two gaffers and two Bermudans to conclude the contest. On corrected time *White Heather II* managed to win the trophy by 2 minutes 25 seconds from *Astra*; *Cambria* making a creditable third place. *Lulworth* drifted over the finishing line some 5 minutes later than *Cambria*.

The actual and corrected finishing times were:

	Actual	Corrected
White Heather II	5 hrs 15 mins 57	5 hrs 09 mins 03
Astra	5 hrs 21 mins 17	5 hrs 11 mins 28
Cambria	5 hrs 23 mins 03	5 hrs 13 mins 14
Lulworth	5 hrs 28 mins 08	5 hrs 28 mins 08

The entries of *Astra* and *Cambria* to the class in the 1928 season, whilst obviously increasing the scope of competition, did not make a great impact, especially taking into account the generous time allowances which each received. *Shamrock*'s brilliant showing at Cowes was not continued in the Ryde Regatta but her overall seasonal tally was substantially augmented by the RYS and RLYC results.

[1] Sir William Berry, a newspaper magnate, was elevated to the peerage in 1928, taking the title of Lord Camrose. The naming of his yacht *Cambria* bore some likeness to the title of its owner.

[2] The schooner *Elena* was virtually a sister yacht to Mr Davis's *Westward*. The original owner of *Elena*, Mr Morton F. Plant, was a wealthy industrialist who, having raced *Ingomar* at the turn of the century with conspicuous success, was very impressed with the Herreshoff-built *Westward* and, in consequence, contracted that company to build *Elena* in 1911. The main differences showed in *Elena*'s sharper bow profile and increased sail area. The latter was validated by her greater stability as a function of a deeper lead keel forward, without rounding off, unlike *Westward*'s underwater profile. *Westward* and *Elena* were evenly matched in the 1911 calendar. Following the demise of Morton Plant, *Elena* was purchased by Mr William B. Bell in the early Twenties, when she was entered for the King of Spain's Transatlantic Contest, which she won, incidentally beating off the challenge of the larger rival schooner *Atlantic*.

[3] Their peak sailing speeds must, of course, have been somewhat greater when one considers time losses in tacking whilst beating to windward, rounding marks and tidal impediments.

1929

ASTRA SHARES THE HONOURS WITH *SHAMROCK*

For Cowes folk 1929 was a yachting season of mixed emotions. Firstly, there was the greatest anxiety for the health of His Majesty King George V, who was suffering from a very serious illness in London, as a consequence of which the Admiral of the Royal Yacht Squadron could not report for duty at the castle. In consequence, the Cowes Roadstead was denied the privilege of hosting the royal yacht *Victoria and Albert* and the usual escorting guardships this year, but, nevertheless, a record muster of palatial vessels filled the waterway as if to compensate, keeping the old traditions alive. One of these was the very conspicuous Spanish royal mail 7,000 ton steamship *Reina Maria Christina*, resembling a yacht, glowing in her brilliant white paint. She presented an unfamiliar, but most welcome contribution to the Solent gathering, unhappily and unusually deprived of the royal maritime set pieces.

The Week of 1929 was not, however, entirely denied royal patronage, since it was honoured by the visits of Their Royal Highnesses Princess Beatrice and Princess Helena Victoria. A welcome was further extended to King George of the Hellenes.

Secondly, tradition was enthusiastically kept alive by the big cutters, with the unhappy absence of *Britannia*, which remained under the protection of Mr Teddy Woodland at Marvin's East Cowes Yard. (This gentleman had the reputation of chastising minors whose defiant hobbies of trespass on the forbidden premises were calculated to invoke the wrath of the one who patrolled with a menacing cudgel. I seem to remember that he never failed to give chase, but his aggression was consistently outpaced. This particular portion of Marvin's premises was sited on a former brickyard, which was functional in early

Victorian times. There was a huge pond incorporated in the up-river portion formed by the pit where clay had been excavated at one time. Before the end of the last century, local people used to skate on the ice at the Brickyard Pond in winter time.)

The Royal Southampton Yacht Club of Calshot staged its Regatta on Saturday, August 3rd preceding the Cowes programme using the facilities of the Royal Yacht Squadron. The race for yachts exceeding twenty-one metres received the entries of *Lulworth, Shamrock, White Heather II, Cambria, Candida* and *Westward*. The event was enlivened by an accident to *Shamrock* in the full view of the crowds of spectators on the Cowes esplanade. Sir Thomas Lipton's 23 metre *Shamrock* was reaching through the lines of vessels moored in the Roadstead, in third position, when she was struck by a vicious southerly gust, causing her to heel suddenly whilst passing Mr Eustace Blundell's yawl *Octavia*, which was anchored close by. *Shamrock's* crosstree and rigging fouled *Octavia's* topmast, which was carried away.

Damage to *Shamrock* was repaired over the weekend. The race, which was practically a reach over the course of forty-five miles, was won by the schooner *Westward*.

The beginning of the 1929 Cowes Regatta Week was memorable for the excitement accidentally aroused by a further incident which intruded upon the peace of the Sunday evening prior to the programme of RYS events. The mini-drama for those of us on shore, and to a greater degree the trippers returning to the mainland, was played in the vicinity of the western end of the harbour fairway, within full view of the Squadron club house.

The Southampton-bound paddle steamer *Princess Elizabeth*, commanded by Captain Bray, was on its normal outbound manoeuvre, reversing from the West Cowes pontoon terminal, making a turn to go ahead across the Solent, when she was thrust into Sir William Burton's yawl, named *Rendezvous*, by a strong ebbing current. The yacht, which was lying at anchor off the castle club house, suffered a smashed bowsprit. The *Rendezvous* swung around to catch her stern on the starboard side of the 'paddler'[1] before bouncing clear. Happily, there were no casualties reported in this incident.

The Big Seven of 1929 were minus *Britannia* but plus another Bermudan newcomer, *Candida*, built for Mr H.K. Andreae, a banker whose nickname was 'Sonny'. He had previously owned and raced the 19 metre yacht *Corona*. As a first-class helmsman, he was owner-skipper, backed up by a mate named James Gilbey, a winter fisherman from Emsworth. H.K. Andreae had acted as the Hon. Treasurer of the Yacht Racing Association for some years.

Lulworth's owner, Mr Alexander Allan Paton, CB, was elected to membership of the Royal Yacht Squadron on Monday, August 5th 1929. His cutter proudly flew the white ensign once more, and the crew boasted of their new affinity with the club, with the RYS lettering incorporated on their jersey uniforms.

The 1929 season showed a more balanced approach to handicapping, with *Lulworth* no longer penalised by the same arbitrary scratch rating as *Westward*, as they were in the 1927/28 seasons when *Shamrock* and *White Heather II* received an allowance of 9 secs/mile. In addition to the scrapping of this absurdity, *Lulworth* was favoured with the reappointment of Skipper Archie Hogarth, whose skill had contributed to so many of her earlier successes. It seemed that she might, once again, participate in competitive opportunities of a more equitable nature.

The schooner *Westward* was still the scratch vessel sailing under greatly reduced penalties of time donations. The three big cutters, *Lulworth, Shamrock, White Heather II* were racing substantially on level terms once more, as they had done in the 1924/1925/1926 regattas, each of them receiving a miserly 1 sec/mile from *Westward*. (Such an allowance proved totally inadequate when racing together with the wind predominantly on the beam.)

Of the Bermudans, *Candida* received 6 secs/mile and Cambria 6.5 secs/mile (originally 12.8 secs/mile in 1928) from the scratch vessels.

The three surviving cutters of the original Big Five, *Lulworth*, *Shamrock* and *White Heather II*, shared the seasonal honours very closely, with *Shamrock* topping the trio. Both *Lulworth* and *Shamrock* each made forty starts whereas *White Heather II* made forty-five.

Sir Mortimer Singer's *Astra* managed only eight starts by which she succeeded in gaining four firsts and two seconds, putting her top of the season on a 'points for flags-to-starts' assessment of performance, thus demonstrating a most unlikely overall result against full seasonal participation. In other words, whilst *Astra* should not be deprived of honours due, the paper success was strictly a function of the few races which she sailed, combined with the advantages of 5.5 secs per mile allowed her by *Lulworth*, *Shamrock* and *White Heather II*. The schooner *Westward* gave *Astra* 6.5 secs/mile. With nine first and ten second flags to her credit, the 23 metre *Shamrock* might arguably share a claim to the season's star honours.

From my 1929 jottings of some events in the Cowes Regatta, I find that the opening day was endowed with a mixture of elements perfectly suited to the sport. Despite the enforced absence of the sovereign and his cutter *Britannia*, not forgetting the accustomed backdrop of the *Victoria and Albert* with her guardships, the shoreside attendance at the start of the Royal London Yacht Club race for yachts exceeding twenty-one metres was as great as ever – in fact, it seemed impossible to find a pitch in the immediate vicinity of the RYS castle at 9.30 a.m. on the first morning. The battery of the latter provided its usual service to the RLYC. The majority of observers near the club house scarcely moved away until the finish of the big class. The events were controlled by Mr Norman Clark Neill and Mr Gerald Watson (secretary).

The first prize was the sum of £80, plus an award of the Cayley Memorial Challenge Cup (a trophy given by the family of the late Mr C.T. Cayley, a former commodore of the RLYC).   Second and third prizes were £35 and £15 respectively.

The entrants and their time allowances were:

Mr F.T.B. Davis's schooner *Westward* (scratch), Mr A.A. Paton's *Lulworth* (39 secs), Sir Thomas Lipton's *Shamrock* (39 secs), Lord Waring's cutter *White Heather II* (39 secs), Mr H.K. Andreae's Bermudan *Candida* 3 mins 54 secs and Lord Camrose's Bermudan *Cambria* 4 mins 14 secs.   The Bermudan-rigged *Astra* owned by Sir Mortimer Singer failed to make the line.

Despite a reduced field of entrants, the start was spectacular in the extreme.   The course sailed took them twice round the Solent Bank and North-East Middle buoys, a distance of thirty-nine nautical miles.   With a stiff head wind, they set off on the starboard tack, passing over the line almost simultaneously in a westward direction, except that Mr Andreae, in his eagerness, had cut his timing too closely and with the echoing effect of a second gun the blackboard displaying No.8 in white figures was speedily hoisted on the squadron flagstaff, recalling the *Candida*.   She recrossed the start line only one minute later, providing a convincing demonstration of her manoeuvrability.

The order at the start was led by *Cambria*, was followed by *Shamrock* (in the weather berth), *White Heather*, *Lulworth*, *Candida* and *Westward*.   The three cutters and the schooner carried their full topsails; light weather canvas typically bent. In the close haul to the Solent Bank Buoy *Lulworth* demonstrated her windward superiority once again to be first round the first mark, followed in order by *Shamrock*, *Westward*, *Cambria*, *Candida*.   *Lulworth* led *Shamrock* by over a minute on the run back through the Roads with spinnakers set to port; the schooner *Westward* placed some three minutes behind *Lulworth*.   *Cambria* was in fourth position, nearly eleven minutes astern, whilst *White Heather II* came fifth and *Candida* sixth, nearly fifteen mins behind *Lulworth*.   It was probably due to a turn of a foul tide, which retarded *Candida*'s progress rather more than her small time loss in recall. In running to the North-East Middle buoy *Shamrock* overtook *Lulworth* to become just twenty-six seconds ahead at the end of the first round, the times being:

Shamrock	12 hr 16 min
Lulworth	12 hr 16 min 26
Westward	12 hr 21 min 20
Cambria	12 hr 26 min 29
White Heather II	12 hr 26 min 38
Candida	12 hr 29 min 21

Shamrock's lead was short-lived, however, when she was overtaken by *Lulworth* in the early part of the second round. *Cambria* was in trouble with her spinnaker boom at a later stage and gave up before the end. *Lulworth* went on to establish a substantial lead over *Shamrock*, which was 2 mins 25 secs behind the leader at the finish, but there was little doubt that Hogarth had enjoyed yet another exciting duel on level terms with Captain Sycamore in *Shamrock* on this day. The corrected finishing times read:

Lulworth (winner of cup + £80)	2 hr 31 min 3
Shamrock (second + £35)	2 hr 33 min 28
Westward (third + £15)	2 hr 34 min 46
White Heather II	2 hr 35 min 24
Candida	2 hr 37 min 6

On the following day a strong west-south-westerly. breeze, combined with teeming rain and a thick sea mist, dampened the spirits of those ashore and afloat alike. The seafront became practically deserted as an effect of incessant rain and poor visibility and the normally popular King's Cup race was raced in conditions so unpleasant that only a handful of onlookers remained to see the finish. The cup was won by the Rt. Hon. John Gretton's 153 ton ketch *Cariad*, with Major Hunloke at the helm. *Cariad* had taken the coveted prize on four occasions, in the years 1905, 1910, 1912 and 1921, under the ownership of the Earl of Dunraven.

Tuesday's race for the big handicap class, defined as for yachts of between twenty-one and twenty-four metres, was sailed for RYS prizes of £80 first, £20 second and £10 third. *Shamrock* was a non-starter, leaving only five competitors.

Mr F. Davis's *Westward* allowed Mr A.A. Paton's *Lulworth* and Lord Waring's *White Heather II* 40 seconds each, Mr H.K. Andreae's *Candida* 4 minutes and Lord Camrose's *Cambria* 4 minutes 20 secs.

It was an uninspiring start, with the fleet well behind the line at the boom of the cannon. *Lulworth* was first to cross, followed in order by the schooner *Westward*, *Cambria*, *White Heather II* and *Candida*. The forty mile course described two rounds of the Solent Bank, North-East Middle and South-East Middle buoys. At the western mark *Cambria* took the lead, only to be shortly overtaken by *Westward* and *Lulworth* profiting from a southerly wind as they made the reach toward the North-East Middle mark.

Lulworth was a minute or so astern of the schooner when *Cambria* retired from the contest. *Candida* was sailing well to hold third place and at the end of the first round the times taken were:

Westward	12 hrs 27 mins 19
Lulworth	12 hrs 29 mins 3
Candida	12 hrs 29 mins 15
White Heather II	12 hrs 30 mins 37

Despite the advantage which *Westward* had demonstrated over the cutters, there remained only a little more than three minutes between the first and last vessels, but the schooner handsomely trebled her lead during the second round, as the conditions were substantially in her favour. *Candida* was performing exceptionally well, sailing an inshore course with a moderate flowing tide on the final leg, when she succeeded in passing *Lulworth* just seventeen seconds ahead of her topsailed opponent.

Westward took the first gun to receive a winning flag, the actual and corrected finishing times reading:

	Actual	Corrected
Westward (first)	2 hrs 20 mins 33	2 hrs 20 mins 33
Candida (second)	2 hrs 27 mins 45	2 hrs 23 mins 45
Lulworth (third)	2 hrs 28 mins 2	2 hrs 27 mins 22
White Heather II	2 hrs 37 mins 58	2 hrs 37 mins 18

Racing of the big handicap class was resumed on the Wednesday morning, which broke bright and clear for continuation of the RYS Regatta, favouring the 10 a.m. start when a fresh westerly breeze was blowing. *Shamrock* rejoined her fellow competitors once more. Unfortunately, the fine morning defied its early promise and some ominous clouds gathered towards midday, resulting in a showery afternoon.

The race was officially programmed for yachts between twenty-one and twenty-four metres for squadron prizes of £80, £20 and £10. The course known as the Queen's was sailed twice round.

The schooner *Westward* sailed scratch allowing *Lulworth*, *Shamrock*, *White Heather II* 46 secs each. The Bermudan *Candida* was allowed 4 mins 36 secs and *Cambria* 5 mins 45 secs. Sir Mortimer Singer's *Astra* did not take part.

Lulworth and *White Heather II* crossed the start almost together at the leeward end of the line and made for the north shore, out of the strong tide. The others followed in the order of *Cambria*, *Shamrock* (to windward of her), *Candida* and *Westward* bringing up the rear. The fleet was grappling with a dead beat over a foul tide to the East Lepe buoy, during which *Lulworth*, with her usual close-winded character, showed to advantage, rounding the weather mark over a minute ahead of *White Heather II*, *Cambria* three minutes behind her, followed in order by *Candida* and *Shamrock* with *Westward* some twelve minutes astern. On the return run to the Warner Lightship, all spinnakers were set to starboard. As they passed the club house *Lulworth* was leading *White Heather II* by 73 seconds, with the order of the others unchanged.

In the beat back to the line from the Warner, *Lulworth* had stretched her lead to seven minutes ahead of *White Heather II* by the end of the first round.

At this juncture *Candida* overtook *Cambria* to find herself in third place, some seventeen minutes behind *Lulworth* whilst *Shamrock* came three minutes later, just twenty minutes astern. The first round times were:

Lulworth	12 hr 30 min 22
White Heather II	12 hr 37 min 35
Candida	12 hr 47 min 29
Cambria	12 hr 48 min 24
Shamrock	12 hr 50 min 30
Westward	12 hr 50 min 49

Lulworth was absolutely at the peak of her form on this day, with her course chosen to perfection, certainly a tribute to Archie Hogarth's skill.

During the second round Captain Sycamore (the skipper with the 'Captain Kettle' style beard) displayed his determination to successfully challenge the Bermudans, taking the emerald cutter into third place.

At the end of the second round *Lulworth* had added another five minutes to her lead, winning very comfortably from *White Heather II* by some twelve minutes.

The corrected finishing times were as follows:

Lulworth (winner)	4 hr 11 min 55
White Heather II (second)	4 hr 24 mins
Shamrock (third)	4 hr 42 min 24
Cambria	4 hr 54 min 41

Westward   4 hr 57 min 49
Candida no record

Thursday's racing for the big class of yachts exceeding 21 metres was entered by *Lulworth, White Heather II, Candida, Cambria, Westward* and *Shamrock* for town prizes of £80, £20 and £10 over the course of the South-East Middle, North-East Middle and Solent Bank buoys, twice round, some forty nautical miles. *Westward* sailed scratch, to allow *Lulworth, White Heather II* and *Shamrock* 40 seconds each, *Candida* 4 minutes and *Cambria* 5 minutes. The very light north-westerly breeze was scarcely detectable at the start, when the 10 a.m. signal sounded, the whole fleet being substantially downward of the line. *Shamrock* managed to inch over the mark some thirty-three seconds late, then came *Cambria* with *Candida* to weather, followed by *Lulworth* and *White Heather II*. The schooner *Westward* trailed over two minutes astern. The reaching wind which extended around the course was insufficient to give the schooner an edge, as it might have almost certainly done had it blown with greater force. The smaller Bermudans were seen to be enjoying the faint airs, as also was *White Heather II*, the gaffers setting every stitch of canvas. When the yachts made the return reach through the Solent, *Cambria*, with an inshore position to leeward of *Candida*, was leading by forty-five seconds approximately. *White Heather II* came next, 1 minute 27 seconds behind the leader. *Shamrock, Lulworth* and *Westward* came widely separated in that order. *White Heather II*'s skipper found a slight bonus from the elements as a fluky breeze piped up, giving her some encouragement in challenging the Bermudans. As was quite often the case, Captain Mountifield had a nose for discovering the most favourable airs and tidal bonuses the Solent could provide, when needed. *White Heather II* overtook *Cambria* and later *Candida* to make a sporting finish for first place. *White Heather II* received the first gun at the termination of the first round, arriving fifty secs ahead of

Candida.   Whilst the time allowances were halved for one circuit, *White Heather II* had an insufficient margin over *Candida*, which took the first flag on corrected time.   *Westward* found herself unable to derive any inspiration from the flat elements and retired before the end of the contest, as she was left hopelessly behind.   After her brilliant victory over *White Heather II* and *Shamrock* on the previous day with an abundance of air, *Lulworth* had to be content with a last placing.

Her hopes had been thwarted by the conditions, as also had *Shamrock*'s.   *Cambria* flew a protest flag alleging an infringement of the rules by *Candida*, but it was not processed.

The actual and corrected finishing times taken were:

	Actual	Corrected
Candida (winner)	1 hr 54 mins 6	1 hr 52 mins 6
White Heather II (second)	1 hr 53 mins 16	1 hr 52 mins 56
Cambria (third)	1 hr 59 mins 10	1 hr 56 mins 40
Shamrock	1 hr 58 mins 2	1 hr 57 mins 42
Lulworth	2 hrs 7 mins 59	2 hrs 7 mins 39

Six of the over 110 tons (TM) ensemble competed on Friday, Cowes Regatta Day.   Prizes of £80, £20 and £20 were sailed for.   There was a beat to the East Lepe mark against a light south-westerly wind initially, which substantially freshened later.   As the fleet crossed the start line to the westward, the Bermudan *Candida* was first over, some thirty-two seconds after the gun, with *Lulworth* to windward of *White Heather II* and *Westward* in echelon formation, *Cambria* was next, followed by *Shamrock*.   *Lulworth* took the lead quickly, overtaking *Candida* with *White Heather II* challenging for first place.   On the broad reach passing through the roads returning to make the Warner Lightship *White Heather II* overtook *Lulworth* and led her by twenty-five seconds as the yachts passed the RYS club house.   *Candida* came twenty-two seconds behind *Lulworth*.   *Westward* was in fourth position, nearly two minutes after *White Heather II*, *Cambria* was fifth, and *Shamrock* was well astern of the fleet. Handicap concessions, with *Westward* the scratch competitor, were based upon 46 seconds each for *Lulworth*, *Shamrock* and *White Heather* whilst *Candida* enjoyed 4 minutes 36 seconds and *Cambria* 5 minutes 45 seconds for the forty-six mile distance. On the return westward from the eastern mark, the schooner profited from a gathering beam wind to take the lead nearly one minute ahead of *White Heather II*, which occupied second place. *Lulworth* in third position was two minutes behind the leader. *Candida* came fourth and was timed approximately four minutes from *Westward*, with *Cambria* close behind. *Shamrock* showed nearly seven minutes after the schooner at the end of the first round.

There was no change of formation during the second round, during which *Westward* stretched her lead to finish three minutes ahead of *White Heather II* as the first gun was fired.

A protest was lodged against *White Heather II* by *Lulworth* but was not upheld.

The finishing times noted were as follows:

	Actual	Corrected
Westward (winner)	2 hrs 44 mins 9	2 hrs 44 mins 9
White Heather II (second)	2 hrs 47 mins 3	2 hrs 46 mins 17
Lulworth (third)	2 hrs 48 mins 59	2 hrs 48 mins 13
Candida	2 hrs 55 mins 3	2 hrs 50 mins 27
Cambria	3 hrs 2 mins 40	2 hrs 56 mins 55
Shamrock	3 hrs 3 mins 26	3 hrs 2 mins 40

The Royal Victoria Yacht Club Regatta of 1929 staged an interesting event for the Royal Thames participation at Ryde on Monday, the opening day, with a circuit of the Isle of Wight for yachts exceeding twenty-one metres competing for prizes of £80 first, £40 second and £20 third. Unfortunately *Westward* as the scratch yacht did not appear on the starting line; her programmed allowances were for *Lulworth*, *White Heather II* and *Shamrock* 54 secs, *Candida* 5 mins 24 secs, with *Cambria* 5 mins 51 secs. Full light weather canvas was ventured at the 10.30 a.m. start. The commencement was relatively dull, owing to the flat and variable wind conditions. The time for the full distance was well in excess of previous records for this event, although, as the cutters emerged downchannel, the wind piped up. The yachts crossed the start line in an easterly direction and sailed in the order of *Shamrock* (Sir Thomas Lipton), *Candida* (Mr H.K. Andreae), *White Heather II* (Lord Waring), *Lulworth* (Mr A.A. Paton) and *Cambria* (Lord Camrose). Both *White Heather II* and *Cambria* set their spinnakers almost immediately, but to little advantage it seemed, as progress for the fleet was extremely slow. *Shamrock* held her lead for the greater part of the early course, whilst *Lulworth* managed to work through the fleet to reach second place as the wind freshened along the south of the Wight. The two leading cutters were later seen to be in a tremendous battle for supremacy, but, after rounding The Needles to pass into the more sheltered waters of the Solent behind Hurst Castle, *Lulworth* forged ahead to hold a leading position over *Shamrock* and win first prize by the small margin of just forty-one seconds. This was a classic example of how wonderfully matched the two rivals were over nearly eight hours of sailing time, much of it in open water. The official finishing times for the race, with adjustment for time concessions, were as follows:

Lulworth	6 hrs 26 mins 17
Shamrock	6 hrs 26 mins 58
Candida	6 hrs 36 mins 2
White Heather II	6 hrs 53 mins 53
Cambria	7 hrs 1 mins 13

It will be seen from the table of results that, in beating to the westward along the Channel coastline, the course undoubtedly favoured the more weatherly vessels, with their inherent abilities to sustain the lively chop usually experienced off St Catherine's Point, the Atherfield Ledge, and, of course, entry to The Needles Passage.

Tuesday, August 13th, 1929 saw the Royal Thames Yacht Club's concluding events in the Ryde Regatta Week. There was a very light easterly wind at the start which appeared to be variable, but the breeze later became more pronounced in volume, settling to south-west.

The five cutters, *Lulworth, White Heather II, Shamrock, Cambria* and *Candida*, were joined by the schooner once more, to sail a course of forty-two sea miles for prizes of £80 (first), £50 (second) and £20 (third), making a 10 a.m. start.

It was a most uninspiring spectacle at the start, which took some minutes to get under way. The green-hulled cutter *Shamrock* crept over the line nearly a minute late, then came *Cambria* some 40 seconds later, next was *Lulworth* 2 minutes adrift, to be followed by *Candida* 3 minutes behind, and *White Heather* 4 mins 30 seconds in arrears.

Westward was seen to be struggling to achieve some 'way on', well in excess of five minutes astern, but her fortunes were destined to improve, as they would need to do for a vessel already sailing scratch, and then to become compounded by initial lateness penalties. Although *Shamrock* was first to cross, there was insufficient weight in the breeze for her to consolidate her position and, as she came about to indulge in some tacking manoeuvres, she lost ground ending up at the tail of the fleet. Dame Fortune had not forsaken her, however, as a freshening true breeze was first to strike her and she was able to retrieve the lead again, making progress on the reach to the Nab End buoy at the eastern mark of the course. With the wind conditions in which she revelled, the schooner profited in turn by the change of wind direction, shortening the distance to Sir Thomas Lipton's cutter. The two Bermudans were next in procession, followed by *White Heather* and *Lulworth*, set to challenge her white contemporary. Making the reach on the return in a westward direction, *Shamrock* was overhauled by the schooner which had an advantage of 1 minute 46 seconds over the former at the Ryde West Middle buoy, shortly to complete the first round. Meanwhile, *Lulworth*, with full canvas spread, was not to be left behind and improved her position, overtaking *Candida*, *White Heather II* and *Cambria* to attain third place. At this time *Westward* led *Lulworth* by 5 minutes 50 seconds, *Candida* 7 minutes 4 seconds, *White Heather II* 7 minutes 52 seconds, and *Cambria* 10 minutes 15 seconds.

At the end of the first round the timings were:

Westward	12 hrs 38 mins 37
Shamrock	12 hrs 41 mins 56
Lulworth	12 hrs 44 mins 28
Candida	12 hrs 45 mins 15
White Heather II	12 hrs 47 mins 14
Cambria	12 hrs 52 mins 52

During the second round, the positions remained unchanged, but *Westward* increased her lead to nearly ten minutes over *Shamrock*. The advantage of some two and a half minutes which *Shamrock* had held over *Lulworth* at the end of the first round was eroded to fifty seconds at the conclusion of the match: once again the schooner had been favoured by the wind direction. *Lulworth* had to be content with a third flag; a loss of two minutes at the start robbed her of a probable higher placing.

The actual and corrected timings were:

	Actual	Corrected
Westward (winner)	2 hrs 44 mins 28	2 hrs 44 mins 28
Shamrock (second)	2 hrs 54 mins 53	2 hrs 54 mins 11
Lulworth (third)	2 hrs 55 mins 53	2 hrs 55 mins 1
Candida	3 hrs 4 mins 5	2 hrs 59 mins 53
White Heather II	3 hrs 4 mins 14	3 hrs 3 mins 32
Cambria	3 hrs 9 mins 48	3 hrs 5 mins 15

The two day regatta under the sponsorship of the Royal Victoria Yacht Club opened at Ryde on Wednesday, August, 14th, 1929. Whilst the early morning skies did not appear to offer a great deal of promise, the threat of rain passed and the day was endowed with brilliant sunshine throughout. There was not sufficient wind to promote really spirited racing and the finishes were very late. The breeze, although lively at the start, came from the north-west and quickly eased.

The first event was sailed for the Ryde Town Cup, with second and third prizes of £30 and £10 respectively, for yachts exceeding twenty-one metres, over the forty-six mile long Victoria course. The six entries consisted of *Westward* scratch, allowing 46 secs to *Lulworth*, *White Heather II* and *Shamrock*, with *Candida* getting 4 minutes 36 seconds allowance and *Cambria* 5 minutes 45 seconds. A scarcely spectacular start was made from Ryde pier head, *Shamrock* crossing the line immediately after the gun was fired, with *Westward* on her weather. *Lulworth* and *White Heather II* lost some valuable time, each being some forty seconds late in getting away. *Cambria* came later whilst *Candida* was seventy seconds in deficit. *Lulworth* made up some time on the beat to the Ryde West Middle buoy, coming just astern of *Shamrock* as they rounded. *Westward* followed, leading *White Heather II* with *Cambria* and *Candida* behind. The yachts ran with spinnakers set to port as they turned the Outer Spit mark. From the Nab End mark it was a beat to complete round one; the times noted were:

Shamrock	2 hrs 15 mins 52
White Heather II	2 hrs 16 mins 36
Lulworth	2 hrs 18 mins 46
Westward	2 hrs 23 mins 55
Cambria	2 hrs 43 mins 46
Candida	2 hrs 46 mins 34

Protest flags were flown by *White Heather II*, *Cambria* and *Candida*, and the last-named retired after one round.

The race continued for a second round, which was rather unexpected, considering the times taken to cover twenty-three miles from a 10.45 a.m. start. An average speed of less than 6½ knots made by *Shamrock* was an indication of the paucity of air; also it was nearly 6 p.m. when the winning gun boomed from the pier head and the majority of spectators had forsaken the seafront to partake of high tea. (This often included strawberries and cream, crab, lobster or prawns.) No such luxuries were available to the crews, whose activities for a further two hours had to be centred on mooring and stowage of sails and gear. However, some compensation was later enjoyed by the convivial meetings of rival crews in the taprooms of The Royal Squadron Hotel or Yelf's Hotel, both of which remain in Ryde's Union Street.

During the second round *Lulworth* was seen to be fast making up her deficit behind the leaders to overtake *White Heather II* and challenge *Shamrock* for first place, but the emerald cutter's victory was not to be denied. Sir Thomas's *Shamrock* won the 'mug' with fifty-eight seconds to spare.

Actual and corrected times were:

	Actual	Corrected
Shamrock (cup)	5 hrs 57 mins 30	5 hrs 56 mins 44
Lulworth (second)	5 hrs 58 mins 28	5 hrs 57 mins 42
White Heather II (third)	6 hrs 1 mins 35	6 hrs 0 mins 49
Westward	6 hrs 17 mins 2	6 hrs 17 mins 2
Cambria	6 hrs 34 mins 5	6 hrs 28 mins 20

Clearly the schooner was disadvantaged on this day, sailing without her preferred wind direction; indeed, the scarce breeze had exercised the patience of all contestants.

Thursday, the concluding day of the 1929 Royal Victoria Yacht Club Regatta, though gloriously fine and sunny to provide ideal conditions for the ice cream and lemonade vendors, deprived the yachtsmen of air. Whatever wind could be discovered was extremely light and, as a consequence, the race was limited to only one round. The course was identical to that of the previous day. Although there did not seem to be any perceptible movement of air on the esplanade, the manoeuvres of the yachts indicated that a faint breeze might be coming from the north-west. An indication of the strength of the elements was confirmed by the winner taking some five hours to sail twenty-three sea miles (4.60 knots).

The race for yachts exceeding twenty-three metres was programmed for the RVYC International Gold Challenge Cup with £80 added as first prize, £30 second and £10 third. Competitors were Mr F. Davis's *Westward*, Mr A.A. Paton's *Lulworth*, Sir Thomas Lipton's *Shamrock*, Lord Waring's *White Heather II*, Mr H.K. Andreae's *Candida* and Lord Camrose's *Cambria*.

Westward sailed scratch to make time allowances of 46 seconds to *Lulworth*, *Shamrock* and *White Heather II*, *Candida* 4 minutes 36 seconds and *Cambria* 5 minutes 45 seconds, over a full two round distance.

The Bermudans, *Cambria* and *Candida*, led over the start line, closely followed in order by *Shamrock*, *White Heather II*, *Lulworth*, and the schooner *Westward*. A beat was progressed slowly to the western mark against a foul tide. Before rounding, a number of changes in position were seen. Progressing downwind to the eastward appeared more an effect of the tide than sailing. As the yachts passed Ryde pier the order was noted as *White Heather II*, *Candida*, *Cambria*, *Lulworth*, *Shamrock* and *Westward*.

Lulworth overtook *Candida* and *Cambria* as the fleet returned from the Nab End, but there was not enough wind for *White Heather II* to be seriously challenged. Whilst *Lulworth* took the second gun, she had an insufficient margin to claim second prize as *Candida* saved her time by 1½ minutes.

The finishing and corrected times were:

	Actual	Corrected
White Heather II (cup+£80)	3 hrs 45 mins 18	3 hrs 44 mins 55
Candida (2nd+£30)	3 hrs 48 mins 31	3 hrs 46 mins 13
Lulworth (3rd+£10)	3 hrs 48 mins 15	3 hrs 47 mins 52
Cambria	4 hrs 03 mins 43	3 hrs 57 mins 58
Shamrock	4 hrs 0 mins 46	4 hrs 0 mins 23
Westward	4 hrs 3 mins 6	4 hrs 3 mins 6

These records of the 1929 Solent Regatta events, outlining the relative performances of the big handicap class yachts, afforded Mr Paton an opportunity to reappraise his cutter's characteristically competitive edge, following the dismissal of the unbalanced handicap penalties suffered in his first year of ownership, and with Hogarth once more at the helm. Although one seagull does not make a summer, the related points tally for the 1929 Cowes–Ryde events provides a convincing testimony to *Lulworth*'s inherent challenging status. (The table is based upon four points for a first, two points for a second and one point for a third flag.)

	First	Second	Third	Points
Lulworth	3	1	4	18
Westward	3	0	1	13
White Heather II	1	3	1	11
Shamrock	1	3	1	11
Candida	1	2	1	9
Cambria	0	0	1	1

Meanwhile, the local results served to rekindle the enthusiasm of a lad whose association with the great cutter was decidedly remote, but she, nevertheless, remained a favourite to which he was entirely devoted.

---

[1] Unlike a twin screw steamer, with its built-in ability to select differential propeller rotations, a paddle steamer was severely lacking in manoeuvrability.

I remember crossing on one occasion from Portsmouth to Ryde in a fierce sou'west'r on the paddler *Southsea* when she had to make four successive attempts to berth at Ryde pier head, arriving twenty-five minutes late for the journey, which had the result of doubling the advertised crossing schedule.

1930

LULWORTH BOWS OUT WITH FLYING COLOURS

With royal patronage restored, the Cowes Regatta Week of 1930 regained its traditional atmosphere once more. The famed yachting festival was presided over by the royal yacht *Victoria and Albert*, which arrived well in advance of its programmed festivities to bring the King and Queen on Tuesday, July 29th to Cowes prior to the official yachting week. With the *V & A* and its company came the battleship *Warspite*, a sinister apparition of Britain's naval might, which had performed this duty in 1924, also the destroyer *Westminster* and the minesweeper *Albury*, tender to the royal cutter. Hundreds of floating palaces supported the event, strung out in tiers through the Solent stretching between Egypt Point on the western esplanade to Osborne Bay, limiting the eastern anchorage. To name but a very few, these vessels included the 2,220 ton steamer *Rover*, owned by Lord Inchcape, Lady Yule's 1600 ton turbine-powered yacht *Nahlin*, with smaller diesel-engined vessels such as Sir William Burton's *Calita* and Sir Gervase Beckett's *Romany Rye*. Acres of gaily coloured bunting displayed by so many ships provided a truly carnival titillation to delight the multitude of spectators.

The 1930 season was, in all probability, one of the greatest of first class cutter racing, with a maximum of seven yachts competing. There remained four representatives of the Beken Big Five with gaff rig (proudly defying the latest stark cult), the valiant cutters *Lulworth*, *Britannia* and *White Heather II*, plus the schooner *Westward*. In addition, there were the Bermudan--rigged cutters *Astra* and *Cambria*, which heralded the entry of yachts to the 1928 Second International Rule in that year, plus *Candida*, which joined the class in 1929. Prior to the Solent

Regatta fortnight, the assembly was used as a trial fleet for the latest Americas Cup challenger, *Shamrock V*, designed by Charles Nicholson for Sir Thomas Lipton and built to the American 'J' class rule with a Bermudan rig, known as the Universal Rating Rule of America, attributed to Herreshoff.

It has to be remembered that *Shamrock V* was the only 'J' class vessel in existence in the UK at that time (the summer of 1930) and that racing under 'J' class rules did not commence in these waters until 1931 and even then with only one purpose-built yacht competing with three conversions.

The record of *Shamrock V*'s performance in the 1930 trials is undeniably impressive, if somewhat distorted, bearing in mind the handicap penalty under which *Lulworth* sailed scratch (together with the schooner *Westward*, similarly rated). In spite of this built-in disadvantage, *Lulworth* succeeded in beating *Shamrock V*, winning on four occasions before the latter went to the USA. John Nicholson, in his book, *Great Years in Yachting*, recalls the inability of *Shamrock V* to outpoint *Lulworth* in a light wind when racing in the 1930 Clyde Regatta. He states that, whilst *Shamrock V* was "pretty fast off the wind", she was not "as good to win'ard as his father had hoped". The new Bermudan-rigged *Shamrock V* was seen on many occasions to be "tuning up" with the veterans of the big handicap class on Solent waters early in the 1930 yachting season. She subsequently made appearances in some coastal regattas before voyaging to the USA, escorted by Sir Thomas Lipton's palatial yacht *Erin II*, on which so many of his friends and acquaintances enjoyed the most generous entertainment. (*Erin II* was engined by three Parsons turbines; her former name was *Albion* when she was first launched in 1905.)

The yachting grocer was unavoidably conspicuous by his absence from the Cowes and Ryde Regattas this year, as his challenger had already departed for battle with the American Defender (*Enterprise*) in mid-September.

The once familiar sight of Sir Thomas's 23 metre *Shamrock* was sorely missed by followers of the Big Five in the 1930

Solent events. Her absence signalled the unhappy
disintegration of a fleet which had competed so bravely, making
up a most remarkable chapter in the history of British yacht
racing. *Shamrock*'s absence in 1930, like that of *Britannia*'s in
1929, obviously upset the balance of competition between the
established topsailed five.

Disregarding the anomalies created by handicap
arrangements of doubtful validity, 1930 was undeniably
Lulworth's season. Whilst *Shamrock V*, of a different class,
recorded more wins in her trials, *Lulworth*'s performance
relative to her established big class competitors was quite
outstanding, recording practically twice as many wins as any of
these. The schedule reads:

	Owner	No. of Starts	FLAGS		
			I	II	III
Lulworth	Mr A.A. Paton	45	11	6	5
Candida	Mr H. Andreae	35	5	9	7
Britannia	HM the King	26	5	4	1
White Heather II	Lord Waring	45	6	6	5
Cambria	Lord Camrose	49	2	14	5
Astra	Sir M. Singer	15	1	1	5
Westward	Mr T.B.F. Davis	14	5	2	3

It will be noted that *Cambria* made the maximum number of
possible starts, totalling forty-nine against *Lulworth*'s forty-five,
the latter missing four opportunities to race on account of a
collision and consequent repairs following the unhappy incident
when the twelve metre *Lucilla* tacked across her bows.

For Lord Waring, 1930 was the year when his business
interests took a severe setback following the 1929 Wall Street
Crash, resulting in *White Heather II* being placed on the sale
list at the end of the yachting season. It was not until the 1932
season that *White Heather II* was raced again under a new
owner, and then it was for just one season.

Sadly, Sir Mortimer Singer, the one-time owner of
Lulworth, took his own life in 1930. As a pioneer aviator, he
had suffered a crash damaging his spine, leaving him in almost
permanent pain, resulting in that most distressing of afflictions:
insomnia. His later yacht *Astra* (built by Charles Nicholson's
company in 1927) was subsequently purchased by Mr Hugh
Paul to compete in the 1931 season, following a brief period in
the hands of Sir Howard Frank.

The Singer Sewing Machine was one of the marvels of the
age, and practically ubiquitous – it was found in almost every
household before 'off the peg' garments became the norm. It is
a very sobering thought to realise that a gentleman such as Sir
Mortimer Singer, who enjoyed immense wealth, was to be
driven to an extreme of desperation by the 'poverty' of
insomnia.

In 1929/30 there was a college of trendily-minded exponents
of the sport, albeit those whose fortunes fell substantially short
of 'J' class yacht ownership, who were bitten by the cult of
getting together with the Americans in big class cutter racing.
This sounded undeniably – as it was – like the chorus of
idealists. The British policy had been to build yachts of lasting
quality and to periodically update them, adapting where
possible to suit the historic rule changes, but still maintaining
such traditional ornate features as gaff rig on the older vessels.
These big class yachts were all individually owned, maintained
to the highest UK standards and raced under handicap ratings,
if only suffering some imperfections in those respects.

For all the euphoria about getting together, this bluntly
meant that either Britain or American must 'call the tune'.
Furthermore, the American yachts would be built and raced by
wealthy syndicates, able to indulge in a 'throw-away' policy.
In 1930 we were committed by the YRA to the latest rule to be
adopted in this country, known as the 1929 International Rule;
and so with the impending fifth challenge for the Americas Cup
led by Sir Thomas Lipton, YRA representatives visited New

York to arrive at a mutually acceptable rule to establish nirvana in the yachting sphere.

The outcome was, of course, that the YRA had to reluctantly yield. The Americans insisted upon the establishment of their own 'Universal Rule' with the exception of a few minor concessions to the YRA. We accepted the American rule, which was adopted from the beginning of 1931. With *Lulworth*'s subsequent exclusion from continued competition, I felt at this time that an unforgivable error had been perpetrated. Here we were – with only Sir Thomas's *Shamrock V* being built to the American Universal Rule – with three truly beautiful gaffers (plus another in reserve) which had sustained the British sport for so long, together with three modern Bermudan competitors built to a recent but now extinct formula, facing exclusion from the big class. It was by no means certain that their owners would either be able, or willing, to bear the expense of 'near conversion' to the latest American rule. In any event, only a doubtful compromise could be reached.

History later instanced the fallacy of our acceptance at this time, for the one example of getting together was not made until the year 1935, with a single visit to England by the American cutter *Yankee*.

Furthermore, following the international economic repercussions of the Wall Street fiasco, it was hardly the time to be contemplating expensive and frivolous modifications to the big cutters when, more especially, the country was ominously sliding into a trade recession of no mean proportions, which was eventually remembered as the Great Depression.

However, despite the foundations internationally accepted for the new 'J' class, the final year of participation by *Lulworth* with the big cutters was for her a most eventful and remarkably successful one, although her misfortune in the 1930 Cowes Regatta probably robbed the topsailed cutter of an even greater score.

The time allowances given by *Lulworth* in 1930 to the Bermudans were: *Astra* 9.0 seconds per mile; *Cambria* 9.5

seconds per mile; *Candida* 8.5 seconds per mile; *Shamrock V* 5 seconds per mile.

Obviously the handicappers were, once again, being very unsympathetic to Mr Paton's *Lulworth*. One might have expected a 5 seconds per mile allowance to have been donated by *Shamrock V* because of her advanced technology, seeking balanced competition.

Mr Paton, a director of both the Liverpool and Martin's Bank and also the Royal Insurance Company, was obviously a very shrewd businessman and he came to the conclusion that the expense of converting *Lulworth* to comply with the American rule could not be justified.

The Universal Rule of America adopted by the UK from 1931 onwards was expressed:

$$\text{To establish a rating} = \frac{\text{LWL} \times \sqrt{S}}{\sqrt[3]{\text{displacement}}}$$

$$\text{LWL} = \text{Load Waterline Length}$$
$$S = \text{Sail area}$$

(Note: This rating assessment was never applied to *Lulworth* (ex-*Terpsichore*) as her racing career ended before the 'J' class was adopted in the UK.)

Whilst *Lulworth* was undoubtedly monopolising the contests towards the end of the 1930 coastal season, the Week at Cowes did absolutely nothing to contribute to her summer total of flags in the big handicap class. Her absence at the start line on the opening Monday and again on Tuesday (when she was entered with a gaggle of vessels with lesser tonnage for the King's Cup contest), in combination with her misfortunes on Wednesday, conspired to put her out of commission for the remainder of the 1930 Cowes Regatta. This seemed incredible for a lad whose sentiments were focused upon a repeated local demonstration of her leadership. However, her eventual outstanding tally of flags taken whilst competing at alternative coastal venues in the

1930 season handsomely compensated for the immediate local disappointment.

The Solent weather during Cowes Week sometimes rivalled the more frequent stormy conditions of the Clyde Regatta. Scarcely deterred by blustery conditions on occasions when sou'westers, oilskins and wellingtons, not forgetting umbrellas, dictated shoreside fashion, the yacht owners, in consideration of their crews and riggings, were seen to exercise a logical prudence – disappointing though it proved to spectators. An instance, which I recall, of decidedly 'dicey' conditions prevailed on Monday, the first day of the Week's racing fixtures. The weekend had certainly not lent much encouragement to the prospects for sport. The Royal Southampton Yacht Club's Regatta for the big cutters on Saturday preceding Cowes Regatta Week had already displayed bad omens for the most intrepid of yachtsmen. They had battled with a strong south-westerly breeze, sometimes gusting at storm force, fetching up a rough sea, whilst many of the competing yachts remained at their moorings. The Calshot event was certainly not very rewarding to those on shore. All yachts taking part had crossed the start line, reefed down, whilst *Britannia* was seen without her topsail; *White Heather II* and *Astra* did not start. *Lulworth* was withdrawn early in the race, as also was *Cambria*, leaving the seaworthy schooner *Westward* to take the honours, with *Britannia* coming second and *Cambria* a game third.

In light of Saturday's experience, Monday's race, programmed by the Royal London Yacht Club (starting from the Royal Yacht Squadron line), caused owners of the big class cutters to exhibit extreme caution, with only two vessels competing in the event for yachts over twenty-one metres rating. The general feeling must have been swayed by the possibility of an accident to crew or gear, putting a yacht out of action for the remainder of the week. Only *Westward* and *Candida* braved the start line whilst *Lulworth*, *White Heather II*, *Britannia*, *Astra* and *Cambria* remained at their moorings.

The contest between Mr Davis's schooner *Westward* and Mr Andreae's *Candida* was not exactly plain sailing. The mishaps which each of them suffered in all probability justified the reluctance of their contemporaries to take their places at the start. *Westward* retired after rounding the Solent Bank buoy on the wrong side, and was seen with a torn mainsail, just to compound her difficulties.

Candida's Bermudan mainsail had to be lowered following a split which rendered it useless. She continued with the substitution of a trysail and jib and was stopped at the end of the first round, being awarded the Cayley Memorial Challenge Cup together with the premier prize of £80.

Just to lend further confirmation of the ferocity of the elements on this day, my notes include an outline of the effect upon the handicap race for yachts of any rig between 40 and 110 tons TM. The prizes offered were £40, £20 and £10 for first, second and third flags respectively. There were five entries, but the owners of *Hispania*, *The Lady Anne, Nanette III* and *Dorina* considered discretion the better part of valour and forsook the start line. This left only Mr Hugh Paul's yawl *Sumurun* to take the 10.15 a.m. starting gun. She was promptly away, with a skeleton rig reduced to a couple of headsails plus mizzen. Making one round of the sixteen mile course (West Lepe, Calshot Bell Float and Ryde S-E Middle buoys) the winning gun was fired for her at 12 hr 50 min 28 secs to take first prize for a sail over. Despite her drastically reduced canvas, she made an average of approximately 6.20 knots for the course, assisted by the truly ferocious blow.

The race for the King's Cup was held as usual on the Tuesday of Cowes Week, attracting nearly twenty entries from yachts of widespread tonnage. This was, of course, an extraordinarily large fleet of contestants which included only two of the first class yachts, namely *Lulworth* (which had previously been victorious in the races for the sovereign's trophies at Cowes in 1925 and on the Clyde in 1928) and Lord Camrose's *Cambria*, of 1928 vintage.

Other entrants of smaller tonnage which had previously won the royal cup were *Coral* (1926 and 1928), *Rona* (1927), *Moonbeam* (1920 and 1923) and *Cariad* (1905, 1910, 1912, 1921 and 1929).

The field was complemented by a number of smaller yachts, some of which were *Pretty Polly, Celia, Cetonia, Adastra, Elk, Jolie Brise, Amasis, Rosemary IV, Varuna* and *Carlotta.*

With the exception of *Carlotta, Varuna* and *Elk*, which were gallantly struggling to cross the start line, the majority of contestants made an excellent showing against a strong current.

Cambria was first over the line, followed in order by *Lulworth* to windward of her, with *Rosemary IV, Pretty Polly, Adastra, Cetonia, Jolie Brise, Cariad, Coral, Amasis, Carlotta* and *Rona* following in that order. Some sixteen minutes later *Celia* crossed the line while *Varuna* was twenty-four minutes late and *Elk* last over, nearly forty-two minutes adrift!

Fortunately the wind strengthened, blowing from the sou'west, as the fleet headed in a beat to the East Lepe buoy with *Lulworth* in her element, taking the lead to display once more her windward edge. *Cambria* was enjoying a freshening breeze and upholding the honour of the giant class, not far astern, both cutters battling with the incoming tide. The skipper of each of these yachts was patently aware of the need to work out a substantial lead over the brave challengers of lesser tonnage (as the time allowances given were more than generous) if there was to be any prospect of a gun at the finish. Of course, the handicappers were unlikely to put themselves in a position whereby they might be accused of favouring competitors from the big handicap class. Indeed, the intention behind the race was to extend an opportunity to the widest range of challengers.

It was practically a broad reach back from the East Lepe buoy with *Cambria* only a couple of minutes behind *Lulworth*, both of which appeared from the esplanade to be sailing at near ultimate speed, assisted by the flooding tide. *Lulworth* appeared no sooner in sight than out of it, on her way to the

Warner lightship at the far eastern mark of the course. *Moonbeam IV* followed *Cambria* quite closely, sailing remarkably well. Next came the ketch *Cariad* with *Pretty Polly* in fifth place.

At the end of the first round *Lulworth*, although still showing the way, was just 3 mins 33 secs ahead of *Cambria*, whilst *Cariad* came third, only 10 mins later and *Moonbeam IV* was in fourth place, approximately 9 mins later still. When the tide ebbed from Southampton Water the rates of progress eased appreciably as the yachts made a return from the Warner.

It seemed unlikely at this stage that either of the big class yachts could possibly take the Cup, as their margins over half the course were ominously insufficient and on reflection it is doubtful whether such a hypothetical result would have proven strictly popular. However, to borrow some eloquent lines:

And it's not for the sake of a ribboned coat [burgee],
Or the selfish hope of a season's fame....
Play up! play up! and play the game!

The majority of the yachts gave up before the end of the final round with *Varuna* and *Carlotta* leaving at the end of the first. In the circumstances the results at the end of the first round serve to indicate relative dispositions midway as follows:

Lulworth	Mr A.A. Paton	12 hr	24 min	12
Cambria	Lord Camrose	12	27	55
Cariad	Col. Rt Hon. J. Gretton	12	34	47
Moonbeam IV	Mr H.C. Sutton	12	40	36
Cetonia	Lord Stalbridge	12	45	52
Pretty Polly	Mr T.K. Laidlaw	1	3	8
Coral	Mr F. Chaplin	1	3	57
Adastra	Sir W.H. Dyke–Acland	1	10	39
Rona	Mr W.D. Clark	1	11	3
Celia	Marquess of Northampton	1	13	45
Elk	Lord Glentenar	1	14	33

Jolie Brise	R. & H.C. Somerset	1	20	40
Amasis	{Col. G.R. Newton	1	25	35
	{Capt. A. Leach			
Rosemary IV	Major Gen. P.T. Fielding	1	29	15
Carlotta	Lt. Col. H. & H.C. Guest	—	—	—

During the second round *Lulworth* substantially increased her lead over the rest of the fleet, taking the first gun with just over half an hour to spare from *Cariad*. Although from shoreside observations it appeared that *Lulworth*, with wind on the beam and a fair tide for much of the distance, had never noticeably sailed faster, Col. Gretton's magnificent old 1905 ketch *Cariad*, favoured by similar conditions, took the honours essentially by receiving a luxurious time allowance of some sixty seconds per mile. And so in corrected paper terminology *Cariad* had won the royal vase by saving over a quarter of an hour from *Lulworth*. In retrospect it is felt that the handicappers probably included in their guesswork a prospect of extended windward sailing. It is significant, when comparing time differentials between the first yacht home and the race winner, that some ten minutes separated them after the first round and thirty minutes by the second. This difference was probably due to a shift in wind direction and gathering intensity.

Honour had been satisfied with Col. Gretton's *Cariad* steered by Sir Hercules Langrishe, Bart, taking the King's Cup (for *Cariad*'s sixth time) and to a lesser degree by Mr Alexander Paton's *Lulworth*, whose helmsman, Captain Hogarth, had given such a convincing demonstration of pace-setting. *Lulworth* covered the forty-six mile Queen's course in 4 hours 32 mins, averaging a speed of 10.15 knots. *Cambria*'s finishing time was not announced.

The actual and corrected finishing times recorded for the first four competing yachts were as follows:

	Actual	Corrected
Lulworth (second)	2 hrs 32 mins 25	2 hrs 32 mins 25
Cariad (cup)	3 hrs 3 mins 11	2 hrs 17 mins 11
Moonbeam IV	3 hrs 19 mins 47	2 hrs 44 mins 41
Pretty Polly	4 hrs 35 mins 9	2 hrs 55 mins 32

The second race of the day was a handicap for yachts between twenty-one and twenty-four metres for prizes of £80, £20 and £10 which started fifteen minutes after the King's Cup event. But for the latter preoccupations, *Lulworth* and *Cambria* would normally have been competing with their class. The course of forty miles was twice round the Solent Bank, N-E Middle and S-E Middle buoys. The race was won by *Westward* with favourable reaching conditions, the others finishing in the order of *Candida*, *Astra*, *Britannia* and *White Heather*.

The twelve metre class made a start at 10.30 a.m., being third to get under way. It was a great day for Mr J.L. Lewis's *Lucilla* (newly designed and launched by Charles Nicholson) which proved an easy winner, in contrast to the misfortune which awaited her the next day.

On the Wednesday following, August 6th, I was bathing offshore from Old Castle Point, on the eastern side of the Medina Estuary, when my eyes focused upon *Lulworth*, which was duelling with the schooner *Westward* in the vicinity of the Prince Consort to Castle Point buoys and I witnessed what subsequently proved to be a tragic event. The scene was confused, with a gaggle of twelve metre yachts dicing in the fairway, when the sound of a hoarse and agitated jumble of voices carried over the waters to concentrate my attention, followed by a sharp cracking noise. I could scarcely admit to myself that *Lulworth* had made an abrupt deceleration as I saw one of the twelve metre vessels had become entangled with her bowsprit. Minus a spyglass at the time, I must confess that the scene made little sense, but it transpired that the twelve metre yacht was the *Lucilla* owned by Mr J.L. Lewis, winner of the previous day's twelve metre class.

Whilst I have to declare an inability to appreciate the details of this entanglement from my vantage point at that moment, a fuller explanation was to be derived later. The big handicap class yachts of the over twenty-one metre class were on the return leg from the westward mark on a broad reach with full canvas set to the Warner lightship. *Lulworth* was sailing close inshore in tight formation with *Astra*, *Cambria* and *Westward*. Mr J. Lauriston Lewis's twelve metre *Lucilla* was making for the line on the starboard tack, about to start her race in a westerly direction when she crossed *Lulworth*'s bows; Captain Hogarth was unable to anticipate the situation. Luckless[1] Archie, duty-bound to the helm of his charge, was powerless to frustrate the thrust of something close to one million pounds feet of kinetic energy and was carried forward on a bearing of immediate disaster. *Lucilla* was dragged for quite a distance until *Lulworth*'s progress was finally arrested. The first signs were that it might not be a very serious matter, but *Lulworth* immediately lowered headsails and turned to check her speed in order to lower a rescue dinghy. *Lulworth*'s steel martingale had pierced the hull of *Lucilla*, which rapidly took in water. Meanwhile, *Lucilla*'s crew, with the exception of one man, had clambered on to *Lulworth*'s bowsprit whiskers just before the yachts became separated. *Lucilla*'s damage was so serious that she began to sink and she went down in the deep water of the fairway some five minutes later. It was originally thought that the seven members of *Lucilla*'s company had been rescued, but unhappily, the steward, Mr William Saunders of Burnham-on-Crouch had received a severe blow to the head at the moment of impact, was thrown overboard and drowned before a nearby motor boat belonging to Sir Charles Allom could reach him.

The starting gun for the twelve metre class was fired about thirty seconds after the collision occurred, but the five remaining contestants immediately gave up and flags were lowered to half-mast in sympathy, as news of the fatality became known.

Lulworth could do no more but down sails and retire from the contest with dipped burgee.

The thirty-seven year old *Britannia* went on to win her two hundredth lifetime victory on a day which would ordinarily have been one of great rejoicing had it not been blemished by such a tragedy.

Mr Paton and Mr Lewis were called in by the sailing committee and they were told that it would be required to hold an inquest. The committee would have to postpone requests for statements, the matter being *sub judice*, although they wished to ask Mr Paton whether he would abstain from racing *Lulworth* under Captain Hogarth until the inquest was completed. Mr Paton considered his skipper to be blameless and he felt unable to agree to such an undertaking without prejudicing Captain Hogarth's position. Mr Lewis suggested that a distinction might be drawn to give smaller yachts a priority over the larger ones, so that the big yachts should give way to the smaller. The answer was that the whole question had to be governed by the 'Rule of the Road', plus the YRA rules.

There was quite obviously nothing which *Lulworth*'s skipper could have done to avoid the tragedy, and Captain Hogarth was completely exonerated. With due consideration to the potential danger in later regattas, all yachts over eight metres were required to pass north of the mark boat, except when starting and finishing.

Lulworth was towed to Camper & Nicholson's Southampton yard for inspection and repairs the same day. On the following day a tugboat arrived at the scene of the disaster and made the necessary preparations to raise the damaged yacht *Lucilla* from the seabed, since she was a likely obstacle to navigation.

A subscription list to provide immediate assistance to the Saunders family (a widow and five children), headed by the King and Queen, was generously supported by members of the Royal Yacht Squadron.

Following repairs to *Lulworth* after her unhappy experience at Cowes, she rejoined the class to compete in the Royal Victoria Yacht Club's fixtures at Ryde. The racing was limited to two days, as the Royal Thames Yacht Club had held its normal regatta earlier in July. *Lulworth* did not find much to celebrate on the first day, Monday, August 11th, 1930, even though she participated in a match which she sailed for the King George V Cup. This was a trophy for yachts of twenty-one metres rating and over – a new cup which he had donated (the late Queen Victoria gave four cups between the years 1852 and 1895). The King's own cutter, *Britannia*, did not compete and, whilst *White Heather II* was entered, she did not appear at the start line. Joining *Lulworth* at the start were *Astra* (then owned by Sir Howard Frank, GBE, KCB), *Cambria* (Lord Camrose), *Westward* (Mr F.T.B. Davis) and *Candida* (Mr H.K. Andreae). A stiff south-westerly breeze was blowing and the yachts were programmed to sail a course of forty-six miles eastwards, twice round the Nab End Gas, Outer Spit and West Middle buoys. The schooner *Westward* and *Lulworth* were tied scratch (as if to remind the latter of the agonies suffered in the 1928 season), allowing *Candida* 6 mins 31 secs, *Astra* 6 mins 54 secs and *Cambria* 7 mins 17 secs. All yachts were reefed and both *Lulworth* and *Westward* set jib headers over shortened mainsails.

Candida was first away, followed by *Lulworth*. *Cambria* was recalled, to be turned around within a few seconds. *Astra* and *Westward* were over two minutes late in getting away. After passing the Noman fort, spinnakers were set to starboard by all contestants. *Lulworth* raced to the lead with *Astra* and *Westward* following, each having overtaken *Candida* and *Cambria*. At the end of the first round *Lulworth* was still in the van, having made best use of a broad reach. The noted times at the end of the first round were:

Lulworth leading *Westward* by 2 mins 53 secs
    "   "   *Astra*   by 4 mins 57 secs

"	"	*Candida*	by 7 mins 7 secs
"	"	*Cambria*	by 8 mins 31 secs

With a modicum of luck it seemed that *Lulworth* was strongly placed to take the Cup, for she had been sailing well, but fate struck a cruel blow when her mainsail failed, splitting into ribbons. This left her no option but to retire; the ghost of *Terpsichore* wickedly haunted her still. Her Solent fortnight seemed overshadowed with the spectre of persistent frustration. *Cambria* was steadily left further behind and also retired, her skipper feeling that it was futile to continue in such conditions. This meant that the two Bermudans, *Astra*, of 1928, and *Candida*, of 1929 vintage, were left to battle out the honours with the 1910 Herreshoff schooner. *Westward* easily took the Cup, claiming the gun by a margin of 5 mins 3 secs over *Astra*. The corrected finishing results were:

Westward	3 hrs 12 mins 14
Astra	3 hrs 17 mins 17
Candida	3 hrs 17 mins 41

With only twenty-four seconds separating them at the finish (on corrected time), *Candida* and *Astra* had enjoyed a most memorable struggle.

Racing on Tuesday, August 12th 1930, the second and final day of the RVYC Regatta, brought my boyhood observations of *Lulworth*'s illustrious competitive career to an end, but not without some consolation.

Dame Nature played havoc with the climatic conditions, firstly by producing a typical textbook day, with King Sol smiling down from the heavens, backed up by a fresh north-westerly breeze. (This was a local direction of wind which one grew to traditionally respect over Solent waters.) These conditions were enjoyed practically to the moment of firing the get ready signal when a sudden squall emerged from nowhere, accompanied by heavy rain which gave rise to temporary blindness. The crowds on shore ran for cover, if they could find it, and those armed with umbrellas did not dare to unfold them. The skippers' 'feel' for judging the start line was swamped in the mist, there being no scope for the usual sighting of landmarks.

The course of forty-six miles heading west was sailed by all the big cutters, including Mr A.A. Paton's *Lulworth*, HM the King's *Britannia*, Lord Waring's *White Heather II*, Sir Howard Frank's *Astra*, Lord Camrose's *Cambria* and Mr H.K. Andreae's *Candida*. Mr Davis had a private and undisclosed reason for not entering *Westward*, reputedly never raced on the 12th August. (He could, of course, have been preoccupied with grouse shooting!) The race for the RVYC International Gold Challenge Cup had previously been won by *Lulworth* in the year 1926. On this occasion *Lulworth* sailed scratch to allow *Britannia* and *White Heather II* 1 min 32 secs, *Candida* 6 mins 31 secs, *Astra* 6 mins 54 secs and *Cambria* 7 mins 17 secs for the full two rounds.

As the starting gun was fired *White Heather* took the lead, but was scarcely visible from the shoreside. She was followed by *Astra*, *Britannia* and *Lulworth* in order. *Cambria* and *Candida* were over the line as the Blue Peter came down and were recalled to make a fresh start in that sequence. *Cambria* had the distinction of a reefed mainsail. *Lulworth*, in dashing form with a reserve mainsail, took the lead early in the first round, closely shadowed by *Britannia*. The times taken at the end of the first round read:

Lulworth	1 hr 20 mins 22
Britannia	1 hr 22 mins 7
White Heather II	1 hr 24 mins 5
Astra	1 hr 26 mins 18
Cambria	1 hr 28 mins 40
Candida	1 hr 29 mins 4

Nearing the end of the second round, *Lulworth* was seen to stretch her lead over *Britannia*, 4 mins 20 secs separating them. *Astra* was a further four minutes or so astern. The corrected times, however, found the royal cutter in third position, *Astra* having narrowly saved her time to enjoy second place. And so *Lulworth* performed an encore by winning the Royal Victoria Yacht Club International Gold Challenge Cup once more "and modestly shrugged off the distinction of sailing scratch in the process".

The actual and corrected finishing times recorded for the leaders were:

	Actual	Corrected
Lulworth	3 hrs 58 mins 13	3 hrs 58 mins 13
Astra	4 hrs 7 mins 24	4 hrs 0 mins 30
Britannia	4 hrs 2 mins 33	4 hrs 1 mins 1
Cambria	4 hrs 11 mins 54	4 hrs 4 mins 37
Candida	—	—
White Heather II	—	—

Although at that time I had no inkling of *Lulworth*'s programmed retirement from the sport at the end of the 1930 season, this was the last race in which I glimpsed her participation.

It was, of course, by no means the last race in which *Lulworth* competed, as she sailed on to the West Country regattas; I had no opportunity to witness these but remained drenched in all the magic I had enjoyed from the shores of my immediate environment through the decade.

The result of this race remains for the narrator a fulfilment of a lad's devotion in following the great white cutter's fortunes, which stole so many hours of his daydreams.

It is felt that the *Lucilla* incident probably contributed to a lessening of Mr Paton's enthusiasm for the sport, added to more obvious financial considerations, which together resulted in the final decision to lay up his most successful yacht at the end of the 1930 calendar. *Lulworth* finished the season (and her career) with a proud display of prize flags fluttering from masthead truck to taffrail. These emblems, which signalled the collective seasonal 1930 successes of Mr Paton's great cutter, portrayed a truly dramatic finale, when she revisited her Cowes mooring at the close of the 1930 season. That triumphant galaxy of bright red stars etched upon pale blue bunting spelled the prestige of a valiant cutter defying her undeserved rejection. There could scarcely have been a better way to make an exit than "to score practically twice as many wins for the season than any one of her contemporaries".

Whilst my narrative confesses an unashamedly sentimental bias in *Lulworth*'s favour, balanced against rare evidence and memories, it is undeniable that her aggregate performance record spells out its own story without any literary embellishments, while she was competing with the cream of first-class opposition. For *Lulworth*, September 1930 was in consequence the end of the road. After numerous struggles throughout an eventful decade of racing, this beautiful cutter was destined to race no more. *Lulworth* went on the sale list, having rendered a melodious swansong in leading her older rivals, the cutters *Britannia* and *White Heather II*, as well as the newer Bermudans, *Astra, Cambria, Candida*.

(Of the gaffers only *Britannia* suffered the indignity of conversion to present an unfamiliar and, indeed, a virtually absurd reappearance in Bermudan guise for the next season, after thirty-seven years of topsailed apparel. Quite apart from a change of rig, she was, of course, outside the constraints of 'J' class rulings and had to be accorded a fictitious rating for her inclusion. Additionally, the Bermudans *Astra* and *Candida* were subjected to hull modifications in order to comply with the American Universal Rule. They were not 'J' class yachts, although these outsiders subscribed to the pretence with the aid of some 'botched-up' handicap concessions.)

The virtues of high aspect ratio rigs for the big cutters had taken more than a decade to become accepted. Indeed, Charles Nicholson had pointed the way in the conversion of *Nyria* in 1921, but it is arguable that a Bermudan mainsail presents a stark utilitarian appearance in aesthetic comparison with the once traditional topsailed/gaff mainsail combination.

The classic 'soap opera' had seen its final curtain and, in retrospect, I have to confess to one of the most severe pangs of youthful development when I was so deprived of my dreams. It is difficult, if not literally impossible, to convey what proved a most traumatic experience – having to accept an abrupt end to something deeper than a persistent boyhood fantasy. The summer props of my youth had been ruthlessly snatched away and so in my teens I had been 'press-ganged' into growing-up.

Sic tempora et naves mutantur (thus do times and ships change).

---

[1] This figure has been approximated using the established formula for kinetic energy, accepted as $\dfrac{W \times V^2}{2g}$, and taking the Lloyds avoirdupois gross tonnage for the yacht as 123 or 275,520 pounds, together with a likely forward speed of nine knots (or 15 feet per second). Any influences of tide and skin drag have been neglected.

PART IV

PERFORMANCE TABLES

The building of *Terpsichore* extended far into the 1920 yachting season and, whilst she managed just four appearances at the start line, the post-war challenger was plagued by a series of faults in her spars and rigging. These could have been largely attributed to the haste with which the yacht was finally completed, revealing some teething troubles which would normally have received attention before competing in any races. In fact, *Terpsichore* was not even approaching her targeted specification until the spring of 1921 and, even then, the hand of that legendary yacht designer, Charles Nicholson, had to be called upon to add further design improvements, which were again severely limited in 1922 by both the inadequacy of appropriate competition and of suitable seasonal club racing fixtures. Her early development was extraordinarily prolonged by a variety of influences.

It was not until 1924 that four comparable topsailed cutters, *Lulworth*, *Shamrock*, *White Heather II* and *Britannia*, came together to form an established post-war nucleus of the first class; later joined by the schooner *Westward* in 1925, which sailed with these single stickers until 1930. In order to attempt a rational assessment of relative overall racing successes for the giant yachts, it can only be prudent to disregard the earlier seasons of the Twenties and focus attention upon the period 1924-1930 inclusive to define a relatively consistent assembly which eventually became known as The Big Five. Unfortunately, *Nyria* dropped out of competition in 1923 and the Bermudans *Astra*, *Cambria* and *Candida* (all, incidentally, of lower ratings) did not arrive on the scene until much later. Their seasonal performance figures are shown in comparison, although distinct from the gaffers.

It will be noted that these performance assessments are a function of flags proportionate to the total of races entered for each vessel, using four points for a first flag, two points for a second and one point for a third. The fact that certain members of the class were laid up for some seasons does not, therefore, constitute any penalty in overall performance for each of the seven consecutive seasons as considered.

Although this formula was generally conceded to be a fair measure of comparative seasonal accomplishment, it can only reflect some evidence for cases where a reasonably large number of contests were sailed through a particular calendar, otherwise it is scarcely logical. The point can be simply demonstrated by taking an extreme theoretical case where a race might have been won in the event of a year's single entry. It would then be suggested that the vessel under consideration had demonstrated an immaculate performance by achieving an unrivalled top score of $\frac{4}{1} = 4.0$!

A fulfilment of the illustration is extremely improbable but not, of course, impossible. However, a specimen of the trend for a typical calendar is exemplified in *Astra*'s 1929 seasonal figure, using a literal acceptance of the formula, when she was able to claim an unlikely top score from only eight starts to achieve a performance figure of 2.50, and the best contemporary result was just 1.425 for 40 starts. (*Astra*'s 1930 figure dropped to a mere .73, making fifteen starts, but this is not claimed to have any particular relevance to her score of the earlier year.)

Whilst the following computation is based upon the number of 'starts', there were several occasions when one or other of the competitors gave up due perhaps to the loss of a man overboard,[1] a dismasting, collision, running aground, gear failure, insufficient wind, stormy conditions, exaggerated handicap rating, late start etc., all of which would have had considerable influence upon the final results as tabulated. However, such effects can only be categorised as 'good or ill luck' and it would be futile to make any attempt to bring contingencies of this sort into related performances.

In consequence, the analyses should not be taken too literally, although they are the best which can be presented using the figures from the table of results (page 318) for the Big Five competing yachts during the 1924 to 1930 seasons (inclusive) and, presenting *Lulworth* as an example, a 'points for flag' summary becomes:

51	first flags	x 4 points =	204	
47	second flags	x 2 points =	94	
25	third flags	x 1 point =	25	
		Total	323 points	

Taking the above figure and dividing by the total number of starts, a performance relationship of $\frac{323}{214} = 1.51$ is established.

By repeating the process, we arrive at figures for the flotilla during this period, reading as follows:

BUILT		ENTRIES	YACHT	RIG	PERF. FIG.
1908		{169	*Shamrock*	topsail cutter	1.59
1920	The	{214	*Lulworth*	" "	1.51
1907	Big	{243	*White Heather II*	" "	1.42
1910	Five	{132	*Westward*	schooner	1.39
1893		{162	*Britannia*	topsail cutter	1.36
1929		64	*Candida*	Bermudan	1.36
1928		49	*Astra*	"	1.27
1928		124	*Cambria*	"	0.82

It will be noted that the 154 ton TM schooner *Susanne* has not been listed in view of her few irregular appearances at the starting lines and, further, the little schooner met with only limited success during the 1924-30 period. On the occasions when *Susanne* participated in Cowes or Ryde Weeks, her presence undoubtedly lent a most welcome embellishment to the scene. The omission does not overlook the sporting spirit of the yacht's company. Like *Westward*, the smaller schooner presented a truly magnificent sight.

Susanne's one outstanding success which springs to mind was undoubtedly the winning of HM King George V's Cup on August 12th, 1925, in a handicap race for yachts of thirty-five tons TM upwards, which was organised by the Royal Thames Yacht Club Regatta, and which entailed circling the Wight from Ryde.

This is recounted on page 211. Despite the prejudicial handicaps of the 1927-1928 seasons suffered by *Lulworth* and the agonising misfortunes of the *Terpsichore* period of 1921-1923, her inclusive overall records considered either for the 1921-1930 decade, or the 1924-1930 Big Five era, with its relatively consistent opposition, describe a brilliant canvas to substantially claim first-class honours.

A glance at the related schedules for top seasonal successes shows:

Seasons Entered	Yacht	1921-1930 (The Decade) seasons	1924-1930 (Big Five Era) seasons	No. of Races Sailed (total)
10	*Lulworth*	4	3	247
8	*Britannia*	2	1	216
8	*White Heather II*	1	1	267
6	*Shamrock* *	2	2	169
6	*Westward*	—	—	132
2	*Nyria*	1	—	60

* The figures include the benefit of the 23 metre *Shamrock*'s 1929 performance, which might arguably have been accorded to the new Bermudan cutter *Astra* (see page 246).

Although the 23 metre *Shamrock* was not an actual challenger for the Americas Cup contests, she crossed to the States in 1920 as a trial horse for the 'tuning-up' of *Shamrock IV*, which had been laid up across the 'herring pond' since

1914. The 23 metre *Shamrock* was sailed across under jury yawl rig by Alf Diaper as skipper, supported by Jim Gilbey (an Emsworth ex-fisherman) as first mate, and Alf's brother Tom as second mate. Some very rough weather was encountered early on, necessitating a return to Dartmouth for repairs. A reference to the Diaper family will be found in endnote 2 on page 141. Without any time allowances being invented for the contests between *Shamrock IV* and the 23 metre *Shamrock*, both sailing on level terms, the cup challenger managed to win only three out of the five trial races which they sailed in the USA.

The 23 metre *Shamrock* of 1908 vintage was not represented in the 1930 big handicap class after performing so commendably in the 1924-1929 regattas. Her owner, Sir Thomas Lipton, utilised his place in the 1930 fleet to establish the worthiness of his last challenger and first British 'J' class yacht *Shamrock V*, to make his final bid for the Americas Cup before she left British waters to battle unsuccessfully with *Enterprise* in the States.

For purposes of performance comparisons *Shamrock V* cannot be sensibly substituted to fill the place of the 23 metre *Shamrock* for the 1930 season whilst considering 'yachts versus yachts'. However, the 1908 version made an indelible mark on the class during the six years in which she competed as one of the Big Five.

I have to say that I always regarded the 23 metre *Shamrock* and *Lulworth* as perfect foils for each other and the comparative performance figures of 1.59 for *Shamrock*, sailing fewer races, against 1.51 for *Lulworth*, at the upper end of the table, suggest a measure of confirmation for my observations during the 1924-1929 period.

Their eligibility to claim positions at the top is further underlined by the maximum seasonal records of thirteen first flags won by *Lulworth* in 1926, tying with *Shamrock*'s total of thirteen firsts in 1928, showing individual performance figures for these two seasons of 2.24 for *Lulworth* and 2.09 for *Shamrock*, when the latter made more starts to show a lower related performance figure. *Lulworth*'s seasonal 'points for flags related to starts record' of 1926 was unequalled by her contemporary cutters during the Big Five era.

In attempting to make a rational assessment of the relative merits of these two yachts during the 1924-1930 period, it has to be reiterated that the re-rating which took place under the 1927/28 rule caused *Lulworth* to become severely overtaxed as she had to allow *Shamrock* a time allowance of 9 seconds per mile, or 6 mins 45 secs over a typical forty-five mile course. *Lulworth*'s competitive chances were obviously deliberately and dramatically diminished at that time. Bearing in mind the masterful status which *Lulworth* demonstrated in the 1925 and 1926 seasons, when sailing on level terms with the big cutters, it can scarcely be denied that *Lulworth* was far too heavily penalised, in the 1928 season particularly. Her allotted status of sailing scratch in parallel with the schooner, thereby forfeiting generous time allowances to her topsailed compatriots, might have been taken as a compliment, but to reduce her ability under such handicaps until she could do no more than manage two first flags in twenty-nine starts was less than judicious on the part of the handicappers. Some further comments with respect to the persecution of *Lulworth* 1927-1928 are highlighted in the next chapter 'Rules, Reckonings and Records'.

Third place in the 1924-1930 Big Five series with a very creditable performance figure of 1.42 was established by *White Heather II*. She demonstrated a very consistent record of first flags for the seven seasons, at the same time making the highest aggregate of starts (243), ranging between nineteen in 1924 to forty-five in the year 1930. Like the cutter *Shamrock*, the benefit of an exaggerated 9 secs/mile bonus was allowed *White Heather II* in the year 1928 by *Lulworth*, following their racing on level terms in 1925/26. *White Heather II* took the class honours in 1924 sailing without added competition from the schooner.

The 1910 schooner *Westward*, built by Herreshoff in the USA, with so many successful race entries pre-1914, enlarged the class to five yachts in 1925. Sailing with small time concessions to the cutters, *Westward* made a conspicuous debut into the assembly of first-class yachts, not only on account of her great display of canvas whilst leading the beauty contest, but by taking eight first prizes in the 1925 season from twenty-nine starts. The effect of the re-rating changes is evident in *Westward*'s gaining of only three first prizes for twenty-two starts in the 1928 regattas. The entry of *Astra* and *Cambria* to the class that year further conspired to stiffen the opposition, with their substantial handicap benefits. *Westward* made progressively fewer annual entries over the seven years, with a minimum of fourteen in the year 1930. It was said that HM King George V expressed an anxiety on one occasion, when discussing improvements to *Britannia*, saying, "She must be able to beat that damned schooner!" The performance figure of 1.39 for *Westward* is only marginally better than 1.36 for the royal cutter. These two yachts enjoyed many a dogfight to the point where, on one singular occasion, *Westward* and *Britannia* finished the race with the committee declaring a dead heat. *Britannia*, like her contemporary cutters, was always conspicuously disadvantaged when the schooner was favoured by a beam wind for the greater distance.

Bearing in mind the inherent windward disadvantage with a double sticker both in pointing and manoeuvrability, Alf Diaper, as skipper of *Westward*, rendered Mr Davis a truly gold-plated service.

Of *Britannia* there is scarcely any need to attempt further comment, as her illustrious story over forty-three years has been most ably described elsewhere by a number of distinguished narrators. During the years of association with the Big Five, the grand old cutter topped the bill for one season, in 1927 – incidentally at the age of thirty-four years. It is only fair to remember the illness of the sovereign in 1929 as a cause of *Britannia*'s inability to take her place with the ensemble in that season and the possible effect of her absence is a subject for conjecture. Despite her age, she proved a formidable competitor during the Twenties in the hands of Major Hunloke, particularly in the heaviest of blows.

---

[1] A Y.R.A. ruling insisted upon a competing yacht's dinghy, cutter or gig to be inverted and securely lashed down before commencement of a race. Obviously, whilst in compliance with this requirement, the lashing had to be 100% secure but knotted to facilitate immediate parting in an emergency. On one occasion during a West Country Regatta in 1930, a member of *Lulworth*'s crew was washed overboard. The 'Lifeboat' became launched within sixteen seconds to pick up the seaman, who was ringed with a lifebelt tossed to him by an alert shipmate.

RULES, RECKONINGS AND RECORDS

In perusing compilations of records for the big handicap class during the Twenties, it is patently obvious (taking the figures at their face value) that the sailing qualities of the first five of these vessels have an uncanny similarity under average conditions. This is particularly so bearing in mind the effects of shoals, tides and eddies, plus the varying directions and intensities of winds experienced in such a variety of venues as Harwich, the Thames Estuary, the Solent and South-Western regattas, the Clyde, Belfast Lough etc. Their skippers were all 'out of the top locker' and, whilst their tactics varied, the results shown by the achievement of flags suggest a relatively even balance of sailing talents, including the successful deployment of crews. Although there was a vast difference in their formal education levels, they were all first and foremost 'men of the sea', taught in the same hard school of experience and reaching comparable passing-out standards.

Lulworth (ex-*Terpsichore*) was afflicted with more changes of ownership than her contemporaries: she was originally owned by Mr Lee 1920-1923 and, following his demise, was purchased by Mr Weld–Blundell to race in 1924-25, next passing into the hands of Sir Mortimer Singer for the 1926-27 seasons and later to the ownership of Mr Alexander Paton 1928-1930. It seems unlikely that her record suffered greatly from these transfers, with the exception of her late seasonal entry in 1928, which was further compounded by the loss of maestro Captain Archie Hogarth. (Whilst *Lulworth* remained on the sale lists, his services were leased by Sir William Berry, and he became skipper of *Cambria* in her year of initiation into the class.)

In any case, the owners were all very wealthy gentlemen, able to provide funds for the demands of maintenance and preserve a prestigious visiting card in coastal regattas, where

Lulworth, *Britannia* and *White Heather II* were privileged to display a white ensign. The 23 metre *Shamrock* flew the red ensign as her racing career had ended before Sir Thomas Lipton belatedly enjoyed membership of the RYS.

The two new Bermudan yachts *Astra* and *Cambria* made a fair entry to the class in 1928, without great distinction. However, in light wind conditions the two smaller yachts were often left behind by the old topsailed cutters and it was considered that an adjustment was needed either to the rating of the earlier yachts or (wrongly) to their rigs, since concessions appeared desirable before the next season.

A conference was held in London at the close of the 1928 season by the YRA committee and it was decided to amend the mast height limitation of the Bermudans to permit a 7.5% increase and the rig allowance for a topsailed cutter to be reduced, with a view to giving *Astra* and *Cambria* improved chances in competing. In point of fact, the difference in performance figures for Sir William Berry's *Cambria* in the 1928 and 1929 seasons was not significant, but *Astra* nominally benefited in the few entries which she made.

The new Bermudans *Astra* and *Cambria* (later accompanied by *Candida*) were fundamentally different in concept from the earlier cutters, designed to perform with substantially greater sail areas. The former made claims for greater efficiency, but could scarcely have taken a first flag if raced on level terms in a fair wind with any one of the Big Five. Battling against the formidable topsailed cutters with their clouds of canvas reaching skywards, the Bermudans invariably found themselves substantially outclassed when running off the wind.

Whilst a percentage of rig increase for the Bermudans could not be contested in principle, it points up the fallacy of the 1928 rule. Further, deliberately setting out to reduce the performance of the gaffers in the same breath was positively 'Gilbertian'. When one considers the philosophy of designing, building and tuning a racing cutter to reach an optimum competitive standard over many seasons and then, having gone to such lengths, proceeding to slow her down by reducing her sail area because of the seemingly inferior performance capabilities of certain competitors (notwithstanding adjustments to time allowances to further redress such a situation), it suggests a somewhat peculiar frame of mind. Bearing in mind the complexity and expense involved in a decision to limit the sail plan as a means of de-tuning a faster yacht, it might have been more economic to fit it with a drogue! The big class was given a new title to read 'for yachts over twenty-one but not exceeding twenty-four metres' rating, in an attempt to narrow the racing class limits. *Lulworth* and *Britannia* came outside these limits. *Britannia* was given a special concession so that with an arbitrary rating the handicappers pretended that she came within the scope of the revised class. It appears distinctly odd that *Britannia*'s nominated 24.20 metres rating still left her outside the 21-24 metre classification! (Rules are made to be broken.) Although this arrangement was an oblique attempt to improve the balance for the future, the unhappy discrimination against *Lulworth* during the 1927-28 seasons could never be historically redressed in the assessment of her overall performance for the Big Five era (1924-30). Nevertheless, despite this bias, her fine record in topping three seasons in seven outshone that of her contemporaries.

Of course, the arguments in the adoptions and changes of rules, plus modifications to such rules and discretionary time allowances, etc., had been going on since the last century, with the great yacht designers Watson, Fife and Nicholson voicing differing approaches to an ideal system, whilst the YRA pursued its own considerations. As an example, Charles Nicholson was substantially opposed to the introduction of the Second International Rule in 1920. Another authority of the day, Sir William Burton, supported Charles Nicholson's objections. Nicholson's attitude could be summarised as an objection to a type-producing rule being introduced to measure a wide range of entrants of varying tonnage and rig. In fact, the earlier BRA rule was generally admitted to be the best for bringing together vessels in a wide spectrum of rating and rig. However, the YRA went ahead with its proposal in spite of such objections and, as time passed, the class was seen from 1924 onwards to emerge with a core of big cutters relatively closely matched in sailing performance, and the giant Herreshoff schooner enjoying a welcome. The smaller cutters, yawls and ketches found alternative sport in classes for yachts with reduced tonnages, eventually leaving the big topsailed cutters to race substantially on level terms in the 1925, 1926 and 1929 seasons.

The Second International Rule of the early Twenties was based upon the formula:

$$\frac{L + \frac{1}{4}G + 2d + \sqrt{S} - F}{2.50}$$

The rating was arrived at by adding four factors, e.g. L = length, G = girth (averaged), d = measurement of hollow in the hull section, S = sail area and F = the freeboard. In practice it becomes evident that the factors L and S are the really prominent ones, both of which are major derivatives of a yacht's speed. The determination of length is found by a complex calculation of the actual immersed length of the yacht when it is heeling at an optimum angle.

Typical 1920/21 comparative ratings for the big class are as follows:

	Rating	Tonnage (TM)
Terpsichore	82.20	189
Westward	95.34	338
Britannia	82.80	221
White Heather II	76.60	179
Nyria	73.00	169

There was an obvious inconsistency in the philosophy and the adoption of new ratings with revised time concessions as applied to the Big Five in the years 1927 and 1928, although Major Heckstall–Smith was at the centre of such arrangements for many years. His treatise of this subject, as expounded on page 130 of his work in conjunction with E. du Boulay, *Britannia and Her Contemporaries*, is curiously at odds with the officially adopted ratings. He suggests that the new Bermudan smaller yachts should rate at 23.70 metres. Insofar as *Cambria* was allocated a rating of 23.20 metres, her classification is scarcely in dispute. Similarly, *Astra's* rating of 23.00 metres is proportionate. However, the major continues with the suggestion, using the same ruling that *Britannia* was twelve feet (12.80 feet, in fact) longer than *Astra* on the waterline and carrying some 2,000 sq.feet of additional sail area, and he "supposes" the rating of *Britannia* to be 26 metres, or perhaps a little more. This assessment must be roundly acceptable, and yet the royal cutter was officially accorded a new rating of 24.20 metres at that time, whilst *Lulworth* was re-rated at 25.70 metres despite *Britannia's* substantially greater waterline measurement when running free.

With the adoption of the 1928 International Measurement Rule these earlier ratings were revised by the modified formula

$$\text{Rating} = \frac{L + \sqrt{S} - F}{2.30}$$

to arrive at new alternative ratings and related time allowances, thus:

	Rating	Time Allowance
Lulworth	25.70 metres	scratch
Westward	25.70 "	scratch
Britannia *	(24.20) "	7.5 secs per mile
White Heather II	23.90 "	9.0 " " "

Shamrock	23.90	"	9.0	" " "
Cambria	23.20	"	12.8	" " "
Astra	23.00	"	14.0	" " "

* See Major Heckstall–Smith's earlier comments.

The 1928 rule was originally devised to govern an introduction to the big class by the two new Bermudan cutters, *Astra*, designed by Charles Nicholson for Sir Mortimer Singer and *Cambria*, by William Fife for Sir William Berry. Whilst the extensive time allowances for the two smaller vessels with reduced sail areas was perfectly reasonable, the anomalies of time allowances created between the existing topsailed cutters made little sense.

The main effects of changing from the 1920 to the 1928 rules can be highlighted in the relief of ratings for *Britannia*, *White Heather II* and *Shamrock*, with *Lulworth* suffering an increase, bringing the last-named level with the rating of *Westward*, which enjoyed both a very much greater sail area and waterline measurement.

In the few races which I was able to witness at the Cowes and Ryde regattas in the late Twenties, I formed the impression that the new smaller Bermudans could never steal the show pictorially from the gaffers and they hardly ever displayed any great tendency to become pace setters. Their initial time allowances of 12.8 and 14.0 secs/mile over a typical forty-five miles course amounted to around ten minutes for each to save its time over the scratch competitors. To exponents of the 'modern' high efficiency Bermudan sail plan, the new vessels did not display the same superior result as had *Nyria* in the earlier part of the decade following conversion to the leg o' mutton rig, when she was allowed only 6 secs/mile under a re-rating of 73.00 to the 1920 rule. (Incidentally *Nyria*'s waterline measurement was less than any one of the 1928-29 Bermudan cutters.)

In causing *Lulworth* the penalty of sailing scratch with the schooner *Westward* and further having to allow her erstwhile opponents *Britannia* 7.5 secs per mile, *Shamrock* and *White Heather II* 9.0 secs per mile, (after competing on level terms for the previous two years) the adjustment was hardly of a delicate nature. If it was felt at this time that *Lulworth* was monopolising the prizes she might have conceded one or two seconds per mile to balance the situation and certainly did not deserve such a sledge-hammer adjustment.

Referring to the 1920 ratings quoted by John Irving, the schooner *Westward* is rated at 95.3 and *Lulworth* (as *Terpsichore*) at only 73.00 in contrast. The act of giving the two yachts a common rating by a change of rule proved to be singularly irrational.

Using the table of relative theoretical speeds, the difference between the cutter *Lulworth* and the schooner *Westward* is quite substantial in percentage terms and to find the two vessels tied scratch can scarcely be reconciled with projected maximum speeds of 12.24 knots for *Lulworth* against 13.23 knots for *Westward* (enjoying an eight per cent advantage). It is appreciated that numerous additional influences such as relative sail areas are involved, but, again, the schooner bent some twenty-five per cent more sail than the cutter.

However, the handicap arrangements for the year 1929 were sensibly readjusted among the three big class cutters, which reverted to sailing substantially on level terms once again. A study of the 1929 seasonal results confirms a victory for common sense in presenting a performance tally as follows:

Lulworth	19 flags in 40 starts
Shamrock	20 flags in 40 starts
White Heather II	24 flags in 45 starts

(These figures have to be taken in the context of *Britannia*'s unfortunate absence.)

Perusing contemporary records which are to hand, there does not seem to be any fair basis for the prejudiced observations regarding *Lulworth*'s achievements made by J.B. Atkins in his mammoth work, entitled *Further Memorials of the Royal Yacht Squadron*,[1] published in 1939. Indeed, there does not appear to be any foundation whatsoever for such a grossly misleading historical note.

In his reference to the passing of Mr Herbert Weld of Lulworth Castle who, incidentally, died in the year 1935 at the age of eighty-three, Atkins comments: "*Lulworth* won a good many races, including the King's Cup in 1925 [he forgot to mention her win at the Clyde Regatta during the 1928 season] and this redeemed her record as *Terpsichore* to some extent, but she was not the equal of the best two or three in the large class."

Comparisons may frequently prove sour but are manifestly unpalatable when these are made on the premise of unsubstantiated evidence and result in a baseless analogy. It is accepted that *Terpsichore*, haunted as she was by ill fortune initially, did not qualify for many medals, discounting her 1922 short seasonal successes, which the earlier part of this narrative freely details, "but Atkins's demeaning reference to *Lulworth* is patently unfounded". Whilst suffering an incredible series of mishaps as *Terpsichore* sailing against an inconsistent opposition, her true ranking became established in the years 1924-1930 as the four big cutters *Britannia, Shamrock, White Heather II* and *Lulworth* (later joined by the schooner *Westward*) formed a solid core of competing first class yachts. A glance at *Lulworth*'s record for that period, racing with these giants, speaks for itself.

Disregarding her 1927-1928 persecution in handicapping, Atkins seems to have overlooked the facts that *Lulworth* (ex-*Terpsichore*) took the class honours for the four seasons of 1922, 1925, 1926 and 1930 as well as winning the King's Cup events both in 1925 and 1928. It is submitted that the 1922 triumph was not in the same category as her later successes, but such opposition as there was (enjoying very substantial time allowances) proved *Lulworth*'s achievement in winning 50% of her few entries in that year one of considerable merit. It was, incidentally, greatly to his credit that Reginald Lee's *Terpsichore* virtually kept the over seventy ton handicap class alive in 1922 until the other big cutters, *Britannia* and *Nyria*, rejoined the circuit in the following year, although this virtue has not been disputed.

Her victories in the two Round the Island events during the Big Five era as outlined on pages 191-193 and 252-253 further testify to *Lulworth*'s patently competitive status.

Lulworth's remarkable record – 27 flags for 27 entries in the year 1925 – seems to have been further disregarded in the ungenerous reference to the great cutter.

It was something of an understatement to mention *Lulworth*'s winning a great many races – in fact, the related totals for the 1921-1930 decade, which incidentally include the manifold misfortunes of *Terpsichore*, are as follows:

Britannia	59	first flags	
Lulworth	59	"	"
White Heather II	56	"	"
Shamrock	44	"	"
Westward	33	"	"

In 1930, her final year, *Lulworth* completed the season with twenty-two flags (eleven firsts). *Britannia*, with fewer entries, finished with ten flags (five firsts), *White Heather II* with seventeen flags (six firsts) *Westward* with ten flags (five firsts), *Astra* with seven flags (withdrawn early from the regattas with just one first), *Candida* with twenty-one flags (five firsts), *Cambria* with twenty-one flags (two firsts).

The writer has the greatest difficulty in trying to reconcile Atkins's sentiments as expressed in this wholly unfair allusion to *Lulworth*'s competitive qualities with his revelations of companionship with Herbert Weld, as claimed in a later publication, dated 1947, entitled *Incidents and Reflections*.

He describes how he met Herbert Weld in Greece (at the time of the Thirty Days' War with the Turks) and mentions him as one of his best friends. He recalls the purchase of the yacht *Terpsichore* by Mr Weld, saying that this gentleman knew nothing about seamanship, nor cared to know, but had the good fortune to find a suitable skipper and won many races. This appears an odd tribute to the commodore of the Royal Dorset Yacht Club, who was evidently interested in the purchase of *Terpsichore* and subsequent election to membership of the Royal Yacht Squadron! Atkins wrote that there was always a cabin at his disposal in the renamed *Lulworth* and when the owner was not aboard the yacht was as good as his own.

It seems particularly unfortunate that Atkins should have deliberately recorded this inaccurate reference to a yacht of outstanding accomplishment in his *Memorials of the Royal Yacht Squadron*, a work of such historic importance.

Whilst retaining her powerful gaff-rigged sail plan throughout her racing career, *Lulworth* was never outmoded by her 'leg o' mutton' mainsailed contemporaries *Astra, Candida* and *Cambria*, which joined the class in 1928/29. As a matter of pure conjecture, it is not unlikely that *Lulworth* may have marginally benefited in performance by adopting the 'modern' rig in dispensing with a probable three tons of weight (comprising a gaff, topsail yards and excess canvas) centred some one hundred and forty feet above her deck. This, in turn, could have effected a reduction of ballast in the order of fifteen tons, but a probable loss of sail area in the order of 22%, combined with an inevitable decrease in waterline measurement, on the other hand, would have discounted much of any performance gain. As she escaped the experiment of such a conversion to sail with the 'Jays', the prospect was never explored.

Quite apart from a claimed improvement in aerodynamic efficiency with the employment of a high aspect ratio mainsail, the suggested superiority of Bermudan rig over traditional gaff/topsail configuration has been an ability to point higher when working to windward. The likely sag of a mainsail produced by the weight of a gaff, topsail yards and greater sail area is not disputed.

However, *Lulworth* was never observed to be pinching to outpoint her rival cutters and, uncannily enough, she consistently defied the theory. This virtue is, in part, confirmed by the noted observations of John Nicholson, as recalled on page 263. Additionally many references are to be found in the records of Solent regattas demonstrating *Lulworth*'s mastery in leading round the first mark on an initial windward leg. Archie Hogarth had a preference for a flat cut mainsail and the cutter's canvases always appeared tightly sheeted.[2] His artistry in the trimming of headsails to optimise a balance in changing conditions was almost certainly a contributory factor in the development of *Lulworth*'s edge.

Lulworth was not singular in receiving attention designed to upgrade her performance in the Twenties, as *White Heather II* and *Shamrock* enjoyed the benefit of many improvements during the laying-up seasons. In addition, a great deal of money was lavished upon *Britannia*, with a number of attempts made to keep her abreast of her contemporaries. Much of the attention which she received was on account of her age, although Sir Philip Hunloke experimented with three differing rig modifications on behalf of His Majesty, not all of which proved beneficial, such details being recorded in other works.

Lulworth's history of participation in the various major yacht club regattas has been shown to be somewhat controversial and these exploits, added to her achievements, resulted in a most colourful racing scenario. In the wake of the improvements initiated by Charles Nicholson in the ironing out of Messrs White Bros.' design anomalies, his efforts contributed to a brilliant canvas, more especially through the latter part of the decade.

The facts are, that from her unfortunate baptism, *Terpsichore*, later *Lulworth*, proved to be the equal of any one of the others. She was unquestionably as good as the best of them.

An outline assessment of related maximum speeds for the big class yachts using the empirical formula = K x √ LWL is tabled below, using uniform data based upon known load waterline lengths with vessels running before the wind in slack water. Obviously, these lengths must be greater when measured with the yachts heeled, but in the absence of records the absolute theoretical speeds are indeterminate. Whilst the probable increase of waterline length in this mode suggests a potentially optimised maximum speed, such an assessment has to be balanced against a boosted skin drag resulting from a greater wetted surface. In a similar context, variations of length to beam ratios must be relevant. However, the calculated figures quoted give a fair approximation of the 'relative' expectations of performance under tideless conditions, with sail areas optimised and the influence in weight of wind disregarded. It will be noted that a common value of K = 1.35 has been used in each case, which assumes that the designers would doubtless have chosen lines to minimise drag, and no attempt has been made to introduce any adjustments for fineness ratios. (A study of the length to beam ratio for each of the Big Five is quoted in the Appendices, page 324.)

Lulworth with LWL = 82.2 feet
Theoretical speed = 1.35 x 82.20 = 12.24 knots

Shamrock with LWL = 75.77 feet
Theoretical speed = 1.35 x 75.77 = 11.75 knots

Britannia with LWL = 87.8 feet
Theoretical speed = 1.35 x 87.8 = 12.64 knots

Nyria with LWL   = 72.5 feet
Theoretical speed = 1.35 x 72.5 = 11.50 knots

Westward with LWL = 96 feet
Theoretical speed = 1.35 x 96 = 13.23 knots

Astra with LWL   = 75 feet
Theoretical speed = 1.35 x 75 = 11.68 knots

Candida with LWL   = 79.4 feet
Theoretical speed = 1.35 x 79.4 = 12.03 knots

Cambria with LWL   = 75.0 feet
Theoretical speed = 1.35 x 75.0 = 11.68 knots

The foregoing speed assessments cannot of course be taken literally, being outline performance derivatives which have to be balanced against a minefield of individual design requirements and considerations to produce an answer which might fairly compete with the yacht's log. Before attempting to review a measure of the background philosophy associated with the production of a 'sailing ballerina, a designer is, of course, primarily confronted with the inevitable hand of Dame Nature, who indisputably holds the trump card.

The spectrum of allocations in motive power combined with the degree of disturbance of water surface are hers to the point where the displacement of a vessel in conjunction with the effect of its lines is introduced to augment swell and chop. The design task is more or less one of harnessing the elements to a racing concept in order to exhibit optimum performance at all points except for the least few degrees off the wind, with sails assumed to be appropriately trimmed.

Having accepted the challenge, a designer is ordered to meet with a specification set out by the YRA ruling of the day and the dictates of Lloyds insurers, commensurate with the aspirations of the customer or his appointed representative.

Whilst such information is intended to provide him some guidance, he is clearly unable to start with a clean sheet of paper, although ultimately he enjoys the 'hot seat', which, even if he is very lucky, may only prove to be lukewarm.

The designer's genius is early extended to the generation of a set of lines using maximum beam measurements which provide no more than adequate stability without employing an excess of ballast. These curves are lofted to allow low entry and exit waterline characteristics and at the same time an eye is sighted to devise frame contours which cheat wetted areas as far as is practicable to minimise skin drag. However, the quality of the end product is invariably a function of the availability in design time.

Lulworth represented the ultimate in the development of big topsailed cutters at the period when the fashion for such cutters and, indeed, the big handicap class itself, was finally discarded. Her worthy topsailed contemporaries were all very much older but there was only slight evidence of any handicaps which might have been attributable to maturity during the Big Five era.

These five yachts could roundly be described as a nucleus of seaworthy vessels, brilliantly conceived to exhibit maximised competitive performance and yet prove sufficiently rugged to make the passage between British coastal regatta venues.

Although these competitors were variously constructed over a somewhat extensive interval of twenty-seven years, to differing rules, but with basic design techniques implicit in the adoption of erstwhile 'jackyarder' sail plans, each met with the most wholesome principles of its respective period; indeed, there were no rule-cheating freaks amongst them.

---

[1] An original late nineteenth-century work entitled *Memorials of the Royal Yacht Squadron* was written by Montague Guest, a club member of those times, and it was this essay which inspired J.B. Atkins to edit a continuing history beyond the former work's 1902 ending under the title of *Further Memorials of the Royal Yacht Squadron*. He describes this narrative

as a parergon, compiled in odd moments, aided by Sir Fisher Dilke and fellow squadron associates.

[2] On more than one occasion during Solent regattas *Lulworth* suffered the embarrassment of a burst mainsail, which might have been attributable to the tightness of 'sheeting in'.

BEYOND THE TWENTIES

Lulworth's racing career ending with the demise of her class left Mr Paton in a difficult situation; his obvious course of action was to place the yacht on the sale list, unless he was prepared to cruise around the coast with a racer for the restricted fun of it. In any case, the engagement of skipper and crew alone was scarcely worthy of serious financial consideration for a ship divorced from its sporting concept. Alternatively, conversion of *Lulworth* to a cruiser would have entailed a great deal of immediate expenditure affording only a fraction of her inherent capacity for 'battle'. Clearly the economic climate of the day did not allow any such extravagances. The prospect of finding a buyer for this unique 'jewel' with now limited use was extremely remote, to say the least. From the ace position which *Lulworth* had established in the 1930 season to relegation as a result of entirely unwitting pressure from the USA was, quite apart from any sentimental consideration, an asset viciously discounted. No buyer came forward as the economic situation worsened.

Not only was *Lulworth* on the market in the winter of 1930/31, but so too was Lord Waring's *White Heather II*, although not exactly for the same reason. Around this period Mr W.L. Stephenson, chairman of Woolworth's, sought entry to the sport, and it was said that he purchased *White Heather II* in 1931 from his old business friend, Lord Waring, as a gesture of assistance towards the latter's increasing financial embarrassment. Following some expensive modifications, *White Heather II* sailed in the 1932 season without conspicuous success.

One may be tempted, in moments of idle conjecture, to ponder Mr Stephenson's alternative option (neglecting his intended assistance to his lordship) of entering big class cutter racing by acquiring *Lulworth* instead of *White Heather II*. In truth, it had to be acknowledged that, with the casting of the die earlier in New York, these two magnificent white cutters were both doomed in terms of continued serious big cutter competition, particularly as they were outside the new class limits. Following a brief boom, the new class itself became extinct some seven years later. The whole scenario had by such time evaporated. *White Heather II* was ignominiously broken up at Gosport when her owner decided to build the steel-skinned yacht *Velsheda* for the 1933 racing season. The 23 metre *Shamrock* of 1908 suffered a fate similar to *White Heather II*'s at Southampton in 1932. At least *Lulworth* escaped the knacker's yard!

It was not until 1935, long after my affair with the gaffers had been concluded, that I caught sight of the familiar outline of *Lulworth*, strangely attired in ketch rig, near her old mooring for the Week. My first thought was, 'At least she has survived the slump, unlike two of her old sparring partners.' From Mr Paton's angle it must have seemed appropriate to convert *Lulworth* to a cruising role, as it was by 1934 patently obvious that no new owner would ever come along to race her again. Her racing purpose had long since perished. The economic outlook was then beginning to show signs of improvement, unhappily for rather doubtful advantages in a national sense.

I cannot, in all conscience, admit that I derived any great pleasure from the sight of that glistening white cutter hull displaying the rig of a ketch, almost certainly in combination with an auxiliary motor below. The thought of a propeller lurking under the waterline, despoiling the aquatic flow whilst under sail, offended my purist nostalgic prejudices, sensible though such an installation must have been in the circumstances. I next began to wonder what had been done to her keel, as a by-product of scrapping that proud mast from which so many prize flags had fluttered. But my interest had become dimmed by this date, as the once great cutter was unceremoniously been pensioned off when her racing flag was been finally lowered in the autumn of 1930.

PART V

EPILOGUE

OR SUBSTANTIALLY BEYOND THE TWENTIES

Sixty years on, early in 1990, my attention was sharply awakened by a very brief television news item showing an old hulk allegedly bearing the title of *Lulworth* being towed from the Hamble River on Southampton Water to Messrs Camper & Nicholson's yacht yard at Gosport for proposed renovation. I had known for some years that *Lulworth* entered retirement as a houseboat occupying a mud berth at Hamble where a certain Mrs Lewis enjoyed the daily sight of seagulls and cormorants.

I make no apology for confessing to the most tremendous excitement at the news: such a possibility seemed scarcely believable to me at this time. Of course, the memories of those early Solent regattas came flooding back and I felt compelled to investigate further by exploring the prospect of getting closer to the activity. The thought that I might eventually witness the sight of this grand old cutter with all canvas bent once again was thrilling if a remote possibility.

Perhaps I should have more readily conceded the overwhelming attraction in the rescue of the only survivor of the Big Five for persons with such enviable enthusiasm, combined with an ability to fund such a project.

After spending a few hours delving into my old notes, I lost little time in an approach to Mr Nick Maris, chairman of Messrs Camper & Nicholson, expressing a nostalgic interest in reviewing the former object of my boyish adoration and from the observation of which I retained an unhappy memory of being savagely parted in the late 1930 season. He most kindly issued an immediate invitation to meet at Gosport, where I was warmly welcomed at the yard. The last visit which I had reason to make to Gosport before the 1940-45 war was undertaken across the harbour from Portsmouth on a steam-engined ferry. Such vessels enjoyed the nickname of 'Gosport liners' amongst my youthful compatriots.

Some time was spent during an unusually fine afternoon in February 1990 on the examination of this historic treasure. A vision of pathos and yet potential is the only description which seemed appropriate in my first sighting of the remnants of the once proud cutter. Obviously, Mr Maris would be facing a very substantial task in reviving her but, remembering her traditional Gosport connections, *Terpsichore* could surely be rebuilt to dance again. She looked strangely at home in a berth which she had first occupied over seventy years ago.

The sight of badly neglected vintage yachts was a common one in my extreme youth when I learned to exercise a pair of oars in a ten foot six dinghy, cruising the River Medina. Gratified as I was to see that proud, defiant bow curve once again, there remained something of an empty feeling. Despite being daubed with hideous fading blue paint, which was smeared over numerous areas of dilapidation on her topsides, the ghost of a gleaming white cutter with classic lines hovered behind, desperately begging an essential pot of gold. I fell to wondering what had happened to all the cups won by *Lulworth* in her prime when my host produced a ladder for access to the deck (yes, the vessel was still afloat, despite the ripe state of the planking) and I ventured down the companion hatch where I saw the once-beautiful built-in furnishings, now severely tarnished but, nevertheless, bearing the mark of superb quality. A glance at the machinery space, which was hardly in the category of an engine room, vied with the sight of cement patches on the deck and the concrete repair to the stern post for 'most horrific impression'. I was compelled to ponder how it was that this treasure of erstwhile magnificence could have been permitted to degenerate into such an object of neglect, but, unlike her contemporaries, *Lulworth* had at least provided a pleasant and unique shelter for many decades.

Mr Maris affirmed the fitness of the steel frames as a basis for reconstruction, further stating that very little structural warping from the ravages of time could be measured. I was delighted to learn that a proposal to restore the original gaff rig was under serious consideration. In addition he mentioned a proposed diesel engine installation to facilitate handling in marinas and harbours when mingling with present-day fibreglass traffic. I had to concede the logic of such a proposal, but suffered a feeling of dismay when I recalled her original purist concept, designed to compete with those elite cutters which were exclusively designed to sail.

However, the visit proved to be one of the most delightful experiences of a lifetime. It all seemed too good to be true that I might once more enjoy the vision of *Lulworth* in cutter rig, beating into the teeth of a force 5 sou'west'r through the Cowes Roadstead.

Exciting though the prospect of recutting this jewel undoubtedly appeared, one's jubilation was tempered to some degree by remembering the fates of *Lulworth*'s competitors. The former pictorial capture of the Big Five by Frank Beken could never be repeated. Of the 1925 pentad, *Lulworth* (ex-*Terpsichore*), which was sadly decayed, remained the sole survivor, since her four playmates had bidden a final farewell in the Thirties or Forties, all of which had been dispatched either by gunpowder or the axe.

Firstly, *Britannia* was sunk by an explosive charge over the Hurd Deep in the English Channel in 1936 in accordance with an express wish in the will of HM King George V. Secondly *Westward* met a similar fate to that of *Britannia* following the death of her last owner, Mr F. Davis, who wanted his schooner to be destroyed in a like manner, again over the Hurd Deep off the Casquets, downchannel, in 1947. Thirdly, *White Heather II*, following conversion to sail with the 'J' Class in 1932, was discarded by a new millionaire owner, to be broken up in the following year. Fourthly, the 23 metre *Shamrock*, built in 1908, was ruthlessly dismantled in 1932 following the demise of her owner, Sir Thomas Lipton, in 1931. (*Shamrock V*, incidentally, built by Charles Nicholson in 1929/30, is still sailing from La Spezia in the Mediterranean.)

As a sequel to my Gosport visit, an enquiry was made some months later to ascertain the status of *Terpsichore*'s proposed resuscitation and I was sharply reminded of some lines from Gilbert and Sullivan's *HMS Pinafore*:

> For it sounds all right in a sailor's song
> But you'll soon find out that it all goes wrong.

A reply conveyed the brutal news that the great cutter's remains had been shipped to a Mediterranean yacht yard for refurbishment. Even accepting that the project might still be executed with consummate skills, an essential interpretation had undeniably been lost for ever.

No matter, for, in truth, the departures of her four major compatriots with such finality, long since, prompted a sober conclusion that *Lulworth* (ex-*Terpsichore*) could not now aspire, in the annals of yachting activity, to become more than a shadow of her illustrious past.

Lulworth's day, as with *Britannia*, *White Heather II*, the 23 metre *Shamrock* and *Westward*, essentially belonged to the illustrious topsail rigged era. Those times were sacrosanct and, as such, beyond physical recapture.

The enticing phantasm which haunted my Gosport reappraisal of this once proud cutter had seen its final curtain. However, there lingered a most memorable flood of white-winged pageants which craved a nostalgic dalliance with the pen in order to register a few examples of those blissful associations when sighting some of the Solent's most bountiful offerings...

APPENDICES

I. SUMMARY OF RACING SUCCESSES OF THE FIRST CLASS YACHTS
1921–1930 (inclusive)

YEAR	Lulworth (ex-Terpsichore)				Britannia				Shamrock 23 metre				White Heather II				Westward				Nyria				Astra				Cambria				Candida			
	1st	2nd	3rd	S	1st	2nd	3rd	S	1st	2nd	3rd	S	1st	2nd	3rd	S	1st	2nd	3rd	S	1st	2nd	3rd	S	1st	2nd	3rd	S	1st	2nd	3rd	S	1st	2nd	3rd	S
1921	2	2	1	13	9	6	0	28	—	—	—	—	8	2	2	24	—	—	—	—	16	7	1	35	—	—	—	—	—	—	—	—	—	—	—	—
1922	3	1	0	6	—	—	—	0	—	—	—	—	—	—	—	0	—	—	—	—	—	—	—	0	—	—	—	—	—	—	—	—	—	—	—	—
1923	3	2	0	14	11	6	6	26	—	—	—	—	—	—	—	0	—	—	—	—	11	4	0	25	—	—	—	—	—	—	—	—	—	—	—	—

(contd)	Lulworth (ex-Terpsichore)				Britannia				Shamrock 23 metre				White Heather II				Westward				Nyria				Astra				Cambria				Candida			
	1st	2nd	3rd	S	1st	2nd	3rd	S	1st	2nd	3rd	S	1st	2nd	3rd	S	1st	2nd	3rd	S	1st	2nd	3rd	S	1st	2nd	3rd	S	1st	2nd	3rd	S	1st	2nd	3rd	S
1924*	4	6	0	16	7	5	0	19	1	0	0	9	7	8	0	19	—	—	—	0	—	—	—	0	—	—	—	—	—	—	—	—	—	—	—	—
1925	9	11	8	28	6	0	6	36	9	7	2	31	7	12	5	37	8	2	4	29	—	—	—	0	—	—	—	—	—	—	—	—	—	—	—	—
1926	13	6	1	29	4	4	3	23	7	7	2	24	7	10	6	34	3	5	4	23	—	—	—	0	—	—	—	—	—	—	—	—	—	—	—	—
1927	5	6	2	27	8	6	2	24	5	11	3	33	8	7	3	29	7	3	3	24	—	—	—	0	—	—	—	—	—	—	—	—	—	—	—	—
1928	2	4	5	29	9	5	5	34	13	7	1	32	5	9	6	34	3	4	1	22	—	—	—	0	5	3	5	26	2	6	5	34	—	—	—	—
1929	7	8	4	40	—	—	—	0	9	10	1	40	8	9	7	45	7	1	2	20	—	—	—	0	4	2	0	8	6	3	6	41	3	11	8	29
1930	11	6	5	45	5	4	1	26	—	—	—	—	6	6	5	45	5	2	3	14	—	—	—	0	1	1	5	15	2	14	5	49	5	9	7	35
TOTAL	59	52	26	247	29	36	23	216	44	42	9	169	56	63	34	267	33	17	17	132	11	1	1	60	10	6	10	49	10	23	16	124	8	20	15	64

S   denotes total number of seasonal starts

*   It will be apparent that 1924 saw the re-emergence of an established big cutter class.

II. SUMMARY OF OUTLINE DATA FOR THE BIG FIVE (dated 1927)

LLOYDS Ref. No.	NAME OF YACHT	RIG	TONNAGE	LENGTH (feet)	WIDTH (feet)	DEPTH (feet)	DESIGNED & BUILT	OWNER	HOME PORT
3271	*Lulworth*	cutter (topsail)	111.55 net 123.64 gross 186 TM	95.5 OA 82 WL	21.80 max.	13.90	H.W. WHITE White Bros. Ltd. Southampton 1920	Sir A. Mortimer Singer KBE	Southampton
5306 123125 LPTN	*Shamrock*	cutter (topsail)	94.02 net 175 TM	96.06 OA 75.77 WL	20.85	11.20	W. FIFE W. Fife & Son Fairlee 1908	Sir Thomas J. Lipton Bart, KCVO	Dublin
6545 1241275 HKMV	*White Heather II*	cutter (topsail)	89.89 net 179 TM	95.60 OA	21.27	10.95	W. FIFE W. Fife & Son Fairlee 1907	Lord Waring	Glasgow
6504 147462	*Westward*	schooner (topsail)	314.70 net 323 TM	109.80 OA 96.00 WL	27.10	14.50	N.G. HERRESHOFF Herreshoff Mfg.Co. Bristol 1910	T.B.F. Davis	Jersey
731 99900	*Brittania*	cutter (topsail)	115.02 net 221 TM	100 OA 87.80 WL	23.30	12.60	G.L. WATSON D. Henderson Glasgow 1893	HM King George V	Cowes

III. SUMMARY OF OUTLINE DATA (OTHER COMPETING YACHTS)

LLOYDS Ref. No.	NAME OF YACHT	RIG	TONNAGE	LENGTH (feet)	WIDTH (feet)	DEPTH (feet)	DESIGNED & BUILT	OWNER	HOME PORT
818	*Candida*	Bermudan cutter	— 173 TM	97.75 OA 79.40 WL	20.50 max.	11.20 14.10	C. NICHOLSON Camper & Nicholson Ltd., Gosport, Hants 1929	H.A. Andreae	Portsmouth
355 149143	*Astra*	Bermudan cutter	83.33 net 164 TM	95.80 OA 75 WL	20.20 max.	11 13.80	C. NICHOLSON Camper & Nicholson Ltd., Gosport, Hants 1928	Sir A. Mortimer Singer KBE JP	Portsmouth
MGWV 805 160319	*Cambria*	Bermudan cutter	85.95 net 162 TM	93.70 OA 75.00 WL	20.50 max.	10.40 13.20	W.& R. FIFE Fairlee 1928	Sir William E. Berry Bart	Greenock

LLOYDS Ref. No.	NAME OF YACHT	RIG	TONNAGE	LENGTH (feet)	WIDTH (feet)	DEPTH (feet)	DESIGNED & BUILT	OWNER	HOME PORT
703	*Susanne*	schooner (topsail)	69.54 net 154 TM	93.70 OA 75.03 WL	19.80 max.	10.25	W. FIFE A. & J. Inglis Ltd., Glasgow 1904	Mr W. Brookes 1920 Mr Robert McAlpine 1925	Originally Kiel Port of survey Glasgow
4268 123305	*Nyria* (ex-*Lady Camilla*)	cutter (topsail) converted to Bermudan	73 net 169 TM	98 OA 73.31 WL	20.20 max.	10.60	C. NICHOLSON Camper & Nicholson Gosport, Hants 1906	Mrs E.R. Workman	Portsmouth

IV.   SUMMARY OF OUTLINE DATA FOR VESSELS OF LESSER TONNAGE COMPETING UNDER HANDICAP ALLOWANCE

LLOYDS Ref. No.	NAME OF YACHT	RIG	TONNAGE	LENGTH (feet)	WIDTH (feet)	DEPTH (feet)	DESIGNED & BUILT	OWNER	HOME PORT
4975 115750	*Valdora*	ketch	106 TM	79.20 68.55 WL	18.10	12.10	W. FIFE W. Fife & Son Fairlee 1903	Sir William Portal Bart	Glasgow
4557 136284	*Samurun*	yawl	92 TM	79.10 63.50 WL	16.65	10.90	W. FIFE W. Fife & Son Fairlee 1914	Lord Sackville	Glasgow
686 114578	*Cariad*	ketch	153 TM	94.70 85.35 WL	19.60	10.80	A.E. PAYNE Summers & Payne Southampton 1903	Earl of Dunraven KP Col. Gretton 1924	Southampton
1882 133119	*Harbinger*	yawl	94 TM	78.80 68 WL	16.90	10.50	H.T. STOW Stow & Son Shoreham	Sir Thomas Dunlop Bart, GBE	Glasgow

LLOYDS Ref. No.	NAME OF YACHT	RIG	TONNAGE	LENGTH (feet)	WIDTH (feet)	DEPTH (feet)	DESIGNED & BUILT	OWNER	HOME PORT
2278 123313	*Joyette* (ex-*Almara*)	ketch	89 TM	75 66.73 WL	17	10.20	C. E. NICHOLSON Camper & Nicholson Ltd., Gosport 1907	Captain Cecil W.P. Slade	Portsmouth
3190 141899	*Moonbeam*	cutter	93 TM	79.50	16.65	10.40	W. FIFE W. Fife & Son Fairlee 1920	Charles P. Johnson JP	Glasgow
5420 119119	*Zinita*	cutter	92 TM	79.50 61.64 WL	16.60	7.85	W. FIFE W.Fife & Son Fairlee 1904	Lionel de Rothschild MP	Cowes
5083 121322	*Vida VI*	auxiliary cutter	80 TM	72.90 60 WL	16.30	11.20	W. FIFE W.Fife & Son Fairlee 1906	W.A. Wylie	Glasgow

LLOYDS Ref. No.	NAME OF YACHT	RIG	TONNAGE	LENGTH (feet)	WIDTH (feet)	DEPTH (feet)	DESIGNED & BUILT	OWNER	HOME PORT
914 124490	Coral (ex-Banba III)	yawl	63 TM	65 61.40 WL	15.40	10.40	F.Shepherd White Bros. Southampton 1902	F. Templeton Mew* F. Chaplin 1924	Cowes
2636 124516	Julnar	auxiliary ketch	135 TM	89.10 83.75 WL	19.05	10.90	W. FIFE Summers & Payne Southampton 1909	Oswald Sanderson	Hull Gosport
1960 131773	Genesta (ex-Bluebird)	auxiliary ketch	80 TM	67.50 63.60 WL	17.25	10.00	H.W. WHITE White Bros. Southampton 1911	Sir Frederick G.P. Preston KBE	Southampton

* F. Templeton Mew was a one-time commodore of the Island Sailing Club.

V. LENGTH TO BEAM RATIOS FOR THE BIG FIVE

Lulworth (ex-*Terpsichore*)	$\dfrac{82.00}{21.80}$ =	3.76
Britannia	$\dfrac{87.80}{23.30}$ =	3.76
White Heather II	$\dfrac{74.80}{21.27}$ =	3.51
Shamrock	$\dfrac{75.77}{20.85}$ =	3.63
Westward	$\dfrac{96.00}{27.10}$ =	3.54

The foregoing ratios are evolved from measurements taken from Lloyds's Registers. Whilst the variations in fineness are relatively small for the cutters, *Britannia* and *Lulworth* might be expected to exhibit greater stability in stormy conditions; *White Heather II* and *Shamrock* probably benefited with lower drag constants to show improved behaviour in lighter airs. The beam ratio used by Herreshoff for the schooner *Westward* was demonstrably well chosen, considering the vast spread of canvas adopted to drive her to the optimised limits at all points.

VI.   OWNERSHIPS OF *LULWORTH* (EX-*TERPSICHORE*) 1920-1930

First   Mr Richard H. Lee
                    1920-1923 (inc.)
                    Original name of yacht *Terpsichore*

Second   Mr Herbert Weld Blundell
                    1924-1925 (inc.)
                    Name changed to *Lulworth*

Third   Sir Mortimer Singer, KBE, JP
                    1926-1927 (inc.)
                    Name *Lulworth* retained

Fourth   Alexander Allan Paton
                    1928-1930 (inc.)
                    Name *Lulworth* retained

Lulworth placed on sale list at end of 1930 racing season.

VII.

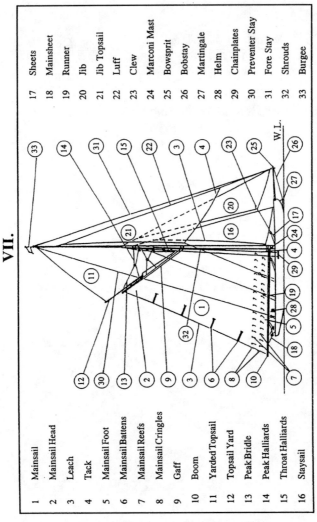

1   Mainsail
2   Mainsail Head
3   Leach
4   Tack
5   Mainsail Foot
6   Mainsail Battens
7   Mainsail Reefs
8   Mainsail Cringles
9   Gaff
10   Boom
11   Yarded Topsail
12   Topsail Yard
13   Peak Bridle
14   Peak Halliards
15   Throat Halliards
16   Staysail

17   Sheets
18   Mainsheet
19   Runner
20   Jib
21   Jib Topsail
22   Luff
23   Clew
24   Marconi Mast
25   Bowsprit
26   Bobstay
27   Martingale
28   Helm
29   Chainplates
30   Preventer Stay
31   Fore Stay
32   Shrouds
33   Burgee

Typical Beam View of Topsailed Cutter Sails and Rigging

VIII. MAPS OF SOLENT MARKERS

Portsmouth Harbour

Gosport

SPITHEAD

Gilkicker Pt.

Calshot Castle

Calshot

Hill Head

E. Brambles

SPIT LIGHT SHIP

N. W. Brambles

W. Brambles

W. Middle

Starbridge

Sand Head

N. E. Middle

S. E. Middle

Peel

Pier

R.V.Y.C.

RYDE

Beaulieu

SOLENT

START

E. Lepe

R.Y.S.
R.L.Y.C.

COWES

ISLE OF WIGHT

Not To Scale

Newtown

Solent Bank

Lymington Spit

Lymington

August 4th, 1921

R.Y.S. REGATTA 1921
Club House, Lymington Spit
N.E. Middle
Twice Round: Total 42 nautical miles

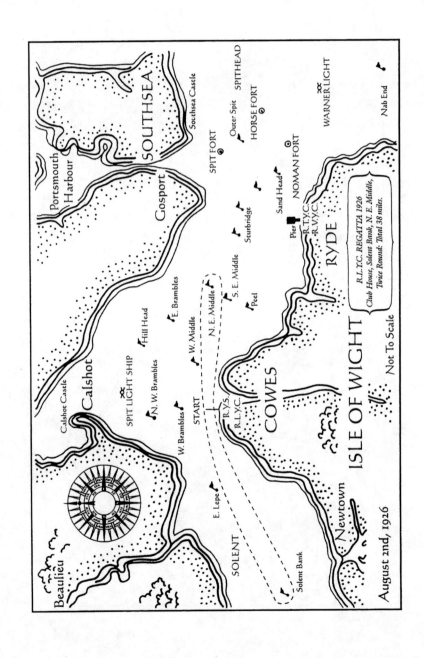

Beaulieu

Portsmouth Harbour

SOUTHSEA

Southsea Castle

SPIT FORT

Outer Spit SPITHEAD

HORSE FORT

WARNER LIGHT

Nab End

Gosport

Calshot Castle

Calshot

SPIT LIGHT SHIP

Hill Head

E. Brambles

N. W. Brambles

W. Middle

N. E. Middle

Sturbridge

Sand Head

NOMAN FORT

S. E. Middle

Peel

Pier

R.T.Y.C.

R.V.Y.C.

RYDE

W. Brambles

START

R.Y.S.

R.L.Y.C.

COWES

SOLENT

E. Lepe

Newtown

Solent Bank

ISLE OF WIGHT

R.L.Y.C. REGATTA 1926
Club House, Solent Bank, N. E. Middle,
Twice Round: Total 38 miles.

Not To Scale

August 2nd, 1926

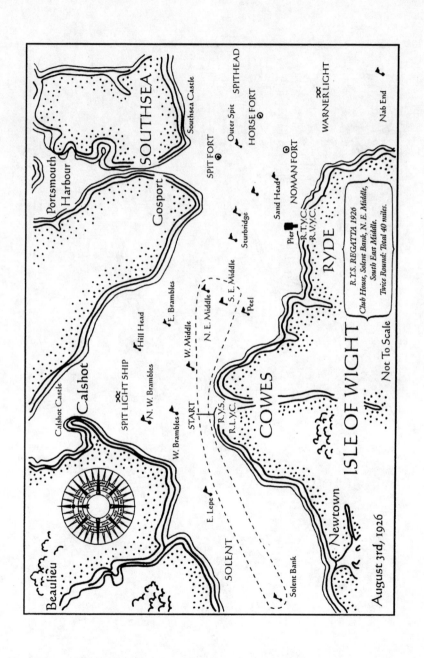

Beaulieu

Portsmouth
Harbour

SOUTHSEA

Gosport

Southsea Castle

Outer Spit   SPITHEAD

SPIT FORT

HORSE FORT

WARNER LIGHT

Nab End

Sand Head

NOMAN FORT

Sturbridge

Pier   R.T.Y.C.
R.V.Y.C.

RYDE

R.Y.S. REGATTA 1926
Club House, Solent Bank, N. E. Middle,
South East Middle.
Twice Round: Total 40 miles.

Calshot Castle

Calshot

Hill Head

E. Brambles

SPIT LIGHT SHIP

N. W. Brambles

W. Brambles

START

W. Middle

N. E. Middle

S. E. Middle

Peel

R.Y.S.
R.L.Y.C.

COWES

ISLE OF WIGHT

Not To Scale

E. Lepe

SOLENT

Solent Bank

Newtown

August 3rd, 1926

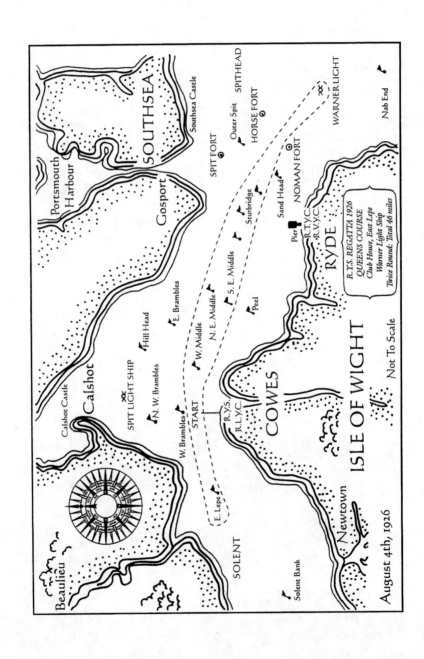

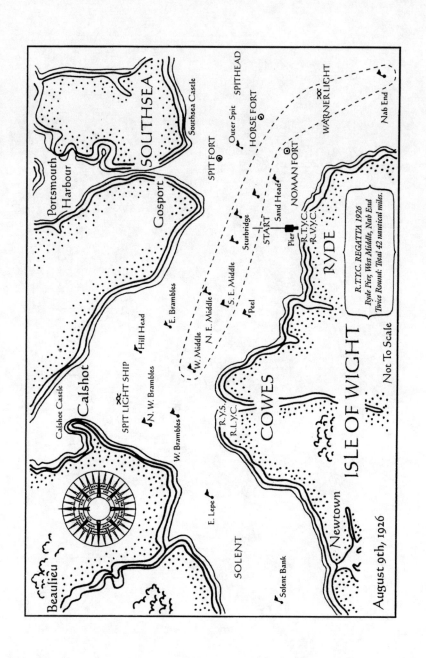

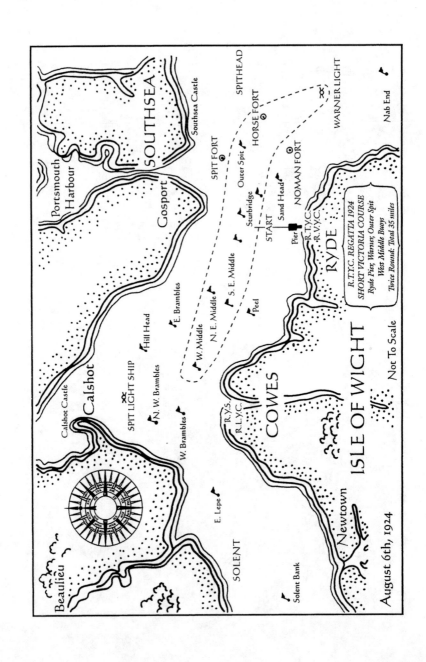

Beaulieu

Portsmouth
Harbour

SOUTHSEA

Gosport

Southsea Castle

SPITHEAD

Calshot Castle

Calshot

Hill Head

SPIT FORT

WARNER LIGHT

SPIT LIGHT SHIP

E. Brambles

Outer Spit

HORSE FORT

N. W. Brambles

Nab End

W. Brambles

W. Middle

N. E. Middle

S. E. Middle

Peel

Sturbridge

START

Sand Head

NOMAN FORT

E. Lepe

R.Y.S.
R.L.Y.C.

COWES

Pier

R.T.Y.C.
R.V.Y.C.

RYDE

SOLENT

Solent Bank

Newtown

ISLE OF WIGHT

R.T.Y.C. REGATTA 1924
SHORT VICTORIA COURSE
Ryde Pier, Warner, Outer Spit
West Middle Buoys
Twice Round: Total 35 miles

Not To Scale

August 6th, 1924

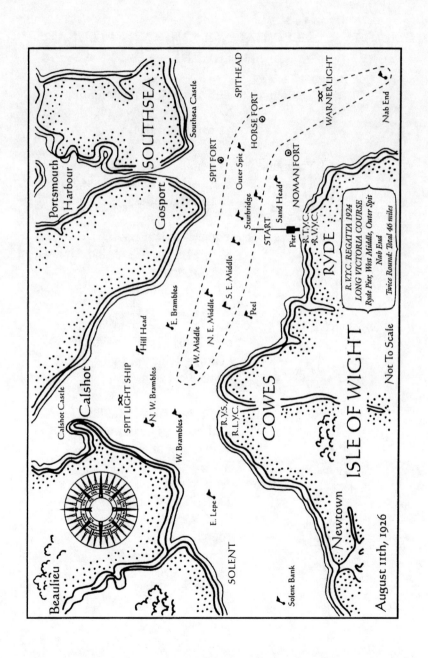

SOUTHSEA

Portsmouth
Harbour

Gosport

Southsea Castle

SPITHEAD

SPIT FORT

Outer Spit

HORSE FORT

WARNER LIGHT

Sturbridge

Sand Head

NOMAN FORT

Nab End

START

Pier

R.T.Y.C.

R.V.Y.C.

RYDE

S. E. Middle

N. E. Middle

W. Middle

Peel

Hill Head

E. Brambles

N. W. Brambles

SPIT LIGHT SHIP

Calshot Castle

Calshot

W. Brambles

R.Y.S.

R.L.Y.C.

COWES

Newtown

E. Lepe

Beaulieu

SOLENT

Solent Bank

ISLE OF WIGHT

R.V.Y.C. REGATTA 1924
LONG VICTORIA COURSE
Ryde Pier, West Middle, Outer Spit
Nab End
Twice Round: Total 46 miles

Not To Scale

August 11th, 1926

IX. TYPICAL SOLENT AND SPITHEAD MARKERS

327   RYS course: club house, Lymington Spit,
                     N-E. Middle buoys, twice round:
                     42 nautical miles.

328   RYS course: club house, Solent Bank,
                     N-E. Middle buoys, twice round:
                     38 nautical miles.

329 RYS course: club house, Solent Bank,
                   N-E. Middle, S-E. Middle buoys,
                   twice round:
                   40 nautical miles

330 RYS 'Queen's' course:
                   club house, East Lepe buoy,
                   Warner lightship, twice round:
                   46 nautical miles

331   RTYC course: Ryde Pier, West Middle, Nab
                   End buoys, twice round:
                   42 nautical miles

332   RTYC 'Short Victoria' course:
                   Ryde Pier, Warner, Outer
                   Spit, West Middle buoys, twice
                   round:
                   35 nautical miles

333   RVYC 'Long Victoria' course:
                    Ryde Pier, West Middle, Outer
                    Spit, Nab End, twice round:
                    46 nautical miles

Note: Courses could be sailed starting east or westwards
depending on the race committee's discretion.

X.   A BRIEF SUMMARY OF SIR THOMAS LIPTON'S *SHAMROCKs*

Sir Thomas Lipton owned six *Shamrock*s, which he built between 1899 and 1930.

The 23 metre *Shamrock* of 1908 vintage, said to be Sir Thomas's favourite, was designed and built by William Fife and Sons of Fairlee, Scotland to compete in British coastal waters. This yacht was the one which raced in the big handicap class during 1924-1929 (inc.) referenced in this narrative.

The five *Shamrock*s which bore the numbers I to V were built exclusively as challengers for the Americas Cup to race in US waters.   Although the narration of their exploits is extremely well documented elsewhere, an outline of their histories is included for clarification.

SHAMROCK I
Designed by Wm. Fife and skippered by Archie Hogarth to meet the Herreshoff cutter *Colombia* in 1899.

SHAMROCK II
Designed by George Watson and sailed by E.A. Sycamore to meet the American *Colombia* in 1901.

SHAMROCK III
Designed by William Fife Jnr., and sailed by Captain Robert Wringe against the Herreshoff *Reliance* in 1903.

SHAMROCK IV
Designed by Charles Nicholson in 1914 and sailed by Sir William Burton in 1920, meeting the Herreshoff cutter *Resolute*.

SHAMROCK V

Designed by Charles Nicholson and skippered by Ned Heard to meet the Starling Burgess-designed *Enterprise* in 1930, the last of Sir Thomas's unsuccessful challenges.

Sir Thomas Lipton was somewhat belatedly elected to membership of the Royal Yacht Squadron in the year 1930 and he crossed the Great Divide shortly after.

XI. THE BEAUFORT NOTATION – WIND FORCES

	denotes			Wind loading in lbs per sq.ft
0	Calm			.020
1	Light air; just sufficient for steerage			.044
2	Light breeze	1–2 knots	}	.079
3	Gentle breeze	3–4 knots	} full canvas	.123
4	Moderate breeze	4–5 knots	}	.492
5	Fresh breeze	5–10 knots:	single reefs	1.107
6	Strong breeze	10–15 knots:	double reefs	1.970
7	Moderate gale	20–25 knots	}	3.067
8	Fresh gale	26–29 knots	} triple reefs	6.027
9	Strong gale	30–35 knots	}	9.900
10	Whole gale	40–45 knots	}	12.304
11	Storm	50 knots:	trysails	49.200
12	Hurricane	80–100 knots:	no canvas	

* The quoted wind forces are measured clear of sea level and must become progressively greater at altitude levels above deck.

XII.   POSTSCRIPTS

P.S.   It was in May 1995 that the writer enjoyed the pleasure of meeting Harry Spencer, a specialist in the manufacture of rigs for classic sailing yachts.

Whilst visiting his Cowes harbour wharfside business premises, I was privileged to inspect a truly magnificent hand-crafted complement of major riggings, fashioned exclusively in support of *Lulworth*'s programmed reconstruction, centred on La Spezia.

These items comprised a seemingly colossal, Marconi-style, fabricated sitka spruce mast, of socketed two-piece design, measuring 168 feet foot to truck, together with all associated spars and a full set of highly finished hardwood pulley blocks. Here were so many brilliant examples of local design concepts and craftsmanship, demonstrating a modern approach to the maintenance of a traditional requirement; in truth, a virtual masterpiece, with a rendezvous at the crossroads of science and art.

P.P.S.   In September 1995, Harry Spencer was left with his contribution towards *Lulworth*'s refurbishment.   The projected revival of the yacht itself had not materialised.

His complement of spars and rigging needed storage space to allow continuing workshop capacity.   In order to solve his problem, the giant mast, with its attendant riggings, was erected pointing skywards on the immediate quayside.

By an accident of fate, a most appropriate memorial, a tribute to a magnificent cutter, had presented itself.